OTHER BOOKS BY JOHN EHLE:

Fiction

The Widow's Trial

The Last One Home

The Winter People

The Changing of the Guard

The Journey of August King

Time of Drums

The Road

The Land Breakers

Lion on the Hearth

Kingstree Island

Move Over, Mountain

Nonfiction

Trail of Tears: The Rise and Fall of the Cherokee Nation

The Cheeses and Wines of England and France,

    with Notes on Irish Whiskey

The Free Men

Shepherd of the Street

The Survivor

DR. FRANK

DR. FRANK

*Life with
Frank
Porter
Graham*

by John Ehle

Franklin Street Books, Chapel Hill, 1993

Published by Franklin Street Books. For permission to quote please write to:
Permissions, 119 East Franklin Street, Chapel Hill, NC 27514.

Copyright © 1993 by John Ehle
All rights reserved under International and Pan-American Copyright Conventions.
Published and distributed in the United States by Franklin Street Books.

ISBN 0-9638915-0-2

Library of Congress Catalog Card Number 93-73743

Manufactured in the United States of America
First Edition

For Galen Wagner,
who initiated this
dear labor.

We all had a guiding light. Frank Porter Graham.
We all looked to his idealism.
We all shared his spirit.

Terry Sanford

Oh, I want to tell you, he was something. Isn't it true here, fifty years later, he walks across that campus, as much a force, as alive as the sun in the sky. When all others are forgotten, there he is.

Bill Friday

I just want somebody to present Frank Graham as a human being.

Arnold King

CONTENTS

AUTHOR'S
ACKNOWLEDGEMENTS
AND PREFACE

Well over fifty people have been interviewed in recent years in the making of this book, and I am indebted to each one. What they told me has been woven into the story, some in a line or two, others in many, but all needed by the whole. Among them are,

In Chapel Hill, Douglass Hunt, Arnold King, Bill Friday, Gladys Coates, Fran Weaver, Ida Friday, Elmer Oettinger, John Sanders, Frances Ferguson, Carlyle Sitterson and Mrs. Sitterson, George Esser, Rhoda Wynn, Stuart Sechriest, Georgia Carroll, George Hogan, Mack Preslar, Colin Soloway, Nell Pickard, James Wallace, Jane Grills Richards, Robert Rubin, Letsy Preslar, Spike Saunders, Nell Pickard, Borden Mace, Ione Markham Linker, Candace Owens, Grace Mace, Charlie Jones, George Watts Hill, Frank Pendergraft, Ione Markham Linker, Guy Johnson, and the widow of the campus cop who used to tour the Chapel Hill cemetery with Dr. Frank, Mrs. Jack Merritt;

In Durham, Terry Sanford, Leslie Banner, Jake Phelps, Bob Ehle, Margaret Rose Sanford, Galen Wagner;

In Winston-Salem, Winfield Blackwell, Sophia Cody, Bill Bondurant, Tom Lambeth, Ruth Julian, Alex Ewing;

In Charleston, Hugh Cannon;

In New York City, Eli Evans, Dr. Jerome Tichner;

In Eden Mills, Ontario, Leon Rooke;

In Cleveland, Ohio, Homer Wadsworth;

In Raleigh, Elizabeth Buford;

In Southern Pines, Sam Ragan;

In Washington, D.C., Wayne King, Bill Cochrane, Ernestine Robertson Hagan;

In Asheville, Max Cogburn, Wilma Dykeman;

In Greensboro, Hubert Robinson, Jr.;

In Berea, John Stephenson;

Atop Grandfather Mountain, Hugh Morton;

In London, England, Nona Porter.

I interviewed several relatives of Marian Graham. Initially one of them told me, I don't think Marian would like to be in a book. She came to realize Marian had no choice. Her relatives were, at any rate, pleased to be of help, and I am in the debt of Elizabeth Matheson, Rebecca Warren, Florence Nash and Jacqueline Nash.

I interviewed two daughters of Alice Neal, Pearl Caldwell and Frances Hargrave. Alice Neal had been allowed by her family to go only to the sixth grade of school; Frances Hargrave, a generation later, was one of the first blacks who registered at the University of North Carolina Graduate School soon after the racial barrier was lifted.

I talked with the only nephew of Dr. Frank, Graham Shanks of Washington, D.C.

In 1961, I interviewed in her office Daisy Lippner, Dr. Frank's United Nations secretary, and talked often with Dr. Graham, himself, usually about the State and University, meeting him for lunch on occasions, and even tried to write a magazine article about him. Dr. Frank found the article embarrassing, as he told me, and never returned it. (It is now in the Southern Historical Collection with his papers). I believe he was embarrassed by the evidences of his generosity that were included. He said, I don't think anything about doing these things. Months later, in Chapel Hill, he told me, If you write a book about me, you can use the article in that.

His suggestion that I write a book about him is out of character, but is confirmed in detail in my journal for 1961. One possible explanation is that recently he had read my book about James Gusweller, *Shepherd of the Streets*[1], a biography this one resembles in style, and he was aware that only academic books might be written about his life. I'm not sure that will cut the mustard, he told me.

Well, of course, we need different types of books about him. We have different readers. The biography by Warren Ashby, *Frank Porter Graham, A Southern Liberal*[2], is most helpful. The book you hold in your hand will take its place somewhere in the spectrum. I hope it will attract the young generation. At first, they will wonder what all the social fuss is about, time and work having changed the more dire situations, but they will be able perhaps to adjust; Dr. Frank was often in dangerous straits.

The style I've chosen for the book is informal, friendly, as was Frank Graham in all the occasions I knew him over a period of twenty-five years. He did not write in an informal style, as a rule, and his writings as used here stand in contrast; therefore the major pieces have been reproduced from their originals as much as possible, and not edited. Readers can read them, or easily refer back to them.

A chronology of Frank's life can be found at the end, as well as a few examples of his thought from his writings. The reader who is drawn to know more and read more about Dr. Frank is encouraged to visit the Southern Historical Collection and the North Carolina Collection, both housed in Wilson Library in Chapel Hill.

I have written three biographies previously but am by trade a novelist, and certain of the novelist's methods play a part here, which I think is helpful and desirable. Fiction, however, is not used here; the book is in all respects based

[1] William Sloane Associates, New York, 1960

[2] John F. Blair, Publisher, Winston-Salem, 1980

on careful research.

I am indebted for the help of my researcher, Lynn Roundtree of Chapel Hill, who principally used the Southern Historical Collection, the North Carolina Collection and the Alumni Bureau in Chapel Hill, to my researcher at Duke, Kay Bowman, and at the Winston-Salem library, Stella Anderson. And yes, too, to the helpful, downright considerate staff of the Franklin Delano Roosevelt Library at Hyde Park, N.Y. I found there over twenty telegrams sent by Dr. Frank to FDR, all of them congratulatory and support-ive.

Typists for the five drafts of the book were Barbara Sale and Nikki Byers, of Winston-Salem, and my secretary, Catherine Marks.

I asked several readers to judge the book as it grew and, as is my style, became more lean. (Some years ago I received two reviews in a single mailing; in one I read that my novel was not much on style, and in the other that the novel was a masterpiece of simplicity of style). Readers of the various drafts were, from Winston-Salem, Lil Meredith, Anne Forsyth and Elizabeth Wood; from Chapel Hill, Borden Mace, David Moltke-Hansen, Leslie Banner, John Sanders, Rhoda Wynn, Joe Herzenberg; from Bluefield, West Virginia, Judy Johnson; from Washington, D.C. Shirley Cochrane; and from Buladean, North Carolina, Michael Joslin. Their opinions were helpful without exception, although not all are reflected in the book.

As I finish this book, I have several bits and pieces here which beg to be included, as does one important item from Arnold King. One bit is from a college roommate at Chapel Hill who said he often found Frank hanging from the lintel of the dorm room doorway, trying to stretch, to make himself taller. Another was that Billy Carmichael, noticing Frank was again launch-ing an attack on entrenched Southern thought, would say, There goes Frank getting up on his little ole portable cross again. Then there was State Senator Clarence Stone, who, after listening for awhile to Frank's rousing defense of the University, was wont to say, All right, Frank, let's put Traveler in the barn and get on with the discussion.

Then there was Arnold King, close friend of Frank's telling me Frank was frustrated most of his life. He saw the big picture so big, King told me, that he couldn't handle it, and he championed some impossible causes. His priorities would have been different, King said, if he had had children, as he wanted. He said Frank was the most tragic figure in our recent history and the closest to a genius we've produced in this state in recent history.

I agree he was a genius by whatever definition, even when stripped of the garments of the legend which he has become. As for failure, well he was to me a wonderful success. Nor did I sense he was frustrated all his life. When I, a student, knew him as president of the University, and in latter days knew him in New York City, Raleigh, Hillsborough, and Chapel Hill, he was secure and radiated confidence, and had plenty of positive advice and hope to share. As I understand it, Dr. Frank as a young man saw the future clearly, the future for his own generations and beyond, far beyond even that of his hoped-for, never-to-be-born child's. He knew that change would be painful for the South, but that change was inevitable and predictable, and he was willing to stand out front and take a portion of that pain, and lead, and cause others to do so. I don't think Dr. Frank ever thought that, within the span of his life, he could succeed with industrialization and race changes in the South, causes that were left in his hands, but were not within his grasp.

No doubt those who sought an orderly administration became at times frustrated with him, Frank having a way of delegating authority, then personally intruding; as were people frustrated while protecting the historic core of the University disciplines, professors whom Dr. Frank thought were slow to change and to make the university systems more attuned to the needs of the people; and frustration descended also on the one who would keep the universities out of harm's way in social change. All these people -- and they were not the same in all three categories -- might have become frustrated with Dr. Frank, who was making his own victorious way.

Arnold King has died since our four hours of recorded sessions about Dr. Frank. He knew Dr. Frank as well as anybody I interviewed. I wish he were with us still to represent more fully his views.

Let me add one thought I have which needs to be put inside these covers, something the reader might want to consider: Dr. Frank was an American of Scottish descent, and was proud of it. As such he was a Calvinist and an American patriot; the Scots serve Calvinism and patriotism well. Also, a male Scot is likely to have his own work outside the family, and often is dedicated to education, as well as religion and country. He does at times sacrifice himself and his family for them. That Dr. Frank is a Scot strikes me as a key to understanding him.

Two further, final notes. One: I chose not to use quotation marks. In a biography of this type, relying on incidents and on hundreds of statements of acquaintances and family, such marks seem to me to intrude. Wallace Kuralt, the publisher, has agreed to these deletions. All statements attributed to individuals named earlier in this acknowledgement are accurate word for word, and come from recordings.

Two: In its working drafts this manuscript was tentatively titled <u>Frank Graham of Chapel Hill</u>. And so it was; for the most part it was restricted to him in that place of privilege and beauty. We did venture out with him to Indonesia and India and the United Nations in New York City, but always we kept an eye, as did he and Marian, on their special place, which, except for his sense of self-denial, would have been for the last decade of life his and her home. He rests there now. And his spirit remains on campus and in the village, even after decades, challenging, revitalizing. To some, endearing.

John Ehle

Winston-Salem

2 July 1993

INTRODUCTION

These words are for those who were not acquainted with Frank Porter Graham:

He was a saint.

Those who knew him will not have to be told.

He was one of the greatest Americans of the Twentieth Century, no doubt, and the most remarkable human being I ever came across, self-less, sunny and brave. In all his life, did he ever think a dark thought or act on a selfish motive? I never heard a murmur of it and cannot imagine it.

I believe the Church requires evidence of miracles, however, before elevation to sainthood. Frank Porter Graham performed miracles, too. In the midst of the Great Depression of the 1930's, he took the leadership of a poor University in a desperately poor state and transformed it -- by tact, diplomacy, outright wheedling and steady strength of character -- into a model of public higher education and a light for the nation. If building a great University when and where he did it wasn't miraculous, then miracles don't exist.

He was a Christian. In a time when so many "Christians" reveal themselves on television as pinch-faced bigots, it is good to remember the genuine item, an open-handed lover of the world who could express his religious faith and his abiding feeling for his country this way:

In this America of our struggles and our hopes, the least of

these our brethren has the freedom to struggle for freedom;
where the answer to error is not terror, the respect for the past
is not reaction, and the hope of the future is not revolution;
where the integrity of simple people is beyond price and the
daily toil of millions is beyond pomp and power; where the majority is without tyranny and the minority without fear, and all
people have hope.

That vision could have been enunciated only by a patriot intimately
acquainted with the Sermon on the Mount.

Nobody who reads the stories in this fine book by John Ehle will be
able to mistake Frank Porter Graham for one of those passive saints rest-
ing beside still waters. No, this one drove a speedboat, darting furiously
around the estuary, creating a huge wake and rocking all the other boats
wherever he went. Ignorance, poverty and intolerance were among the
home-based craft that got a thorough rocking. They are still on the pond
in Frank Graham's native North Carolina, but they have not quite recovered from the good swamping he gave them.

If North Carolina is, among a good many of its citizens, a shade
more liberal and kindly state than some of its southern neighbors, that is
a legacy of the University president, U. S. Senator and speedboat driver
we once had.

Nobody could quite keep up with him, but hundreds of people he
knew were swept up in his great wake. I think of Bill Friday, Terry
Sanford, Albert Coates, John Sanders, Allard Lowenstein, Tom Lambeth,
Tom Wicker, Jim Wallace, Joel Fleishman, Eli Evans, and the author of
this book, John Ehle himself, and many more I did not know but have
heard of, all men and women whose lives were touched and changed by
Frank Graham's life, and who went on, thus touched and changed, to
lead in politics, to head up corporations, to direct great universities and
foundations, and to write and think and serve their state and nation.
Frank Graham had no children; we are all his children.

In my own family, every brush with Frank Graham is well-remem-
bered. My father came to the University of North Carolina from Massa-
chusetts in those hard Depression years, hired a man with a mule and
wagon to transport his trunk from Carrboro Station to the campus, and
soon became aware of the diminutive professor of history known then as
"Mr. Frank." This professor scurried everywhere, seemingly always late
for an appointment. It didn't take long for my father to understand that
Mr. Frank *was*, in fact, always late because of his habit of stopping to
talk with everybody he met, grasping new students by the arm and inquiring about their hometowns, their ancestors, their ambitions and their
general welfare.

My father was graduated in the year of Frank Graham's election to the University presidency, and, thinking to make a little money and have a little adventure, he organized a geology field trip from Chapel Hill to California. This expedition went broke in the Sierra Nevada Mountains and was forced to send a telegram to the new University President requesting a cash advance to get home. From somewhere, President Graham came up with the requested amount, and when the caravan of trucks and buses straggled back to the campus, he was the first the welcome it, eagerly inquiring about the success of the trip, never mentioning the money.

In my turn, I, too, came to Chapel Hill to school, and after me, my brother Wallace, publisher of this book. Frank Graham had recently left the campus, but each of us found something in the air of the University, a kind of generosity, a certain tolerance, a disposition toward freedom of action and inquiry that bound us both to this one place as to no other. This was the atmosphere that Frank Porter Graham created and left behind him.

As editor of *The Daily Tar Heel*, I cncountered Dr. Frank at a function in Raleigh one evening. "I have been reading your editorials," he said. This surprised and pleased me. "Sit down here," he said. He drew a chair up to mine and took me by the arm as my father remembered his doing all those years before. "You are being a little hard on President Gray," he said. Persuaded, as I was, that Frank Graham's high standards were being compromised, I had been exercising the student editor's prerogative of raking the new administration of Gordon Gray over the coals. "You are free to write what you like," Dr. Frank said to me like a gentle parent, "and President Gray doesn't always do things just the way we used to do them. But try to see what he is up against. Try to put yourself in his place, you see, and understand his problems, and try to help him when you can. He has a tough row to hoe." Then he asked after my family. *The Daily Tar Heel* may have been a little easier on the new administration after that. Dr. Frank had bothered to give even a teen-aged editor a dose of his most famous tonic, sweet reason.

Years afterward, I witnessed a staggering display of his prodigious memory, about which thousands of stories survive. Mine goes this way: I was vacationing on the Outer Banks with my two daughters. We were invited to attend the annual Daniels family reunion on the grounds of the Methodist Church at Wanchese on Roanoke Island. There we ran into Dr. Frank, also paying his respect to the Daniels clan. "This is Lisa," I said to him, "and this is Susan." He passed a minute or two talking to these little girls of mine before turning to greet others in the huge crowd. The next year, we were back at the Daniels family reunion, and so was he. He walked up to my daughters, extended his hand to them, smiled, and said, "Hello Lisa, hello Susan."

So this is a book about a man who once, through a crowded year, remembered the names of two little girls, who once delighted his nieces with stories and who rescued runaway balloons at the beach, who took the arms even of his detractors and wrung from them their life histories and their grudging friendship, a scholar, visionary and activist whose goodness and courage still works its inspiration in his native region, a man who wanted to be a baseball player and, willy-nilly, became a saint instead.

If we ever become so self-absorbed that we forget about Frank Porter Graham, we will have forgotten everything noble about our past. John Ehle deserves our thanks for keeping his memory alive and shining.

-- Charles Kuralt

DR. FRANK

CHAPTER ONE

IN THE EARLY 1930s in the South, particularly the old plantation sections of eastern North Carolina, whenever a lady was not married by the age of thirty, she was classified as a maiden aunt, a family helper, a spinster, or at least a spinster-to-be. Marian Drane, who was rather pretty and well formed, was thirty-two.

When she had graduated from Saint Mary's College in Raleigh, the yearbook, *The Muse,* said this about her:

> We're proud of Marian. Not only does she attain the Honor Roll and understand 'N Philosophy' but she also lends poise and dignity to our class when we appear in public. Appearances are deceptive though -- those are only her company manners. When within the sheltering walls of Senior Hall she is a leader in the fun and frolic of our class. In addition to all this, she is our class beauty, and, moreover, has been voted 'Most Courteous' for two years. Still, we can't praise her for that. She can't help it. That's just her all over.

Marian had spent her adult years since college taking care of her father, Robert Brent Drane, the rector for fifty-six years of St. Paul's Episcopal church in Edenton -- the second oldest town, and one of the prettiest, in North Carolina. She had worked at the library and had taught second grade quite successfully. The teaching particularly had given pleasure, and had in a sense afforded foster motherhood.

Even so, she was undeniably thirty-two and unmarried. And now that her ill father was being forced into retirement, she was more obligated than ever before to make a choice. And she did want children, did long for the love and responsibility of a family.

But what to do, what to do?

Her pretty sisters Katherine Perry and Eliza Webb were married and had growing children. They proved that a parson's daughter could have courtship and husband. Fair enough. However, one might admit the daughter left to take care of her widowed father did inherit a more difficult situation.

She had met Frank Graham in Chapel Hill, the President of the University, a lordly title for such a friendly person. Her father would be inclined to approve him. In fact, she had on February 24th, of that year, 1931, written Mr. or Dr. Graham -- she didn't know which -- about that visit:

> Dear Mr. Graham.
> I had such a good time in the Piedmont -- and I want to thank you for adding so much to my pleasure while I was up there. Your dinner party was lovely -- and I enjoyed seeing you in Hillsboro and at the Gimghoul Castle. I only hope that breeze and drizzle from the tip top of the tower didn't give you a relapse. We should have had more sense!
> I was so thrilled that the Appropriations Committee recommended that your request be granted. I do hope that question will soon be settled to your entire satisfaction -- and that of every friend of the University.
> I'm remembering April 11th, and am looking forward to it.
> > With kindest regards,
> > Sincerely,
> > Marian Drane
> > Are you a doctor?
> > Edenton --
> > Feb. 24 --

He's -- why he must be forty, her sister told her, and is known to be a bit of a troublemaker, he is out to remake the world, or at least his part of it. Older sister, Eliza for one, liked her world as it was.

It was true Frank Graham even as a professor had sometimes been criticized in letters to editors and in everyday conversations, but recently, in 1930, Mr. Winslow and Mr. Battle had, along with other trustees, voted him to be president of the University of North Carolina, a worrying job in the Depression -- or at any other time -- and had increased his fame.

If Marian at thirty-two had a developing problem, Frank Graham at forty-five had a more pressing one, not only from age but also because of his recent, 1930, appointment. Joking -- or only half-joking with a friend, Lee Wiggins -- he had admitted to three needs to qualify him for the post: a hat, which he could buy, a car, which would be provided, and, more important, a wife, and he didn't know how to go about finding her. He was known to forget his hat on occasions, and didn't drive, and was a Scottish Presbyterian bachelor who had devoted every week of his life to his work, very little time left for social pursuits. He had told a friend he had found by means of an hour's workout in the gym he could somewhat relieve his sexual drive.

Two men who had helped Frank into the presidency, attorneys Kemp Battle and Frank Winslow, had ideas about a wife for Frank. Both were part of the landscape in Eastern North Carolina, were from wealthy families who had benefitted from their generation-by-generation connections. Frank Graham had been a fellow student at Chapel Hill some twenty years before, had been president of their senior class in 1909 -- indeed had held most all the offices.

Whenever Frank Winslow and Kemp Battle got together, which was every summer day they were at the shore at Nags Head, the Outer Banks of North Carolina, they had occasion to mention him, a favorite friend. They had met first at the Warrenton High School at Warrenton, which was run by Frank's uncle, John Graham, where Frank had gone to study classics in the senior year of high school. Kemp recalled Frank had arrived at college having already memorized the names and addresses of every upperclassman; maybe he had studied the previous yearbook.

He was editor of the student newspaper until his eyes complained. They had been weakened by a childhood disease. Also, Frank was forever getting pneumonia, which he called the grippe, which appeared to be an illness that ran in the male side of his family.

Even so, he was tough as old hickory. Played football, baseball --
Loved baseball the best. Wrestled -- liked to wrestle.
Used to carry a baseball in his pocket.
All the time. Never without it.

Both Winslow and Battle were on the Board of Trustees of the University. They had championed Frank, who was a full professor in the history department, for President of the University.

Frank didn't want it.

Might not want to marry, either, the two cronies decided, seemed to be a confirmed bachelor, but he had the big president's house to care for now and had entertaining to do. Not seemly for the president to be a bachelor, sets the wrong example. They wondered if Marian Drane could do Frank Graham's work alongside him.

Probably could; she had handled her father, Dr. Drane, for years, which should qualify her. Both had known her since she was a baby and they were boys of ten, twelve.

Attractive. Dependable. A very private person, considering the nature of being a president's wife.

So they talked day by day, and enjoyed their speculations. Winslow invited Frank to come visit Nags Head this summer, 1931, as he had done before during the recess. Come early and entertain Miss Marian Drane.

Should we actually mention Marian to him?

Marian Drane. Pretty name. Yes, let's do.

Parson's daughter. Family of churchmen for generations back.

Yes, tell him. He knows full well he needs a wife. Has that big house, all the entertaining -- tell him. Lay it on the line. His sister Kate's not wanting to keep house for him forever.

Should we mention any bishops? There must have been at least one among the Drane churchmen. After all Frank is Scottish you know, both sides of his family Presbyterian.

No, better not mention any bishops to Frank.

Frank Graham's first romantic journey to Nags Head to meet Marian was cancelled. He wrote Frank Winslow July 30, 1931, as follows:

This simply breaks my heart. I have been almost living for that Nags Head trip. After a year's absorption in this present job which takes me all day and night and not to see the person on the other side of the Chowan River who is also going down on Saturday simply takes the ground out from under me right now. I must stick here and hold on and do the best I can.

He wrote Mrs. Winslow, this second letter delivered a few days later:

Please ask back the lady by the Chowan River and not let her get away or be kidnapped. This is my special and confidential charge to you.

In late August the work in Chapel Hill had relaxed enough for Frank to reschedule the vacation.

The route from Chapel Hill to Nags Head lay through Elizabeth City. There a ferry took cars over to the Outer Banks, and Winslow and Battle had sent Frank the ferry schedule for a Friday, had underlined the final sailing, realizing he would not make the earlier ones.

However, on the way down Frank stopped in Fayetteville, his birthplace and the resident city of several relatives, and at Rocky Mount, the home of the Kysers, Emily Royster Howell Kyser having a revolving salon for visitors interested in vigorous conversation of a light, but not frivolous, vein, mostly about the state's leaders and this "Great Depression" which had inflicted throbbing pain on the nation and especially on the South. Also, this was the house of Jean Kyser, whom Frank had courted several years ago, a mild, gentle escorting. She had loved him.

Mrs. Kyser was as lively as ever. Frank stayed longer than planned. He had told his black driver he would be here half an hour, and two hours passed. Then, as he was leaving, Mrs. Kyser began telling about her son Kay's recent success, told yet again the story of Kay's leaving Chapel Hill with his college dance band and driving to New York in an old Ford, which he parked on Times Square. He and his band members attached to it a boat's anchor -- oh, it must have weighed a hundred pounds, she said, which they left on the sidewalk. Half an hour later, on his return, Kay found reporters taking pictures, so he posed, and the next morning went into the biggest booking agents' offices. I arrived just yesterday, he told the agents, and I'm in the newspaper today, and am eager to go to work.

The usual route to Nags Head led northeast to Elizabeth City, then east to the ferry, then south along the Outer Banks, but Frank saw on the road map that the more direct route lay through Columbia, North Carolina, and Tyrrell County, so he chose that way. His driver knew no better, and they headed out into the marsh of a great swamp.

Several times previously Frank had tried driving a car, but the cause and effect relationship of mechanical contrivances eluded him. Early in his driving experiences he had had a wreck, while talking to passengers in the rear seat.

Also, his eyes were weak and should be saved for reading. Further, with a driver he could use travel time effectively, as now, by stretching out his short body on the back seat and going to sleep.

They arrived at the ferry with horn blowing and the driver shouting for the boat to wait for them.

Frank had a method of greeting people, making friends. Frank hurried to meet the people. He never met a stranger. My name is Frank Graham, what's yours? He grabbed hold of people's arms, held to them, never satisfied with shaking hands. He gleaned names. And where are you from? What was your mother's family name? Where was she from? Do you know Matt Wolfe there? He wanted to know every person aboard. There were only about thirty, a mere mind-snack for him. And he would remember them, their names and family backgrounds for years and years. A miracle, always something special to witness, as even his driver recognized, it was a form of magic watching Frank work. Work it was, too, never doubt that. Work and pleasure. Life and blood to him. He was hard at it. He would need all those people before his time ran out.

In her mind Marian had remembered him as a formidable person. Actually, he was small. Her guess would be 5'4", and 125 pounds at the very most. In fact, he was boyish in size. Sad eyes, wide-spaced, bushy brows. His ears were deeply cupped, outstanding. Balding. Head a bit large for his small body. There he stood near the road, being greeted by the Winslows -- all of them, the children as excited as the adults.

His clothes were office attire. A crisp white shirt and tailor-cut suit. He held a straw hat in his hands. His black attendant was standing off behind him.

If asked to pick out of a group of five the one who was the world-shaking president of the University of North Carolina, Frank Graham might be the last chosen. He resembled a small-town merchant in his Sunday best, over-dressed for vacationing here at the beach.

They met for dinner at the Winslows' house, she and her father, and she recalled years later they were all seated after dinner on the oceanside porch, Battles and Winslows, her father and Frank. Directly she noticed she and Frank were there alone. The others had gone indoors. Frank was talking. He was a great one for questions. Wanted to know all about her life, her work, her father's work, her mother.

He walked home with her and met her sister Eliza and her children, and spent time talking to her father. However, he stayed late enough to pass everybody's bed time. Hour after hour he and she talked. It was late, indeed, when he thought to leave.

Quietly, so as not to awaken the others, they crept to the door. The door stuck when she opened it, making a loud, cracking noise, awakening everybody.

Next night was much the same, except they ate at the Battles' and she did less talking about herself and more about her visit to Paris, and about a few disappointments at Versailles, and her working toward mastery of the French language. Again, he took her home. It grew late, but no noise at the door this time. Frank left through a window.

On successive nights, the window came to be known by the children as Mr. Frank's window.

First day he wore the business suit. He had packed beach clothes but had not remembered to bring the suitcase. Rather he had brought it but found it was not his. Must belong to one of the students living in his house.

He tried borrowing Winslow's shorts, but they were baggy on him. Battle and Winslow sorted through clothes their teenage children had left. There was a serviceable pair of shorts, which he put on, but no shirt.

And my, was he hairy! His back was very like a bear's. Marian commented to Eliza that he had more hair on his back than on his head.

Hot liberal thoughts have burned away the hair on his head, someone suggested.

One afternoon Marian took tea onto the beach. The two of them sat on the sand under an umbrella, and he sipped a swallow or two. Later she was to learn Frank didn't use tea or coffee. The children who had played ball with him gathered around and ate the cookies. One of the balloons got free of the three-year-old, Frances, who was brother Fred Drane's daughter; it was lifted high, it went sailing eastward, only to dip low over the water. Frank dashed into the water, swam against the tide and rescued it, to wild applause from the children.

He spent more time at Nags Head than planned. After leaving, even before the month was quite out, he returned. This time he was a guest at the Dranes' house, was provided with the best room, the largest one with a view of the ocean, assigned that by Dr. Drane, himself, and he was guaranteed mornings of quiet while he did two or three hours work.

By the end of summer, Frank had come to be a friend of Dr. Drane and his family, and dear to Marian. He was friend as well, for that matter, of storekeepers and officials, lifeguards and boatmen, and all the children. In fact, little Frances embarrassed Marian by climbing into Frank's lap and calling him Uncle Frank. That embarrassed her but seemed to delight Frank.

The marvel was it also pleased Dr. Drane.

Even though Dr. Drane liked Frank, he did find him annoyingly able to avoid certain critical issues important in evaluating a prospective son-in-law. Christian doctrine, for instance. Dr. Drane had talked with all the beaux of his daughters about Christian doctrine.

Frank would reply to questions by stating what he believed, a personal statement including God and the brotherhood of man. The Nicene Creed was not there. Dr. Drane faced Frank about it, about the

Virgin birth and the physical rising from the dead and ascension.

Frank appeared to be sympathetic, but not committed to the Creed so much as to Dr. Drane's right to believe it.

When pressed, Frank with devotion repeated his own Creed, which might be Presbyterian, but wasn't Episcopalian. Even so, there was no argument possible. Frank did not ever argue. He merely gently restated his own view, without criticism of anybody.

Equally difficult for Dr. Drane to persuade Frank to be less... less newsworthy. Frank often made public comments about the Negro for instance. Leave them alone, they are coming along; Dr. Drane for a number of years had ministered to the Church of St. John-the-Evangelist, Edenton's Episcopal parish for blacks.

He had watched sympathetically the growth, the improvement, the betterment of men and women, black and white. He held no animosity toward any man, but the present cultural attainment of the Negro was, to his mind, inferior to that of the white. Also, Frank was often found representing the cause of organized labor, another form of slavery, as anybody could judge. Was it necessary, he asked Frank, for an educated American in the twentieth century to be embroiled in such matters?

Frank's reply began in ancient Greece. Actually, as Dr. Drane recalled, it began in Athens, came at last to Rome, arrived in England and finally the United States, a parade of progress which included an entire episode devoted to the Declaration of Independence and to the pioneer movement of America, with elaborate praise of electricity. This new source of power appeared to represent a method to free laborers. All this progress was arriving in North Carolina today with a sweep that no one could stand against.

Dr. Drane told Marian he didn't dare ask Frank anything else about it.

Frank also visited the Dranes in Edenton, sometimes merely for an hour or so, occasionally overnight. Never did he fail to spend time with Dr. Drane, and he appeared to enjoy visiting the church and the churchyard. Astonishing, his questions: his enthusiasm for the single stained glass window, his curiosity about every tombstone. Dr. Drane told Marian that Frank was more interested in the dead than most people were interested in the living.

Here, this tombstone, Frank wanted to know who it was, this name carved in the stone. What did he do for a living? How many times did he marry? How many children did he have?

If anything, Frank was too avid in asking about a certain defaced tombstone. This particular act of chiseling Dr. Drane had done himself, in order to remove offensive tributes to the physical charms of a young lady, wife of a parishioner. It had proved an annoyance to walk past those poetic distractions. With hammer and chisel Dr. Drane had censored the phrases.

Always Frank asked about children, seemed to be respectful of the miracle of having one's own children. Marian noticed that, too, and responded warmly to the attitude. Hand in hand they followed Dr. Drane through the graveyard listening to the lectures on the lives ended here, and the births, and how people had died, and what humor they had.

Some people had no sense of humor at all, Drane once told them. My own is of late muffled.

Then in the rectory, all one night Frank never went to bed. When Marian came downstairs for breakfast, Frank was in the library. She told Dr. Drane he had gone to sleep reading his sermons.

Many others have, he said. However, never could anyone have done anything to please the rector more. Even going to sleep while reading them was a tribute. It showed a commendable attitude.

Enough to make any rector weep. Especially an elderly man, retiring. In my will -- I'm drafting it, he told Frank -- I've told my executor to burn my sermons.

Dr. Drane had made such drastic decisions throughout life, most all the decisions in his home had been made by him. Marian and the older children all had chafed under his rule. She was one who had not been terribly fond of him while growing up. Bluntly, caustically he had corrected their manners, their habits, their use of English. He would not have countenanced "terribly fond" for example, the term being in conflict within itself. Any questionable use of a word would send the user to the unabridged dictionary, which was kept open in the dining room.

He taught Marian skills of gardening, and saw to it that she learned those of a seamstress. In both she was taught strict attention to quality. Her brothers were taught carpentry, cabinet making and sailing. Dr. Drane, himself, sailed a skipjack for pleasure.

A founder of the Roanoke Island Historical Association, he delved into local, as well as ecclesiastical history. Every August 18th, the date of Virginia Dare's birthday, he would take a boat-load of Nags Head cottagers over to Roanoke Island to hold "Divine Service" at the site of the Lost Colony's settlement.

Once Marian had returned home to care for him, she came over the years to love him more. He was difficult, but he was consistent. Yes, and often dear. He was controlled by his own sets of convictions and methods. He answered mail on receipt and so, he insisted, should everyone. He answered all questions instantly. For fifty-six years he had presided over his flock, exhibiting piety in his own life, expecting piety in his children.

The young man will be buried in the church cemetery, Dr. Drane told the parents of a son who had killed himself; he will not be carried into the church. Yes, there will be a service in the church yard.

He always knew exactly what he thought was right and he stuck by it, no matter what, and in that he guided his children, as well. He did have to tolerate differences in their political views. Eliza, the oldest daughter, was conservative, was set in establishment ways, while Marian, the youngest, was liberal, and was the most willing of the daughters to serve others self-sacrificially, as she had demonstrated for years.

Indeed, Dr. Drane's possible confusion about Frank's religious views is understandable. Frank's religious dogma was not revealed, never defined. Sometimes he advised students to follow the light within; as to the Protestant church, it was a distinguished institution which he avidly supported as a pillar of democracy. His dedication to human rights virtually amounted to a moral factor in his life. He fervently believed in the worth of each individual -- it never occurred to Frank that the person he was meeting might be a scoundrel -- and he believed he should and could help each person develop into a responsible and morally sound individual. His biographer, Warren Ashby, wrote of him:

> His religious connections and moral sensitivities were qualified by a sense of history. Whenever an issue arose, he found it demanded that he view it historically in the light of the western democratic tradition, and it became natural for him to reach out for the religious, political, economic, and social past that flowed into the present. His feelings were for people and social movements in history, not for ideas and philosophy or sensuous qualities and art. The sense of history became a divining rod for understanding the present, a rod that ever turned toward the most significant movements of the moment.

During the months of visits and letter-writing, Frank's affection for Marian increased apace, and so did the warmth of her letters to him.

In an undated letter, doubtless in 1931, she even refers to her and Frank's secret, which one supposes might be their plans for marriage:

2. Dr. Robert B. Drane of Edenton and his daughter, Marian.
North Carolina Collection, UNC Library, and Dr. Louis Rubin.

My Sweetie,

I am a good girl to keep right on writing to you when I don't get a line from you! That shows how much I love you.

Sara and I went to Norfolk today and had a successful time with our shopping. I bought some lovely evening slippers that make me taller than ever. You don't care though, do you?

Robert is crazy to tell our news. He says it's hard for him to keep his mouth shut. When can we let him tell? It's up to you.

Must stop now and go and mail this. I wonder if you've gone to Blue Ridge today. But how can I know? You haven't told me!

I love you just the same. Have you been looking at that lovely moon tonight? I wish you could come here Sunday.

My dearest love to you.

    Devotedly,
    Marian
Thursday Night

    Monday Night
My dearest precious,

Your letter thrilled me through and through. You are an angel to think all those beautiful things about me. It's going to be a terrific strain to keep you fooled always! But it's marvelous to have you feel that way, and I just hope I can in some small way live up to them and deserve them.

I was thinking about you last Friday night and devoured what the News and Observer had to say. I think Mr. Daniels must like you pretty well, doesn't he? Katharine and I were afraid to read the paper Saturday when the headline jumped out at us "Graham states that he will not retreat"!! Did you see Sister and Cheshire? They must have wielded a powerful influence if the crowd really applauded you as many minutes as Josephus said they did!

Kemp Battle was pleased by the way the courtship was progressing. He and Frank Winslow had a history of influencing Frank's life, from student days to the present virtual certainty, an engagement of marriage.

Thursday night

My own darling - own sweetist
I've decided if I can't see you
every night (or day!) at least
I can write to you every night -
If you ever read this - which
you may never, because I'm
not a writer (its not my
profession or craft - I don't
want or can't compete with
your glorious talent -) but
at least I shall have a
record of my feelings for you -
to read when I'm alone -
or lonely - I shall be sometimes
but it can be done - if you
love me truly..

3a. First page of letter

I wonder if you realise
how many fathoms deep
I am in love with you -
I would lay down my life -
dramatic perhaps - but true!
I would adore to be a good
wife for you but I have
mis givings . You might
find some one better for you -
I wish I was your perfect
mate. I've just been reading
this stupid astrology book
it says I'm not. But
that in its self is a
challenge! I think we
would make wonderful
marvellous babies - & I'm

3b. Second page of letter

willing certainly to give
that a try! Even if we
didn't marry I know
our babies would love
us. I want to marry you.
but I don't want to mess
up your life. We both know
how precious life is – & that
it must not be wasted – So
let us be quite sure – that
You can enhance mine
& me Yours. We are both
remarkable & precious people.
& must not waste each
others resources. But I do
love You. Do please – that we

3c. Third page of letter

can live together for
a time - at least. I
believe you love me -
And on this happy &
confident note I shall
say good night my darling.
I wish you were in my arms
& that I held you last night
& I am blessed.

3d. Unsigned letter to Frank, apparently never sent, from Marian's papers. The deep affection she held for Frank and the intimacy of their relationship and her selflessness regarding him are evident in this letter which, she says, "You may never ... read." *Papers of John Ehle*

CHAPTER TWO

LAST YEAR, 1929, when Battle and Winslow had worked to make Frank president of the University, he had resisted that far more than he resisted Marian Drane. He declared he did not want to be president, even after a hundred friends from all across the state clamored for him to be chosen.

A few days before the trustees meeting he sent telegrams to Battle and to Winslow and to Otho Ross in Charlotte -- Otho was Frank's doctor and a powerful trustee -- and about fifteen others, stating that their effort to elect him would not do.

Frank's telegram of June 3, 1930:

> SEE IN PAPER A DELEGATION GOING BEFORE TRUST-
> EES COMMITTEE TO PRESENT MY NAME. PLEASE USE
> YOUR INFLUENCES TO STOP THIS. DEFINITELY AND
> CONCLUSIVELY WITHDREW MY NAME IN STATEMENT TO
> GOVERNOR IN LETTER TO CHAIRMAN OF TRUSTEES
> COMMITTEE AND IN RESPONSE TO ALUMNI TRUSTEES
> AND FRIENDS AND STAND ON THAT STATEMENT OF
> WITHDRAWAL A DECISION I MADE WHEN SUBJECT WAS
> BROACHED TO ME ON TWO OCCASIONS IN OTHER
> YEARS. I CAN BEST DO MY WORK FOR THE UNIVERSITY
> AND THE STATE AS A TEACHER AND CITIZEN. SINCERELY
> HOPE ALL WILL UNITE ON CONNOR WHO IS REMARKABLY
> EQUIPPED TO BE A STRONG AND PROGRESSIVE LEADER.

Frank approached Kemp Battle, personally begged Kemp not to burden him with this presidency. With all its money-raising problems, Frank knew very well that at this time the very existence of the institution was in danger. North Carolina was among the poorest of the forty-eight states, and the General Assembly was facing one crisis after another over funding for schools, highway maintenance, the prisons, the colleges, the university...

Also, Frank publicly, enthusiastically supported Professor Connor for president. One of the best teachers on campus, Robert Connor was, alongside Frank, a professor in the History Department. He had been

4. The President's Walk, a gravel path through the University Arboretum on the main campus. *Archibald Henderson,* The Campus of the First State University, *UNC Press*

State Archivist and Secretary of the Board of Trustees. A trusted friend and advisor, he had suggested Frank go to Columbia for a master's degree and to the University of Chicago to work toward a doctorate. Frank had finished the course work and needed now to buckle down and do the dissertation. The topic he had chosen had to do with the influences of electricity on the industrial revolution, a monumental task, indeed.

Friends told Frank nobody could ever fulfill a challenge of that magnitude, but Frank was in love with the topic. The doctoral degree mattered greatly to him. He had law training and was licensed, he had a master's degree, but wanted the doctorate. Frank was from a family of educators none of whom had ever gone that far. His father was a teacher and school superintendent. Frank had four sisters who were school teachers, he had two brothers who were teachers, he had two uncles who were teachers, and, as he said, about ten cousins who were teachers.

Frank asked Kemp Battle to withdraw his name, should he be nominated. Battle refused. He argued that Frank could come to the Trustees meeting, it would be an open session on the campus June 9th. He could withdraw his own name.

Frank wouldn't dare go near.

Finally, Battle promised, and at once regretted doing so. To save the situation he told other trustees that the meeting must forego nominations, since he would have to withdraw Frank's name should it be entered. Governor O. Max Gardner was to be Chairman of the meeting, and he consented to this tactic.

As he well knew, a $20,000,000 state bond issue, all for education, had been completed, which Frank had led; Frank more than anybody else had gone town to town, drumming up support for it. The Governor appreciated that, liked Frank and could see the University's chances of surviving this desperate Depression improve with him in charge.

Trustees who favored Professor Connor argued that Frank was too young and was controversial, having only this year been reprimanded by the university's president, Harry Woodburn Chase for publicly supporting textile strikers in High Point. He was always in difficult straits and would drag the University in, too.

At the trustee's meeting, Governor Gardner proceeded to a discussion of the candidates, calling on a committee to name and discuss possible ones. There were Professor Connor of History, Professor Archibald Henderson of the Mathematics Department, Frank and several others. Once a vote was called for, Connor received twenty-six of the forty-two needed, Graham received twenty, Henderson received ten, others sharing the remaining twenty-seven.

The Governor called a recess, affording time for lobbying. During the lobbying, arguments were advanced solemnly, pronouncements were made:

Henderson has more to do now than any one man can handle.

Graham will most surely take the University into the jaws of controversy.

Connor was deprived of the presidency last time because he was then a trustee; therefore he deserves it now.

Graham doesn't yet have a doctorate.

Neither has Connor.

Graham doesn't want the job.

By the third vote Graham and Connor were neck and neck. Once Governor Gardner called for the fourth count, Frank Graham won.

It took half an hour to find him. He was apprehended on his way to town. The trustees were outside, under the oaks, and there received him. Frank went at once to Governor Gardner and beseeched him to call another ballot. Editor Josephus Daniels and Judge John J. Parker, both friends of Frank's, assured him he was needed here and now to save the University. These are tough times, we need you, Frank -- such comments were repeated.

The Governor said the state couldn't afford to get a qualified president from outside, a statement Frank might have taken to be a back-handed compliment.

Frank knew many of the trustees and asked them by name to spare him this. He wanted to teach his courses, he said, and finish his degree.

None of his friends would help him, it seemed.

About an hour after the election, the trustees ushered him into the Pharmacy Building. Frank kept muttering that he didn't know what to say. "I want Professor Connor to be president," he told them.

"Be a Marine, Frank!" somebody told him, recalling his World War I branch of service. Governor Gardner introduced Frank as the choice and asked for a unanimous vote.

Frank asked if there wasn't something that could be done.

I've not mentioned duty to you, have I Frank? the Governor asked.

Frank said, Well... with your help... He sank down on a front row seat. And God's, he said.

Sorry speech, Kemp Battle said at the time. Poorest acceptance speech he had ever heard.

At a celebration ball, Mrs. Connor's eyes were almost closed shut from crying. Connor's defeat was, indeed, a pity for her and her husband. The best teacher on campus, Arnold King says he outdid the Ph.D men in quality of his teaching and his publishing; he had written four or five books; everybody had thought the trustees would choose the older, more experienced person.

Frank was never to finish his dissertation. Mr. Frank, as many students called him, was to become Dr. Frank after Columbia and other universities and colleges gave him honorary degrees. Whether he ever in this world could have completed the examination of the chosen topic is anybody's guess; in a letter written earlier to Dr. Hamilton, chairman of the History Department in Chapel Hill, he discussed research he was doing in Washington, D.C.

> I am getting into my subject pretty well now. I have been trying to work out the evolution of power -- water, wind, steam, oil, gas, gasoline, electricity -- and its economic, social and political implications so that I can understand what electricity did when it came. It's hard digging but fascinating and will give me another and fresh point of view in teaching I trust.

Marian's sister Eliza, who lived at Hillsborough, less than fifteen miles from Chapel Hill, had a commodious house, the first rooms built in 1790 when this village was an important government center; it was, too, a beehive for anti-government "Regulators" before the Revolution. Eleven of these revolutionaries were hanged for an armed revolt in 1771, well in advance of Concord and Lexington. The Battle of Alamance and the hangings had been pretty well forgotten, as had the beautiful, storied town, except by the several hundred local residents.

Eliza's was a great house -- with large lawns and gardens, a magnificent front porch -- was a wonderful place to visit, and Marian found good reason now to do so, to place herself near Frank, who took advantage of her presence. Traveling back and forth from Chapel Hill, he was often in and out of the house through doors and windows.

Hubert Robinson, as Frank's driver, kept a diary to register his trips, and the week of January 19, 1932, is cited:

January 19 Mr. Graham and student to Winston-Salem
  21 Mr. Graham to Raleigh
  23 Mr. Graham to Charlotte
  24 Mr. Graham to Greensboro
  28 Mr. Alexander Graham from Greensboro
  Mr. F. to Hillsboro
  30 Mr. G. to Hillsboro

On one trip Frank forgot Hubert Robinson had driven him to
Hillsborough and accepted a ride back to Chapel Hill. After an hour or
so Hubert found out about this and went on home. It was not the first
time, he said. Frank was an out-and-out genius, but not in everything.

Marian visited Chapel Hill, too, but did not always tell Frank. On
one occasion she had the car stop in front of the president's house and
had marveled at the august size, imposing pillars, the lines of trees, the
low garden walls which had been built before the Civil War by
President David Swain to keep the free-ranging cattle off his lawn.

The house was a challenge to any prospective bride, most
assuredly. Beautiful. Stately. It did appeal to her, the challenge, both the
house and her dear Frank.

Few people were invited to attend the wedding in Edenton. Dr.
Drane, recovered from an illness, came over from the house,
prayer-book in hand, the service in mind, and he faced a near-empty
church. Where is everybody, Marian? he asked.

We wanted a small ceremony, Papa, Marian told him.

Actually, the date for the wedding had been cancelled twice
because of Frank's work. The General Assembly was conforming to the
state requirement of a balanced budget, and one way was to cut the
appropriations for public schools and colleges, including the University,
to a degree threatening their survival. Representing all the schools was
Frank, the diminutive president of the most prestigious school, and he
represented education by means of one-to-one meetings, taking hold of
the legislators, making friends, hanging on to them while he talked. In
addition to one-person-at-a-time lobbying, Frank had statewide strate-
gies. He contacted leaders in senators' home counties, called for an
avalanche of letters and telephone calls, the letters arriving while more
friendly senators took the floor to lock up debate until weekend recess,
to allow time for the letters to arrive.

He would speak to legislative committees with eloquence, an
experience new to even veteran legislators. A light seemed to radiate
from him. He was in command, yet never did his voice rise. His words
fell with Biblical rhythm.

Saw you got the Frank Graham treatment this morning, one
grinning member of the House might say to another. Did he tell you
about the wise men of ancient Athens, as well as present-day children
looking to you?

Twice Frank worked through his wedding weekend. Each time he
put in emergency calls to Marian.

Hey, Sitterson, he called to a student at the University who was in Raleigh for the weekend, come here.

The student quite happily crossed Fayetteville Street to shake the President's hand.

Aren't you from Kinston?

Yes, sir, young Carlyle Sitterson said.

Do you know Senator Hardy?

Yes sir. He lives just two doors from my parents' house.

I want you to do something for me.

Yes, sir, young Sitterson said eagerly.

I want you to talk to him about the University's budget.

Sir? The budget? Well, I'll do it when I see him.

No, that'll be too late.

Well, what should I do?

I want you to go to the Sir Walter Hotel and go to his room and tell him the University and the public schools have to be saved from the budget cutters, it's a matter of life and death to them. You understand?

Yes, sir.

And young Sitterson did just that, as directed.

As the third date for the wedding approached, Frank told Governor Gardner he and Marian Drane had postponed their wedding so often he couldn't do so another time, and the Governor promised to get the budget set by Friday. And he did so, with the University and public schools taking a cut, but less than had been predicted. For the drive to the wedding, Frank climbed into the car beside his black driver, Hubert Robinson, who had packed Frank's clothes for his honeymoon trip. For the wedding Hubert had bought Frank a new suit, a new shirt and a pair of shoes from the boy's department of a store on Fayetteville Street, Raleigh.

On the way to Edenton Frank bought the wedding ring.

In a hotel room he changed clothes while Hubert read him again and again the instructions that Dr. Drane had sent for the wedding. At precisely five till four o'clock, Hubert parked the car in the street in front of the church.

Starting up the steps, Frank stopped. Hubert, I don't have a belt, he said. Let me have yours.

Hubert sacrificed his belt.

Marian's sister, Katharine Perry and her son Bennett, who was four, niece Rebecca age seven, Frank's sister Kate and her husband, Shipp Sanders, Marian's maternal aunt Marian Skinner, the sexton, and Hubert Robinson, the one clasping his trousers, these were the witnesses at Marian's and Frank's wedding. Hubert drove Frank and

5. McCorkle Place on the Chapel Hill campus, viewed from South Building, with Wilson Library in the distance, on a snowy morning in 1930. *The North Carolina Collection, UNC Library*

6. The President's House on Franklin Street.   *The North Carolina Collection, UNC Library*

7. The house of Marian's sister, Eliza, in Hillsborough.
Courtesy Elizabeth Matheson

Marian and their luggage to the train that was to take them to Canada, and their honeymoon.

This was July 21, 1932.

That Robert House, executive secretary of the University of North Carolina, and his wife, Hattie, were not invited was surprising to observers of the University administration. Bob House had been a friend of Frank's since Bob's student days, and during the year Frank had been president the two had worked out this system: Bob House did whatever needed to be done that Frank didn't want to do. Each knew what the other thought, each knew the procedure, the laws, the appropriate attitudes, whether approached by a student or professor or trustee or newspaper reporter -- whatever the matter, it conceivably would be one Frank Graham or Bob House could solve. A student or the parents of a student, seeking a place to rest, might wander into Bob House's office or Frank's; the door to each was always open.

Kemp Battle wasn't at the wedding, nor was Frank Winslow. Nor were most of Frank's brothers and sisters. Whatever the social slights and oversight, friends pardoned Frank quickly, because they knew he simply couldn't fit everything and everybody in.

I imagine he forgot his hat, too, one person commented, discussing the slight.

Somebody said this must have been Frank's shortest speech to date: I do. Frank was widely known for his long speeches. His inaugural speech had lasted an hour and fifteen minutes, longer than the audience had expected; however, the speech was a landmark in education.

One critic told Dean House, Frank's "I do" didn't give anybody time to leave.

Bob House replied that not one person had left Frank's inaugural, either.

That was another characteristic of Bob House, he always took up for Frank Graham.

Frank probably grabbed hold of his bride right away, one friend speculated, a reference to Frank's taking hold of people he knew or didn't yet know. Men he would grasp by the hand or forearms, women by the forearms or shoulders. He had told Marian she would just have to get used to his taking hold of women. He had always been like that.

Bob House and his wife, Hattie, lived across the street from the President's house, and on arrival after her honeymoon, Marian made friends with Hattie.

Nearby lived the head of the Pharmacy School, Edward Vernon Howell, who was known as Uncle Vernon. It was his niece, Jean Kyser, at age sixteen, who had had a dinner date with Frank; her mother and uncle had allowed her to have her first date with him. If there's any man on God's earth I would trust her with it's Frank Graham, Howell said.

Marian as the President's wife was the new leader of the women here, the faculty wives.

Elizabeth Lay Green. Her husband, Paul Green, was a playwright who had recently won the Pulitzer Prize for *In Abraham's Bosom.* Elizabeth and Paul had been in college with novelist Thomas Wolfe, whose first novel, *Look Homeward, Angel,* was a topic of conversation locally.

There was Bessie Roberson Woollen. Her husband, Charles Woollen, was university business manager and director of athletics and was very important to Frank, who was not adept at money matters, as Marian learned at once and to her dismay.

Anna Louise Odum, wife of the famous head of the Department of Social Welfare, Howard Odum, one of the stars on the faculty. He was charting social changes in the South, including changes in Negro and white relationships.

Penelope Wilson, wife of the University Librarian, Louis Round Wilson, a historian of the University. He and Frank could talk for hours, given a chance, and Marian found she and Mrs. Wilson could talk only ten minutes, and that about the Episcopal Church that Marian attended. Anyway, the Wilsons were leaving soon for the University of Chicago.

Loretta Hannigan Koch, pronounced Kotch, not Coke -- that, too, to be remembered -- her husband, Fred Koch, founder and head of the famous Carolina Playmakers, Professor of dramatic literature and playwriting.

Mary Durland Greenlaw, occasionally in town. Her husband, Dean of the Graduate School; the Kenan Professor of English and co-founder of the University Press.

Blanche Pickard Patterson, who ran a dining club for about fourteen men which was called the Old Soldiers' Club, although its name was the Faculty Club, and which Frank had joined during his single days. All members were bachelors, except one divorcé -- a rarity in Chapel Hill -- and one widower.

Sadie Hanes Connor. She and her husband are leaving for Washington. He is still hurt not to be the University president, and she is hurt not to be the first lady. Handle with care. Her husband is to become Archivist of the United States, head of the new National Archives.

Kate Sanders. Frank's sister, the one who had taken care of Frank's house for the first year of his presidency. When Frank had told her he wanted to marry, she whooped with joy. Shipp Sanders had wanted her to marry him but she had been unwilling to leave Frank, knowing he needed someone to take care of him and that huge house. Shipp teaches Latin and Greek.

Mary Gatlin Cobb, her husband, Collier, in Geology. Elizabeth Chesley Baity, her husband, Herman, Dean in the Engineering School. Adeline Mitchell Bernard, wife of William, Professor of Greek. Margaret Flinn Howe, her husband, George, Professor of Latin Languages and Literature. Lovena Pickard Wilson, wife of Thomas "Tommy" Wilson, the University's Registrar. Elsa Couch, her husband, John, a Botany professor. Laura Mace Abernethy, wife of Eric Alonzo Abernethy, the University's first physician.

And so forth and on, ever so many, with the stack of calling cards on the hall table growing like a wild plant.

    Mrs. Gustave Harrer
    Mrs. Wm. Dougald MacMillan, III
    Mrs. James Penrose Harland
    Mrs. Richard J. M. Hobbs
    Mrs. Floyd Harris Edmister
    Mrs. James Bell Bullitt
    Mrs. English Bagby
    "Sorry I missed you."
    Mrs. Urban Tigner Holmes, Jr.
    Mr. and Mrs. Robert Wallace Caldwell
    Mr. and Mrs. William Norton Dey
    Alice and Billy. "So sorry to miss you all."
    Mr. and Mrs. Collier Cobb, Jr.
    Mr. Norman Forrster
    Mr. and Mrs. Fletcher Green.

Marian turned over to Hubert the keys to the house, seven sets; they were never used. Frank, along with most Chapel Hillians, never locked a front door. Also she asked Hubert to help her clean and polish the furniture, which was in deplorable condition, as were the linens and kitchenware, except for a beautiful set of plates, fourteen of them, a gift from a wealthy alumnus.

There were two servants. Alice Neal Sheppard, a native of the area, and Hubert Robinson, recently arrived from Montgomery, Alabama.

Hubert was a college graduate. Alice Neal's father, a school teacher, had died here in town when she was a small child, and her mother died when she was twelve. Her grandmother, born a slave of Cornelia Phillips Spencer, a *grande dame* in University Civil War history, did not encourage her to go to school; consequently, she had only six years of education but was smart as could be and an excellent cook. Yes, and a pleasant person. Both servants were congenial, and Marian and Frank often carried on lengthy conversations with them and relied on their judgment.

Frank's parents arrived for a visit -- not at the best time, unfortunately. One problem: all the spare bedrooms were occupied by students, eight students in all, to whom Frank had given quarters because they had no money. Marian moved two students to a neighbor's for a week and cleaned up their room.

Mr. and Mrs. Graham seemed to have stepped out of a picture book on American Gothic. Mr. Graham was stern, was given to judgments and punishment. He was critical of Marian's decision to attend the local Episcopal Church, the Chapel of the Cross, insisting a wife should follow her husband. Marian told him she had decided to remain an Episcopalian and Frank a Presbyterian, and that decision would stand.

He became amused when Marian referred to the particular Lord's Day as the nineteenth Sunday after Trinity. He said he hadn't any idea why there was need for so many as nineteen.

Frank excused his father, recalling he campaigned year after year for money for public schools, for black as well as white students; on counts of respect for education and fairness in race, Frank recommended him. As for his mother, he loved her and admitted it was she who had guided his early life. Marian attributed Frank's and Kate's friendliness and helpfulness to Mrs. Graham, judged after three days of visiting with both parents.

As the elder Grahams' stay neared an end, they both helped carry Marian's sewing machine, and the supply of buttons and thread, to the tiny room at the top of the main staircase. Sewing is a favorite occupation, Marian told them, ranking alongside gardening and reading.

Kate Graham claimed that her parents had been the happiest couple present at Frank's inaugural dinner in November 1931. The event went on for a long time, most of the trustees and faculty were present, and many wanted to speak. Hour after hour seemed to go by. One guest remembered seeing Miss Meta Glass, President of Sweetbriar College, sitting at her table joking with some of her classical friends; she was enjoying it, long as it was. The two others who seemed to be happy for the speeches to go on forever were Frank's father and mother.

Marian was amused by a story told her by Mildred Moses Graves. After that very dinner Mr. Alexander Graham was asked if he was Frank Graham's father?

No, he said. Frank Graham is my son.

Mildred Moses Graves. There's another person to keep happy. Frank's girlfriend of a few years ago, now married to Louis Graves, the editor of the *Chapel Hill Weekly*. If anything, she was more shy, less interested in meeting people than a president's wife could have afforded to be.

8. Frank and his parents, Alexander and Katherine Sloan Graham.
North Carolina Collection, UNC Library

9. Alice Neal, the Grahams' cook and helper. *UNC News Bureau file, North Carolina Collection, UNC Library*

9a. Hubert Robinson, Sr., the Graham chauffeur and helper, in his later years, when he was active in community affairs and became a member of the Chapel Hill Board of Alderman. See Appendix H. *Photograph courtesy Frances Hargrave*

CHAPTER THREE

SINCE FRANK WAS downright friendly and accessible, a small, informal fellow who couldn't drive and forgot the whereabouts of his hat or driver, there is danger of missing one of his main assets.

Frank Graham was brilliant. He was an outright genius. Not only had he a highly retentive memory, almost miraculous in its power, but he had spent decades developing his mind. His encounters with education were complicated, were prolific enough to bring joy to his teacher father. Consider this:

Public schools through high school,

A year at his uncle John Graham's preparatory school, Warrenton Academy, living in his uncle's home, majoring in classics and languages.

Undergraduate college work at the University of North Carolina, where he held every student office.

A year of law, because friends were entering law and he had no pressing goal for himself.

Two years teaching in high school in Raleigh, 1910-1912.

A year at Columbia and getting a master's degree in history -- not difficult to get at Columbia in those days -- 1916.

Two years in the Marine Corps, never close to the war zone in spite of his best effort. Rose to be a lieutenant.

A year as Dean of Students at Chapel Hill, at which he failed, his school spirit anathema to other veterans of the war.

Assistant Professor of History at Chapel Hill.

Then the University of Chicago studying for a doctorate in history, there falling under the spell of Professor William E. Dodd, a native of North Carolina and the first professor to make history of the South his exclusive province, unveiling in lecture after lecture the body and beating heart and weeping soul of his own dear part of America, a region crippled by its historic embrace of slavery, a region wounded near death by a war it lost gallantly -- Frank's father and uncles had fought for the Confederacy -- a region still held in economic bondage by the North, a region feudal in social and economic structure still awaiting the industrial revolution with the changes that would bring to labor and owners, as witness its savaging recently of New England and, earlier, old England. How could the South free itself, cast off the social fetters and the feudal bonds, and in good grace meet the change inevitably coming?

How, indeed? Consider the personalities of the Southerner, his fury when faced with change of racial or work attitudes, the ropes dangling from trees, the prison cells, the tongue of gossip and innuendo. The South, a religion, a mistress dear, a basket of pride. And poverty. The deepest poverty in America.

Slowly the curtain was revealing the future. Frank Graham glimpsed the future, the social and industrial strife beyond -- yes, even beyond England's and New England's, neither of them having had the race problem alongside the industrial one.

He completed his course work for a doctorate in 1923. A fellowship, two-year, was awarded Frank, and he went on to Washington, DC, studied at the Brookings Institution and monitored the Federal government. Then he decided to journey to London to the London School of Economics to seek answers there, meeting classes of Harold Laski, a brilliant economist, and R. H. Tawney, somewhat more moderate in temperament.

He returned to Chapel Hill, to try to lead the South into the new age. Chapel Hill was ideally situated for this. Here were the young male leaders of North Carolina, along with those from other states. The University was the largest and best university in the South by fact and reputation, with an outstanding faculty. It was an ideal site for Frank Graham. In his classroom and in the state he wanted to seek leaders to lead the South intelligently, into its own best future. There had been no one qualified to give him this assignment, so he had assigned himself.

Along the way, others did assign him, or at least invite him to do certain tasks. For instance, starting in 1926, Frank led the Citizens' Library Movement in North Carolina, the first of its kind in the nation. At the time, North Carolina spent four cents per capita on libraries, ranked forty-seventh in the nation. Almost half of the hundred counties had no public library facilities at all. Sixty-eight percent of the citizens had no access to a public library. Also, North Carolina was second from the bottom in the nation in number of newspapers, magazines and books read per capita. Frank pitched in, and by 1929, the movement had established thirty-five school libraries, and six local libraries were opened or in formation.

Again, Frank was selected for state leadership. In 1927 he was elected to the board of directors of the North Carolina Conference for Social Service, where he was able to use his ability in lobbying for a workman's compensation law, better race relations, better educational institutions, better prisons and fairer business methods. In 1928 he was made president of the North Carolina Conference. Indeed, the wheels of government began to respond to the lobbying of the Conference members -- professors, women's leaders, labor leaders. For instance, a bill for worker's compensation was passed into law, the most liberal workman's compensation law in the South.

Then he was assigned an even heavier duty, the University Presidency.

Preparing for his inaugural speech, Frank spent two weeks studying in the University of Chicago Library, gathering material, then he set all books and notes aside and wrote an eight-thousand-word address, accepting the host of challenges facing him and the University of North Carolina. On inauguration day, the warm sun and blue sky conspired to make this the most perfect November day. In Kenan Stadium were faculty, students, many alumni and over two hundred representatives of educational institutions. Opening the ceremony were remarks of Governor Gardner and a prayer offered by Bishop Pfohl, head of the Moravians of Winston-Salem. Frank's speech lasted an hour and fifteen minutes, and was recognized for its greatness.

Alice Neal, the cook, often accommodated Frank's visit to the kitchen. She would laugh at his wearing Marian's bedroom slippers, which were far too big for him, so that he had to shuffle about. He enjoyed the place, the aromas and warmth, and the pleasure of preparing meals. On occasion he would take a seat and ask her to read aloud a speech he had been writing, so he could judge it.

The first time Alice was reticent. Some of the words were unknown to her, so she substituted for each by saying "skip it."

Alice, what do you mean "skip it?" Tell me when you don't know a word, and I'll define it for you.

She told her daughter Frank drank more Coca-Colas than he wanted Marian and other people to know about. He would ask Alice to watch for him, then he would step into the pantry with his Coca-Cola.

Hubert Robinson often recalled the kitchen commotion surrounding special occasions, particularly freshman orientation. As many as four hundred students would gather for punch and cake. These were huge get-together sessions, young people mingling, meeting. Hubert and Alice and Marian spent days preparing for each one.

Terry Sanford remembers his own astonishment during the freshman speech Frank gave his incoming class. Along with the punch and cakes, and among the statements of welcome were prominent doses of Frank's social philosophy:

> I remember his talking about things that were shocking at the time. Talking about sharecroppers. Well, I had never thought of sharecroppers being abused. A tough life, yes. But a system that forced them to be sharecroppers, a 17-year-old boy hadn't known about that even if he came from Scotland County. Certainly hadn't thought very much about the race prejudice as being prejudice as such. They had a place. There weren't any problems as long as they stayed in their place. You came to Chapel Hill, you had these young boys from all over the state who, I think, were having their eyes opened by Frank Graham and by the influence Frank Graham had on the campus -- Corydon "Shorty" Spruill, Bob House, Howard Odum, they were talking about the great, boiling issues we didn't know about until we came there. He was giving me a social conscience that I had vaguely from my mother and father. Not pointedly, not so deliberate, not so controversial. I had been taught not to abuse black people. I had been taught to try to be fair to folks. I had been taught to worry about the boys who lived in the mill section of Laurinburg, but these issues as great issues, social issues, things that had to be done, you got those from Frank Graham's influence at Chapel Hill.

There were several stories Frank often told in his talks to students.

One was about Alice Neal herself. She had been in the Drane beach house during a storm. Three feet of water washed back and forth under the house, and Frank assured her there was no danger. Alice said, I'm not afraid of that three feet of water, Mr. Frank. I'm afraid of those miles of ocean leaning against them.

Another was about his Scot ancestors. After the Battle of Culloden, he said, leaders of the Highland Scots had a choice. They could accept Governor Gabriel Johnson's invitation to come to North Carolina or they could stay in Scotland and be executed. Frank noted they argued about it for forty-eight hours before deciding.

The third was about Cornelia Phillips Spencer, daughter of a great professor, sister of a professor. After the Civil War, using a pseudonym, she wrote newspaper articles criticizing the carpetbagger president and faculty of her beloved university, calling for redemption, for a return to the high standards of pre-war years, when Chapel Hill was the largest and most successful university in the South. For a few years the

10. Dr. Frank and Bob House
North Carolina Collection, UNC Library

University even closed its doors. She continued to write, demanding it
be reopened. Once the opening was assured and a new, better faculty
hired, it was she who walked from the Phillips home to South Building,
leading neighborhood children, and on the top floor they took hold of
the bell rope and rang the bell, for half an hour the sound going out
over the campus and into the hearts of the people.

Frank's views on integration often flashed through. He would obey
the laws, Federal and State, which segregated the Southern society, and
work to change them. And he would remain friends with people of
differing views from his own, recognizing that the South is honest in its
belief, handed down for generations, that segregation is not an evil, but
the only way the two races can live together in harmony.

Paul Green and his wife Elizabeth came by for tea with Marian and
were persuaded to stay for dinner with her and Frank. Marian had
bought a ham shoulder and head of cabbage, and Alice Neal was
boiling them together, a dish Frank liked. Marian had found he liked
everything that was in any way Scottish. Paul entertained them at
dinner talking about the outdoor drama he was writing, which Dr.
Drane and others at Nags Head were commissioning.

Paul was gently hinting that Dr. Drane might be criticized for
insisting that the most significant event was not that this was England's
first colony in America, nor that it was the birthplace of the first
English child born in America, nor was the disappearance from
Roanoke Island of the colonists the most important aspect. Rather, it
was the baptism of an Indian, Manteo, demonstrating that the colonists
had missionary intentions.

The conversation turned to George Bernard Shaw, with whom Paul
had visited in London. Shaw was known on one occasion to have come
out of his dining room praising his dinner, one of the best possible, he
felt.

He had eaten a dozen bananas.

Frank said when he was studying at the London School of
Economics he would sometimes visit the city docks and get bananas
that were about to be thrown away, which satisfied his hunger and his
budget.

As the dishes were being cleared away by Hubert, Paul told
another story about Professor Horace Williams, for whom he had
worked as an instructor in the University. He said Dr. Williams had
asked him to read the manuscript of his new book on philosophy, and
Paul found it needed much work. He avoided Dr. Williams for days.
One afternoon, however, the proud professor saw him on campus and
fell in step beside him. Paul, did you read my book? he asked.

Yes, I did, professor.

What did you think?

Paul could not afford at the time to lose his appointment. Well, I tell you, last night I dreamed my little house was on fire and I was concerned whether to save your manuscript or my new baby.

Dr. Williams stopped on the path, impressed. Paul, which did you do? he asked.

Paul said he was deep into the deception and decided he must continue. I saved your manuscript, professor.

They walked on a ways. Again the professor stopped. Looking off at the horizon line, he said, Paul, you did right.

Marian continued to adjust to the public exposure of her new life. Also, she adjusted as best she could to the secular nature of it. Public service seemed to replace worship and meditation much more than she as a rector's daughter was accustomed to.

Being in a university town was different, too, and that aspect was delightful. In Edenton young people went away, here young people arrived, a fall and spring harvest. Students who had never met were thrown together, held with gentle bonds. Often they were children of parents who had come here one generation ago.

Maturity came eagerly to meet young people here.

Discovery. Confidence. Yes, sometimes alienation.

For one hundred fifty years young people had come here.

No, for one hundred forty years. Young people from all parts of the South and country had brought gifts of themselves. The town hummed with the spirit of youth, and she marveled at it and reveled in it.

Frank's school notebooks were here in the house, his student writings. Here was his address as senior class president, the talk echoing the words of his cousin, Edward Kidder Graham, past university president. Frank had said, The cause of North Carolina is the cause of the University, and the cause of the University is the cause of North Carolina.

Frank's sister Anne came by. She and Henry -- Henry Shanks was a junior professor here in the History Department -- were leaving. Henry had an offer at Birmingham-Southern College and didn't think it proper to ask his brother-in-law to meet the offer. Indeed, he wondered if Frank could afford ever to advance him, a relative.

Betty Smith came by, waved. She was out walking with her daughters. She was one of the Carolina Playmakers and was writing a novel about growing up in Brooklyn.

New life, new work, new beginnings, and departures. It took nerve to be the first lady of a place as rigorous as this. Marian described her everyday life in letters to her father. Her letters also reveal her continued interest in his welfare, and that of her sisters.

Chapel Hill

402 E. Franklin St.

Sept. 7, 1932

Dear Father,

It is fine to have news from you and to know that you and Nanny are getting on comfortably. I hope the weather has improved as to temperature. Last week was so hot, we are appreciating these cooler days more than we would ordinarily.

Frank and I were in Hillsborough Saturday. He left me there and went on to Greensboro for a meeting and came back in the afternoon. We stayed with the family there for supper, and enjoyed our visit very much. They were all well and glad to be at home again after their pleasant month with you.

I will hand my transfer over to Mr. Lawrence today, and will ask him to write you. He uses the old, small chapel for services during the summer, but when the students return, will use the stone church. The Lawrences had us for supper the other night, all six of their children were there. They range in age from seven to twenty.

Frank was very pleased to have your letter yesterday. He seems to be kept busy every day seeing people about various and sundry things. He had hoped to catch up with back correspondence, but he doesn't seem to be able to get to it.

I hope you can get a good driver from Lloyd Burton's filling station. That will be convenient. I hope you and Nanny keep well. I will write to her soon and thank her for the pepper grinder she had sent me.

Love to all, Marian

Later that month she and her sister Eliza drove their father home from Chapel Hill. On September 26, she wrote him about their return trip, and about Frank's schedule.

Frank has to go to Raleigh tomorrow morning, Winston-Salem tomorrow night, and Raleigh again Wednesday. I'm afraid I won't be able to keep up with that rate of travelling. I wish he didn't have so many calls.

The following month she wrote her father that on Sunday she and Frank had visited Hillsborough for a family dinner; however, on October 14th she wrote less happy news:

I went over to Hillsborough yesterday afternoon and found sister sick in bed. She had been examined yesterday morning and the Doctors think that she is suffering from sinus congestion rather than from a tooth. She has felt the pain for the past two weeks, but has had fever this week and she gave up and went to bed after her company left. Dr. Amos would like her to keep quiet for some time and build up. She told me she had written to Nanny that she couldn't leave for Edenton tomorrow.

Mrs. Traylor wrote that she would like to go home about the fifteenth to get some work done. I believe it would be a good idea to let Nanny make arrangements. If she should have trouble I can run down and help out. If you stay in Edenton until after the Bishop's visit in December, do you plan to occupy the Rectory until after that time? Or do you prefer to pack up and make your permanent arrangements there, and move from the Rectory after Nov. 1? I can come down and help any time.

I am enclosing a Program of Founders Day -- Oct. 12. We had a very good day. We entertained the visitors, about thirty five, for lunch. With much love to you all.
> Devotedly
> Marian
> Today is Frank's birthday.
> Chapel Hill,
> October 14.

Marian wrote out a fact sheet about Frank and kept it close at hand, facts about his early years, before she met him. Forty years of his life she must find out about. For instance, he liked as a student to wrestle -- still did -- and was known for two holds taught him by Negro friends in boyhood, the ox dodge and the snake lock. He had been for a year the University's Dean of Students; she had heard he left the job as soon as he could, found he was not cut out for punishing people; he was also too eager to promote the Carolina spirit, had lectured the students about it, dismaying the veterans of World War I who had all the spirit they wanted. Students actually held a procession across campus, and at the old poplars buried a shoe box in which they said lay the damned Carolina spirit.

Here was listed the state's twenty-million-dollar bond campaign he had directed -- a fortune, which had built a major portion of the campus during the past administration, that of President Chase.

Here was his dear picture. A little boy, a young man. From his copy of the University's year book --

Now, how had he grown to be 5' 6'' in the description? That would make Frank only one inch shorter than she. His height was 5' 4'', she knew.

Here were items he had clipped from newspapers, carbon copies of letters he had written, put by in books, on shelves, here and there. One struck her as particularly revealing of Frank's personality, his willingness to engage in a fight, in the days before she knew him. He was willing even to help fight labor's causes at a time when the powerful industrialists virtually dictated jobs and lives of their employees, and affairs of the state.

Peter Hairston recalls on arriving in Chapel Hill as a freshman he found the family had sent a big trunk by rail, as they had for every Peter Hairston going to Chapel Hill from the Yadkin Valley for generations. The trunk, delivered to his dormitory, was left for him on the sidewalk. He was trying to figure out how to get it upstairs to his room when a little man came walking by and offered to help. A strong little man. The two of them got the trunk upstairs, all right. That night at the freshman reception, Peter again met his helper, the President of the University.

Indeed, that is one of many stories about Frank's helpfulness. Sometimes when visitors lost on the campus roads asked directions, Frank would surprise them by riding on their runningboard while directing them to their destination.

He would help in any misfortune, no matter its type. A man losing his hair might get a demonstration of Frank's recommended corrective: bend far over for a few minutes, so that circulation in the scalp will improve.

Losing a hat in a windstorm -- Frank Graham will run and get it. One man, knowing of Dr. Graham's athletic prowess, didn't bother to run after his own hat, blown off in a gust of wind; it would be a shame, he felt, to deprive Dr. Graham of the pleasure of running it down and returning it to him.

At a student dance, it was Professor Graham organizing the young men, making introductions so that there would be no wallflowers.

12. (Below) Frank Porter Graham (at right) as a UNC student, with friends. *North Carolina Collection, UNC Library*

11. Frank's senior class picture (above) from the 1909 *Yackety Yack*. *North Carolina Collection, UNC Library*

Chapel Hill, N. C.

Dec. 10, 1929

Dear Mr. Editor:

      In your issue of November 28 you correct a statement about me which appeared in your issue of August 29. In the former issue it was state that I had been present at a labor conference at Burnsville last summer. In the later issue, as a correction, you say that you have it from a friend of mine that I positively denied being at the conference. In explanation you say that the mistake was in the report on the conference made by a detective agency.

      I was not at the conference and was not expected to be. I was at the Columbia University Summer School at the time. But I do not wish to be put in the light of thinking that there would have been anything discreditable about my attending this conference which was held under the auspices of the state federations of labor of several Southern states. Since an issue has been made of my alleged attendance at this labor conference, let me say that I am perfectly willing to attend a labor conference, and when I do, my attendance will not be the subject for any apology on my part.

      A month after this conference was held, I did make a talk at the commencement exercises of the Southern Summer School for Women Workers in Industry at Burnsville, as reported in the newspapers. Several weeks ago I spoke at the reunion of the alumnae of the Bryn Mawr and the Southern Summer Schools for Women Workers in Industry at the conference on workers' education in Durham, as also reported at the time in one or more of the newspapers. I will attend, if practicable any other conference of workers or business men or church people, or teachers, or any other group of our people who invite me on the chance that I may be able to offer some small word of light or reason. Any so-called labor conference that I have attended, or any talk that I have made, has been open for public print, and any such meeting which I may attend or any talk which I may make will be open for public print.

      I have been talking to groups of North Carolina people for more than a dozen years, and on the issue of my right to talk to groups of workers I stand as one who knows what he owes himself as a citizen of the state.

Sincerely yours,

[Frank P. Graham]

13. Frank was often the target of attacks from the *Southern Textile Bulletin.* Here, while a professor of history, a letter of explanation -- and statement of principle in staunch support of the labor movement. *North Carolina Collection, UNC Library*

14. As a freshman, Hugh Morton called on Dr. Graham at home; Frank, noticing the student was nervous, invited him to come play a game of horseshoes. Horseshoes and wrestling were two of Dr. Frank's passions. This picture was made at that time. Frank won.
Photograph by Hugh Morton

15. Dr. Frank in his office in South Building on the UNC campus, keeping up with events by telegram. *Photograph by Hugh Morton*

CHAPTER FOUR

FRANK HAD NEVER administered much of anything, certainly not an institution. His two campaigns were to benefit libraries, and to benefit schools and colleges. Here he was for the first time with an office and secretary and myriad duties to perform. His office procedure was to give priority to the person who had waited longest to see him. Professors began to complain mightily about being kept waiting on the bench outside his private office door, while Frank spent half an hour with a student. Dean of Students Francis Bradshaw said a week for Frank wasn't complete without four or five freshmen coming through his office.

He would spend hours on a complaint others would dismiss in five minutes. Nell Pickard, a secretary elsewhere in South Building, says she heard that he even replied to circulars. He replied to letters punctually, usually drafting the lengthy, thorough replies in longhand before having his secretary type them. He also worked at home and while travelling, dealing with any individual's needs -- whoever needed him most -- setting the style for the University and leaving the day to day operation to his Executive Secretary, Bob House, who had served predecessor President Chase in that capacity, and Charlie Woollen, the Business Manager, along with their associates. Frank stayed in touch through the personal contacts, usually one student or teacher at a time.

He was the same person with everyone. No favorites. Well, in fact, all were favorites. He simply delighted in people.

One farm lady selling eggs told of stopping at a certain house, and she said a little man came to the door and invited her in. He bought a dozen eggs, then talked to her for the better part of an hour. She liked him well enough to ask at the next house who he was. President of the University! she cried out in astonishment. Why he's just as sweet and common as any man I ever met.

Since Frank dealt with matters brought to him, leaving the bulk of demands to others, he was able to tune the instrument, and to test it. If a student complained to him about a problem, by solving it he would establish a pattern for others. He might also solve a student's problem by admonishing him. Vermont Royster, later editor of the *Wall Street Journal*, says as a student he became furious over treatment his clothes received at the University laundry. He waited his turn, then stalked up to President Graham's desk and plopped down his socks.

Frank examined the socks, took money from his pocket and told him to buy a new pair, without so much as a glance of criticism.

Frank met controversies head-on. He was fearless and tough. A newspaperman wanted to know what opinions he had about Bertrand Russell, the controversial English philosopher, who had been invited to speak on campus. The reporter said there had been demands that Chapel Hill have no more of these so-called incarnations of Paganism. Did he as president of a state-supported institution defend an incarnation of Paganism?

Frank replied with a statement he often used, taken from his inaugural address: Without freedom there can be neither culture nor real democracy. Without freedom there can be no university.

Langston Hughes was brought to the campus by Professors Paul Green and Guy Johnson. This was about the date of Frank and Marian's marriage; indeed, they returned from their honeymoon to find stacks of mail, hundreds of letters in protest.

I. R. Tatum, retired textile manufacturer of Belmont, had on September 8th, 1932, called on Governor Gardner: In heaven's name, Governor, save our state from further predatory acts by these so-called modern educators against things of the spirit.

He brought with him a petition signed by 285 citizens. There were, Frank learned, other letters and petitions flooding the Governor's office as well.

Frank's secretary typed hundreds of letters in reply. And in all he respectfully, kindly, urged confidence in the University, in its wholesome spirit; in all replies he assumed the protesters were writing in good faith. He suggested this would be an opportunity to talk further together.

Professor Guy Johnson himself came to Frank, said he was the one who had invited Langston Hughes to the campus and was ready to take the heat from the protestors.

No, no, don't you do that, Frank told him, they'll demand your resignation. Better to let them attack me. They can't unseat me.

The two men talked further, mostly about what novelist and poet Langston Hughes had said in his lecture. An off-campus literary quarterly, *Contempo*, edited and printed in Milton Abernethy's Bookshop on Franklin Street, had published several of his poems in

16, 17. Milton "Ab" Abernethy with William Faulkner, *above*; Ab and his wife, Minna, operated the Intimate Bookshop and helped create the private magazine *Contempo*, which was often the source of trouble for Dr. Frank with his board of trustees. The appearance on campus of poet Langston Hughes, pictured below *(right)* with Tony Buttita, another founder of the shop and magazine, brought hundreds of letters of protest to the university administration. *North Carolina Collection, UNC Library, courtesy of Minna Abernethy and Tony Buttita.*

honor of his appearance, including *Christ in Alabama*, which declares

>   Christ is a nigger, Beaten and Black - O, bare your back
> and ends with
>   Most Holy bastard of the bleeding mouth:
>   nigger Christ
>   on the cross of the South.

Frank urged his hundreds of friends to write the Governor, affirming faith in the health of the University and the importance of freedom, but to do so in such a way that each one spoke his or her own thoughts; he was careful to avoid appearance of orchestrating a campaign. And when he was told that Florida State had a damning file on one orchestrator of the attack, a man who had attacked their college's freedom, Frank refused to accept the material from them, and to one who wrote suggesting he strike back hard, he replied that the intellectual freedom of this University is going to be preserved with goodwill.

When critics demanded he get rid of the small Communist cell among Chapel Hill students, he replied that in a student body of thousands he would much rather have a handful of Communists out in the open and in the sunlight where they can be confronted in argument. I think democracy and freedom can take care of themselves, he said.

When adversaries found out that faculty member E. E. Erickson had eaten dinner in Durham in the hotel suite of a Negro, James Ford, who was running as Vice President on the Communist Party ticket, Frank dealt calmly with the demands which arose that the professor be dismissed. Dr. Roy W. McKnight of Charlotte declared such an act violated the sensibilities and social traditions of thousands of university alumni and taxpayers, and demanded that the university administration start a house cleaning. Years later Frank reported on the affair:

> Well, one of my dear friends, who was a member of the Board of Trustees, came across the state to visit me. And if I may -- of course your memory isn't always absolutely accurate, but as I recall the conversation in the privacy of our office, he said to me, Now I have been on your side in many of these battles and I think I've got to leave you on this one.
> And he said, I'll frankly say to you -- maybe it's my prejudice. If this man had been a Negro and that was all, I could take it, he said. If he had been possibly just a Communist, I may have swallowed hard and taken that. But now here he's both and I just think that's the limit for us and it's going to be very

damaging to the university and therefore I think we've got to get rid of that man.

And we talked. This man was very sincere. A wonderful man, by the way. One of our finest trustees.

I said, Now let's analyze this. What is the charge against this man? If you analyze it to its basic elements, it is that he ate with another human being, and I don't think we can dismiss a man from the University because he ate with another human being. Whatever you may think about other human beings, you know. One of the charges against Jesus was that he ate with disreputable people, publicans and sinners. And here our professor was eating with a Negro Communist who is running for vice president. But actually what is it that he did? He ate with another human being.

I didn't have any bravado about what I was going to do. I just simply said I was going to stand by him. The first issue, I thought, would be my tenure rather than his. Well, that trustee stayed here overnight, felt the temper of this community. Of course, telephone calls were coming in from everywhere in protest.

And he thought the thing through and he said, Well, we're going to be in your corner on this issue. We know that you are against totalitarianism in any form, that you're for freedom. And really, real freedom is at stake here, and I'm going to be on the side of the university in this case.

To all who wrote him, whether in perplexity, in anger, or in bitterness, Graham replied in detail, always assuming the sincerity and intelligence of the writer, always believing that if the critic could visit Chapel Hill he would see the wholesome spirit of the University, always confident that if he and the critic could only talk together they would find much to agree upon.

When the volume of critical mail that came in daily convinced the administrations in South Building that the University was in jeopardy, Graham asked his friends to write the Governor and to urge others to do so. He asked that they give their impressions of the moral, intellectual, and spiritual life of the University.

With sweet reasonableness he met the criticisms, always with respect for the other's argument, and he held safe the fortress.

Later, when a member of the board decided to resign because a socialist, an English teacher, was on the faculty, Graham wrote the trustee that the faculty by and large is a very conservative body of men and the professor has a right to speak his political and economic views.

In a letter to Mrs. Jessie Kenan Wise, December 8, 1932, he wrote:

> I know I am often subject to misunderstanding and even
> misrepresentations, but I owe it to the great tradition of this
> University to take the blows as they come and as long as it is
> my responsibility to hold fast to those principles which are the
> very intellectual and spiritual stuff of her history and her life.

One student complained because he was being denied admission to
medical school because he was a Jew.

In this day of Hitler and the Nazi claim of Aryan superiority, Frank
was incensed, and at once was vigorously in action. He found that the
student, from out of state originally, had married a Durham resident and
lay claim to being an in-state applicant, that he qualified for admission
and had repeatedly pressed his claim on Dean Manning, even hiring a
Durham attorney, Reuben Oscar Everett. Bob House had reviewed the
application and had urged Dean Manning to approve it, but, having
admitted four Jewish students for the new class, which was the quota he
had assigned for a class of forty, he would not admit a fifth.

Frank invited Dean Manning, a friend for years, to meet with him.
Dean since 1905, Manning had only two passions, caring for his family
and caring for his medical school. It was a two-year school, one of a
handful of that limited type, and its graduates therefore had to be placed
at the major medical schools to complete their training, and for years he
had had a hell of a time placing the Jewish boys simply because the
large schools had quotas.

For instance, Loyola in Chicago, had a quota, Harvard had a quota,
Johns Hopkins Medical School had a quota, Yale had a quota set and
enforced by Dean Wilton Charles Winternitz, born Jewish. He accepted
five Jews in every class of fifty, basing his quota on the percentage of
Jews in the total population, which he believed to be considerably less
than 10 percent. He also set a quota for Catholics at 10 percent.

Manning spent much of each year's time trying to place his forty
upperclassmen in the best medical schools; the reputation of his
program rested on his placing them well, and he was proud of his
record: Harvard, New York University, Johns Hopkins, the University
of Pennsylvania, Rush Memorial College, the University of Maryland,
most of which had Jewish quotas, and most all of which were swamped
under applications from Jews.

He argued his small school could not ignore the policy of the
medical profession nationally.

Frank knew Manning and his wife and three sons. He knew his
brothers, one of whom had been dean of the law school. He hated to

overrule his dean but, as he had been known to say, he knew of no scripture establishing the divine right of deans. This boy's rejection was, pure and simple, a case of institutional unfairness, which he could not tolerate. His meeting with Dean Manning was friendly, the two men disagreed, and the result was Dean Manning stepping down as Dean, returning to full-time teaching.

The Manning-Graham episode was reported in newspapers within and outside the state. Most editorials favored Frank's action.

By no means was all praise, however. The medical world was incensed to have its prerogatives and privacy violated, and more than a few influential state citizens joined the ranks of Graham's critics.

Arnold King recalls sitting in Frank's office not long after William MacNider's appointment as Dean of Medicine. The phone rang, and the raspy, loud voice of the new Dean of Medicine, Dr. MacNider, was heard. Frank, I'm tired of being a God damned dean, MacNider told him. I want out.

Oh no, don't resign, Frank said.

Frank, I want to return to my research.

I'll think of some better solution than --

All these damn papers, schedules --

I'll send you an assistant dean first thing tomorrow.

Patiently Frank talked MacNider into calmer waters. That achieved, at once he phoned Dr. Reece Berryhill, Director of the Infirmary, and told him to report to MacNider tomorrow morning at 8:30, to be his assistant.

Berryhill protested.

Take a title, Frank told him.

Berryhill didn't want to be an assistant to anybody. There was nobody to run the infirmary, he said.

There's Ed Hedgepeth, Frank told him. He's been there for years. He's as good a doctor as you are. I'm putting him in charge there, and you are now Assistant Dean of Medicine.

Right there, Arnold King recalls, Frank settled the whole question: that's how he operated.

Frank moved expeditiously, one might even say impetuously in hiring new professors, too. In the early thirties he began going to Washington to talk to Frances Perkins, President Roosevelt's Secretary of Labor, who came to respect his views on improving the situation of workers, white and black, in the South, and to Eleanor Roosevelt and other New Deal Democrats, and he was likely to hire somebody along the way, in a train station or on a moving train, or wherever. Bob House would be left with the job of fitting the hired person in. House would dutifully telephone the chairman of the appropriate department and say something to the effect, Dr. Kattsoff, you might not have known about this, and I might not have known about this and you might not like this and I might not like this, but Frank has hired a new professor for your department, a Helmut Kuhn; this one, a refugee from Nazi Germany, he met last night on the train.

Now and then the arrangement did not work out. A new Professor of Anthropology was not at all welcomed by Howard Odum, Guy Johnson, Rupert Vance and their colleagues and was excluded. The newcomer posted his course offerings on trees, and met classes for at least one academic semester. He also gave grades, but students noticed these were not recorded on their reports or transcripts. Their appeals for correction left them with a peculiar situation, the Registrar explaining the courses had never been approved. Eventually, the students were given credit by administration decree.

Phillips Russell, the biographer, was another one hired while travelling. Russell had served as one of the few reporters hired by an English newspaper and among his best selling books were biographies of Franklin, Emerson and John Paul Jones. Also, his great aunt was Cornelia Phillips Spencer, the heroine of the Civil War period. Frank liked him and hired him to teach writing.

Phillips was not welcomed by the English Department. In journalism he taught the first year without a contract, or even a letter, and assumed the first year was the whole of his employment. The summer recess he spent in New York City, writing, and in the fall decided he would try to get Frank to put him back on. He was entering onto the campus when he was hailed by a professor who told him he was supposed to be down at the gym registering students.

Phillips went at once to the gym, registered students, met his classes that term, and subsequently taught at Chapel Hill until age seventy, without a contract or even a letter hiring him.

Frank not only hired professors, sometimes he fired them. One day Frank and Arnold King walked to the athletic fields and came upon the football practice just as the new football coach, Chuck Collins, let out a stream of profanity. Frank said it was worse than he had heard even in the Marines. Arnold, did you hear that? That's got to stop, he said.

The coach was a native of the state and had been one of the teammates of the famed ''Four Horsemen'' under Knute Rockne at Notre Dame. At Chapel Hill, he had a winning record, had proved effective since 1926 in picking excellent players, most all of them Catholic students from the Northeast who had failed to make the Notre Dame pick. Chuck Collins was a favorite of the alumni and students.

Soon, however, in 1933, Frank had him replaced, and weathered the storms of indignation. Freedom of speech did not, obviously, extend into an area Collins had occupied.

Frank's most complicated, hot and troublesome administrative problem came early in his term as President. In November, 1930, the Brookings Institution made a report on state government reorganization, advising the Governor to study, as an economy measure, the consolidation of the three institutions, the University of North Carolina, North Carolina State College of Agriculture and Engineering, and the North Carolina College for Women. State was in Raleigh, some thirty miles to the East, and the Woman's College was in Greensboro, about fifty miles northwest of Chapel Hill. At once Governor Gardner saw this as a way to save money, a mighty appeal in the days of the Great Depression, and he proceeded without further study to consolidate.

Frank was skeptical. Each of the three had its President and administration, its own set of departments and faculties, own trustees, and thousands of proud and powerful alumni. Then too, the two younger institutions had experience largely in vocational education, one training men, the other women.

In March, 1931, a bill made its way through the General Assembly specifying that a commission be appointed to study and plan for the consolidation. Frank kept out of the limelight while advising caution. When the commissioners recommended that the Engineering School be transferred from State to Chapel Hill, he managed to be quiet, as the cry of outrage from State alumni awoke the state.

Frank earnestly had asked the trustees not to appoint him Chancellor in charge of this three-headed institution, the other two presidents didn't want a Chapel Hill leader, either. No matter what he preferred, he was selected.

Josephus Daniels, publisher of the *News and Observer* in Raleigh, was one who came to the conclusion that title Chancellor was unsuitable, arguing that Frank was too down-to-earth to have a foreign title, so Frank became President of the three institutions, and the executives of the campuses were made vice-presidents.

The stated purpose of the consolidation was to eliminate waste and duplication. Not much waste was likely to be found. The state appropriations for the three had in the last year or two, during the Depression, dropped from $894,000 to $426,000 for the University, $451,000 to $205,000 for State College, and $465,000 to $200,000 for the Women's College.

This left little room for financial maneuvers, or for placating faculty members by means of bonuses. Nor was there hope in the consolidation process of pleasing most alumni, numbering 42,167 men and women alive at this time.

Optimistically, Frank described his task of bringing union and economy to the three institutions as being a great American adventure. It was to be his, and his alone, to negotiate.

One thrust of the adventure was for Frank to meet the key faculty and administration leaders of State and the Woman's College and make friends, then reach the hard decisions. After considering what each campus might best become, how each could serve from its own place and state of maturity, he led the trustees to take from Chapel Hill its respected program in engineering and gave it to State College. A mighty howl of protest went up from alumni, faculty, current students; also, from powerful banker, John Sprunt Hill, an alumnus and trustee, who declared open war on Frank Graham.

From State College, Frank took the program in commerce and from the Women's College that in library science, which he gave to Chapel Hill.

The Women's College received from Chapel Hill elementary education. Further, he gave them a monopoly on first- and second-year women's enrollment for the three campuses. He added departments of art, classical civilization, and philosophy.

Since only Chapel Hill at that time had a doctoral-level faculty, he decreed that granting of doctoral degrees would be reserved for that campus.

In 1934 he accepted resignations of the chief officers at State and the Woman's College, replaced them with men of his choosing. Bob House was to be the administrator of the Chapel Hill campus. He had these three administrative Deans report to him personally, or on business matters to the financial vice-president. Frank kept his office in South Building, as before, on the Chapel Hill campus. For Greensboro he chose a teacher of twenty-three years, for State a teacher of twenty-four years. None of the three had a doctorate, none was as avid about social change as Frank.

He hired no new staff. He created no bureaucracy. It was done expeditiously, it was fair. And he ended up with three distinct, unique campuses, one modeled on engineering schools such as MIT, one modeled on women's colleges such as Wellesley, and one modeled on his concept of what an American state university should be. All three, of course, had North Carolina accents.

Frank, in record time, had improved administration, faculty and curriculum at all three campuses, had placated most opponents, and, to the consternation of his few trustee enemies, emerged stronger than ever before.

On all three campuses professors looked at him with awe. How does one deal with such a man -- appoint a faculty committee, thank them for their conclusions, reject them by means of appointing another committee, or two, until he got the recommendations he wanted, yet nobody was angry with Dr. Frank.

How could one make a coherent whole of his disparate qualities: he was a philosophical and rhetorical democrat but often served as an authoritarian actor, explaining all the while that he was compelled to do what he did by historical forces.

During all this, there were speeches to make. Seemed as if Frank would not turn down an invitation, either to meet with some group or other, or to address them. Since Frank did not drive, Marian sometimes drove him. This gave her the chance to be with him for an uninterrupted session, but often as not he would use part of the travel time to sleep. Charlie Jones, his pastor, would drive him on occasions. Charlie drove him once to Sweetbriar College, where Frank was to be given a reception. Many people, noticing he had nothing to drink, asked him what he wanted. Punch?

No, nothing, Frank told them.

Then tea?

No.

Coffee?

No.

Coca-Cola?

Well... no.

Finally, to avoid any displeasure, he agreed to drink something. A glass of buttermilk. Alarm set in. Somebody quickly hurried to find the chosen drink for the honored guest.

Members of the faculty were sometimes asked to drive Frank, especially those who were discussing leaving for a higher-paying position. And, of course, more often than not there was Hubert Robinson.

Should Frank find he had more engagements than he could satisfy, he would ask others to cover for him. Bob House might get a call from Asheville, for example, where the night before Frank had spoken. He and Marian were still there. He had agreed to hold a morning session for a Negro group, and he had agreed to speak at five at Greensboro at a women's club meeting and at eight at the Statesville Library. Could Bob get the Greensboro talk for him?

An hour later Frank might phone again.

Bob, I find I can get to Greensboro and had better do that one. Can you do Statesville?

Bob would go to Statesville, and he would be successful, too, having an informal speaking style. He had shepherded the men's Bible class at the University Methodist Church every Sunday, and he had substituted for Frank many times on campus and off. As he knew, chances were Frank would arrive after all. About half an hour into Bob's talk, Frank would enter the room.

The audience would be delighted. With pleasure they would welcome him.

Bob would take his seat and let the master talk. Never heard better. A talk Frank had given before, but one never tired of hearing him. Seemed to be out of a great trove, a bin of truths most everybody could accept, freedom and the founding fathers and the dignity of the University, which was a light for the state, the South, the nation.

Nobody was likely to be offended with Frank's talks, either, for his views were all out of what might be called an American Bible, which borrowed from both the New Testament and from history.

I think that here in the South where human slavery made one of its last stands in the modern world and industrialism is making fresh beginnings, we have the great opportunity to build a civilization that perhaps could be nobler in its human relations -- both interracial and industrial and prophetically international -- than that of any people in the Union or on the earth. And that's my vision, that's my hope for the South -- that it will again become creatively and prophetically the leader of America and a leader in the world. Maybe that's the generation that's to come after us.

From the history of our country, I will mention a few Southerners:

George Washington, father of the country.

Thomas Jefferson, author of the universal declaration of human rights in the Declaration of Independence. James Madison, who framed the Constitution.

John Marshall, who made in Marbury vs. Madison the great decision, that the United States Supreme Court is ultimately the law of the land.

Andrew Jackson, source of the great Jacksonian Democracy.

After the talk there would be half an hour to visit with people who had attended. Friends marveled to watch Frank, who knew ever so many of the people present, and was able to recall in detail previous meetings, to ask if their mother's health had improved, or whatever, and to seek out those he did not know and make them friends, too.

Mrs. Ione Markham Linker worked in South Building in the 1930's, and she remembers Frank and Marian well. She recalls that Marian was gracious, lovely, private. She cared for Dr. Graham but didn't rule him, she says, and he certainly needed caring for.

Everybody liked Dr. Graham, she says, including those who didn't agree with him on his politics. Very dedicated man. Good man. Thoughtful of others. He was a good person to work for, but a difficult person, for he was in and out of the office. He would run around and talk with different people and try to get it arranged -- whatever the matter was. He did have a way of getting things done. Good politician.

Very much a normal human being, she says. Some human frailties and great ideals. No, she never knew him to be angry. Frustrated, yes, but not angry or irritated.

Marian would take him hot chocolate and a cookie each afternoon. On the way to his office she could walk through the arboretum where often Dr. Coker was to be found, he and one or two students there, planting. He taught mornings and worked in the afternoons. Well, he worked in the early morning, too, sometimes, Hubert Robinson had told her. Marian wasn't one for getting out of the house early in the morning, herself, and had to trust to others. Early morning was her own very private time.

Coker would stop whatever he was doing to talk to her. The two would discuss the plants, using Latin names. As she explained to him, her father had taught her gardening and had used the Latin names.

She enjoyed taking the snack to Frank, but after a year he asked her not to continue.

Why not? she inquired, astonished.

Because I've come to look forward to it so, he told her.

Now what was to be made of that? she wondered.

Well, so have I, she told him, and continued.

Money, or rather the lack of it was a lingering problem. Frank was once heard to say, analyzing finances within the University: They talk about imperialism; there is no imperialism equal to academic imperialism at budget time.

Well, his own finances were dire, as Marian realized, as everybody who worked with him knew. He refused to allow the trustees to raise his salary. If he had any money with him, he would give it away to the poor, or to children. The Board of Trustees had to pass a special ruling depriving the President of the right to lend money to students. They might well have forbidden him to bail out students, yes, and others from jail. As the end of the year approached, Frank and Marian would determine how much they could give away to various and sundry groups. Each year the list of Frank's memberships lengthened, from fifty to one hundred to one hundred fifty. To each he wanted to give something, if only five or ten dollars. Among his memberships were some of Eleanor Roosevelt's projects, and these were so unpopular that he believed he must give more. Those dealing with sharecroppers and blacks always got the lion's share.

His salary seemed to Marian to decrease every year. It was $10,000 annually at the start, plus the house and servants' salaries and the car. He was to pay his own expenses for entertainment.

By the third year he was down to $6,200.

He explained that everybody had taken cuts. That was so, but the loss continued to be so even after he had obtained small raises for the faculty and had been given two other colleges to administer as part of the consolidated university.

All for $6,200 a year.

Easier to lobby for faculty raises if I exclude myself, he contended.

Entertaining university guests took up much of their income. Chapel Hill had an inn, but that cost money, too. In any case, Frank preferred to use the President's house. One guest due to arrive was Eleanor Roosevelt.

Marian must bring this dilapidated, great house up to clean and prime condition for the wife of the President of the United States. Hubert could be the butler, Alice could be the cook. Marian supposed she could, and would gladly, be the scullery maid.

Professor Horace Williams saw Marian working in her garden. He doffed his hat, stood stolidly, solidly on the sidewalk. He said, I see in the student newspaper, Mrs. Graham, that Professor Henderson is the only man in the South who understands Einstein's theory. And he is the official biographer of George Bernard Shaw, and is a teacher, and is a surveyor. In all he is thirteen things, or so the student newspaper has reported. Now God himself is only three.

He stood there in the sun for a moment longer, then smiled briefly and went on along the street.

Dr. Drane's health and mental abilities were fading. Marian worried about him and did what he could to see that he was properly cared for in Edenton. Whenever he visited Chapel Hill, she was able to tend to him herself.

Hello, Dr. Drane, Gladys Coates spoke to him one morning, meeting him on his return from the post office. Dr. Drane in retirement was always looking for more mail.

Do you say hello? he asked critically.

I do, but if you object, I won't.

Next person they passed, she said hello.

There you go again, he told her.

Well, Dr. Drane, I have my hello friends and my non-hello friends. I promise never to say hello to you.

He smiled, pleased with that.

Then he began to talk to her. I don't understand the doctor, he said. He doesn't like the good things of life, a glass of wine, doesn't care about his food. We had Sillybub and Sherry jelly and he wouldn't eat them once he found out they had alcohol in them. He said he wouldn't break the law.

They got to Marian's house. He said come on in, I want you to sign my book. Indoors he brought out a book and Gladys signed it.

He said, Is that the way you sign your name?

I'm afraid it is, Dr. Drane. What's wrong?

The loop should go below the line, he said.

Dr. Drane, you are absolutely right, Gladys said. I know you are right.

Dr. Drane would say to Marian, I'm losing my mind.

Marian would say, Papa, you know you wouldn't want anybody to say that about you, and you mustn't say it, either.

Sometimes she would need to go look for him, or send Hubert Robinson to find him. Forgetting the way home, he would be waiting, sitting on a wall. On one occasion, he was sitting on a neighbor's porch, believing that to be home.

He became caustic with Frank, and even with Marian in these latter years.

I'm not afraid of death, he would say. You afraid of death, Frank? What will happen to all your societies? he would ask.

He admitted being proud of his son-in-law's achievements and fame, and regaled acquaintances in Edenton with stories about him and Marian, but he rarely stopped trying to improve him. Improvement to Dr. Drane meant coming into partnership with God and one's own beautiful life, being much more content with oneself and the world than Frank seemed to be. An Episcopalian sought reasons to be satisfied; the

Calvinist sought reasons to be dissatisfied. That at least was one opinion he offered Frank, who appeared to be helpless to reply, except to retreat to the defense he so often used when a reply seemed to be argumentative, which was that he wished he had made lists of all his failures in his life.

That argument amused Dr. Drane, who said it confirmed what he was talking about. Episcopalians have arrived and are more likely to be satisfied than are Presbyterians. They might even list their achievements.

He was concerned about Marian and tried to pry into her private life. As to attending two churches, she admitted she had found it difficult at first to walk along Franklin Street on Sunday morning with Frank, only to leave him as they reached the Chapel of the Cross, where she walked to the left to join her friends worshipping there, while he crossed the street to the Presbyterian Church, where he served as elder. And Lent, she had not known how to abide the university activities during Lent. And why didn't Frank come home on weekends and stay?

Old Dr. Drane would bow his head in sympathy.

His last will and testament he discussed with her. He had only a fair amount of money, but he did have the cottage at Nags Head. All his children loved it, but there was an established practice to give a house to one's wife or, lacking a wife, to the daughter who had served him best, and who had served him last. Even though Marian had left him, marrying Frank, he was leaving her what he highly valued, the cottage. However, he was bound to leave part of his estate to the Episcopal Church, Diocese of East Carolina, so he would in fact leave it to the church, with her having a lifetime tenancy.

It appeared she wasn't likely to have children, anyway. He thought it a father's right to inquire. It was not too late, of course. Did she want children?

Yes. And Frank does, too, she said. Frank had pleased her by saying he wanted a child more than anything in the world, but in a sense he slightly displeased her by designating a son, which she found thoughtless. But an accident as a boy -- he explained to me before we married that he might be infertile, she said.

Do any of Frank Graham's brothers and sisters have children?

One son to a sister, Ann Shanks.

One child for how many brothers and sisters?

There are nine in the family.

See there! See there! he cried.

Marian and Frank were visiting relatives in Monroe. He settled himself down at the living room desk to write, although he was dressed only in his pajamas. Marian looked up, said, Frank, you don't have on enough clothes.

With that, he put his hat on his head, smiled at her, and continued his writing.

Frank was a friendly, conversational storyteller; he enjoyed his stories, and if anybody was made fun of in them, it would be Frank.

One battery of stories had to do with his older brother, Archie Graham, who had in youth been a professional baseball player, ascending even to a brief stint in the major league; this was before Archie left the sport to become an eye specialist. It was to Archie Frank had gone when his eyesight failed him. Back in 1916 he had taken a summer job in a library in New York City, following his MA work at Columbia, and his vision blurred. He visited Archie in Minnesota. Archie took all reading material away and put Frank outdoors at a logging camp on Sturgeon Lake.

Walking through the snow-white countryside, Frank ventured onto the frozen lake only to fall through a thin place, an air hole. His overcoat spread as he went down, which helped him in his struggle to get onto the ice surface. Once there he crawled, then hobbled to the camp where he was allowed to warm slowly, very slowly. One lumberjack told the other men, Here I've been in the camp for months and taken no bath yet, and our visitor goes and takes a bath the second day he's here!

Frank would admit his efforts to get into the Army, Navy or the Marine Corps were rejected by all three branches because of his poor vision; he could read only the largest letters on the chart. And because of his 5' 4'' height and light weight.

Even once he got into the Marines, following repeated tries, an officer receiving a new shipment of men told his sergeant to get rid of the runt. The sergeant had known Frank at Chapel Hill and told his commander Frank could wrestle most anybody and suggested the officer take him on. The officer decided not to wrestle, but to let the little man remain. Frank never got out of the country. He remarked that George Washington reached the height of his career when he crossed the Delaware River and Robert E. Lee when he crossed the Potomac. Well, during the great World War, I had the honor to cross both those rivers.

In talking about his days as enlisted man and officer in the Marines, Frank sometimes told of his going up in a Marine observation balloon and jumping out in a parachute. The jump was highly successful, but the landing -- well, he had no idea how to spill the air out of the canopy, and the strong breeze took him bouncing on a tour of a rocky, brush-covered landscape, depositing him -- one of the Marine's first parachutists -- up against a farmer's woodpile.

He had stories about football, upsetting ones for a little man, tough as he was, and baseball, his favorite sport -- unless wrestling was. Yes, even cheerleading, recalling one game in which Chapel Hill trailed by thirty-three to six, with three minutes left to play, and Frank jumped up and called for greater team support. We can still win! he shouted.

Some of the stories were about labor unions, textile strikes, and ensuing dangers. He said Communists in the North had in 1929 formed the National Textile Workers Union, and at once made plans to organize the South. North Carolina, the chief textile state, was chosen, and the first mill was to be the Loray Mill in Gaston County, near Charlotte. There were ninety-nine mills in that county, and Loray was a key one. Owned by Rhode Island interests, it was operated without concern for its workers or the community. Its superintendent had maintained the level of production while reducing the work force from 3,500 to 2,200, and decreasing pay from an average of twenty dollars a week to fifteen, and even less.

A Communist, Fred Beal, was sent in to organize the mill, a strike was called, and owners and management of other mills in North Carolina went into shock. Once they found out Beal was a Communist, they attacked on that score, and the Communists sent in more Northerners and even announced this was the start of a national unionization of Southern textile workers. Loray management began hiring new workers, strikers returned to work, the strike collapsed, but on the night of June 1, five people -- one of them the chief of police -- were shot, and a crowd of two thousand gathered and by dawn the police proceeded to arrest seventy strikers. The chief died the next day, the Communists were blamed, and Beal and fourteen others were indicted for murder.

And into this maelstrom came Frank, at that time a professor of history at Chapel Hill, helping to secure North Carolina lawyers to defend the accused, even though the Communists among them insisted on New York lawyers. Frank also sent a telegram for publication in the *News and Observer*, July 28, 1929, stressing the obligation to afford a fair trial. Nobody had any idea who had shot the chief of police. Gastonia citizens began to admit he might have been shot accidentally by one of his deputies. In any event, the jury found all the people arrested guilty. Three received five to fifteen years and Beal and the others twenty years.

18. Dr. Frank in the late 1940's. *Southern Historical Collection, UNC Library*

Tough days, rough days. Rougher than any days in the Marines, Frank decided. Nothing amusing about that story. Frank was not one to hold long to the hem of failures, however, unless humor was, indeed, present. We were playing Lafayette, he told Marian and several friends.

Ninth inning, two outs. Three men on base and the score tied. Our last chance up. And Coach Floyd Simmons, to the consternation of the whole team, and the whole student body, chose me to be pinch hitter. You know, I could catch pretty well in the outfield, steal bases and so on, but wasn't much of a hitter.

Choosing me to be pinch hitter was a great mystery.

He put his arm around me as I walked up to the plate, and he said, little one, you understand the situation? Score tied, two out, three men on base.

I said I understood.

He said -- and I didn't tell this for twenty years -- he said, Whatever you do, *don't hit at the ball.*

I took my place at the plate, my baggy pants scarcely revealing where my knees were; the pitcher threw four straight balls and we won the game.

19. Dr. Frank in his academic gowns.   *Photograph by Hugh Morton*

20. Frank, Eleanor Roosevelt and Lou Harris, president of the campus student political organization which invited Mrs. Roosevelt to speak. *Photograph by Hugh Morton.*

1st Page of Will of

Robt. B. Drane, D. D.

R. B. D., Edenton, N. C.

Being now of sound mind, mindful of the uncertainties of
this life, I, Robert Brent Drane, do make, publish and declare
this my last Will and Testament, hereby revoking and cancelling
all other Wills heretofore made by me.

First: I acknowledge the Goodness of GOD all my life long,
which has given me anything to bequeath.

I will that all my just debts be paid including a fair
compensation to the Executors of my Will; and as such Executors
I name my sons, Brent Skinner Drane and Frederick Blount Drane.

Sensible of the kindness of the Church in retiring me on a
Pension, and also, because of my desire that the ministrations
of our Church should be maintained in Dare County, N. C., I give
my Nags Head Cottage and its land to the Trustees of the Dioces
of East Carolina, of the Protestant Episcopal Church, this gift
to take effect upon the death of my Daughter Marian, wife of
Frank P. Graham, during whose natural life the title to this
property shall be vested in her the said Marian. I will that One
Hundred Dollars be paid to the vestry of St. Paul's Church for
care of Drane graves in St. Paul's Church yard, Edenton, N. C.

I will that my manuscript sermons be destroyed.

I will the the residue of my Estate, Real and Personal be
divided equally among my Children and my sister-in-law;
namely: Brent Skinner Drane, Eliza Harwood Webb, Robert Drane,
Katharine Parker Perry, and Marian Graham and Frederick Blount
Drane and sister-in-law Marian Fiske Skinner for and during her
natural life, and at her death to be divided among my surviving
children. In the event that any of my children above named
should be dead without having children, then their share of the

Estate shall be divided among my other surviving children.

I authorize my Executors, in their discretion to sell any of my property and to execute and deliver warrant deeds therefor.

My body I wish to be buried in St. Paul's Church yard, Edenton, N. C., if practicable, by the side, South of my dear Wife's grave, and my grave to be marked by a stone like that at her grave.

In testimony whereof, I have hereto set my hand and seal to this my Last Will and Testament on two sheets of paper, this being the second and last sheet, both being numbered and initialed by me this 28th day of October A.D. 1936, at Monroe, N. C.

Signed, ROB'T B. DRANE (Seal)

22. The Last Will and Testament of the Rev. Robert B. Drane, father of Marian Drane Graham, in which he wills that his sermons be burned and that Marian be given the use of the Nags Head cottage for her lifetime. *Southern Historical Collection, UNC Library*

CHAPTER FIVE

MRS. ROOSEVELT -- ELEANOR -- was to arrive by train, and Frank suggested that arrangements be made for an engine and special car to use the temporary service tracks that years ago had been built for bringing building supplies onto the campus. This had been during the Chase administration when new buildings were being built in the south quad, result of the $20,000,000 bond issue that Frank had campaigned for, and won. The train tracks were temporary and ran from the village of Carrboro, the train's terminal, eastward along Cameron Avenue and onto the campus.

Incidentally, most of this building program had been accomplished at a time of runaway prices, an economic mountain that preceded a collapse in the early 1920's. At the collapse, local prices for sugar dropped from 40 cents to 5 cents, cotton from 50 cents to 10 cents a pound. Students had successively been buffetted by inflation, then came this depression of the early 1920's. The state's economy regained strength, was at an economic mountain peak in the late 1920s, then it crumpled in the fall and winter of 1929 to the worst trough of all, the Great Depression, which grew worse in the early 1930s. Rising and falling appeared to be endemic to the North Carolina economy and were sledge hammers striking the University students. They received double blows since inflation was as serious as depression. Many had to drop out.

The twin railroad tracks were inherited from one of the booms of 1920, and during the bust soon thereafter lay in weeds, dormant. Some use occurred during the boom of 1925-1929, and the tracks rusted from the fall of 1929 on. Frank, however, had plans to start building again, to start now, even now, and the lady arriving was one means of getting the money from the Federal Government. He had the tracks repaired.

The students turned out to welcome the First Lady. The band played, the train backed onto the campus, and Eleanor Roosevelt, Frank, Bob House and Marian stood on the platform waving, a west-borne wind swirling the engine's smoke and hot embers dangerously close to them. Eleanor and Frank, he one of the few Southerners popular with New Deal people, standing side by side.

Eleanor Roosevelt stayed at Marian and Frank's, had the only guest room Marian had been able to furnish with a substantial suite of furniture. There were plenty of flowers; they decked the large living room, the dining room, the stairway landing and Mrs. Roosevelt's room, and because it was such a special occasion for her and Frank, Marian put small bouquets in their own bedroom, one on each side of the double bed.

One niece recalls as a child being taken by her mother to Aunt Marian's great house to meet the First Lady. Her aunt and uncle and Mrs. Roosevelt, along with a few others, formed a receiving line in the garden. They were standing alongside big bushes, and she and other children realized they could be close to the great woman, the First Lady, by creeping along the other side of these to the magic place, hiding about three feet from her. All would have been secret, except the children could not keep from tittering.

What's this, what this? Eleanor would say, swinging around.

The game was up when one of the children decided to ask Aunt Marian if they could go to the movie and stay out late. Their little heads poked out of the bushes.

Of course you may, she said.

What's this, what's this? Eleanor said.

The main purpose of the visit pertained to programs for human welfare that Eleanor Roosevelt championed, which Frank had supported all along. A second purpose was to let her see the University and become its friend, to become an ambassador for the University within the White House. A third was to hold a fundraising ball for President Roosevelt's polio research campaign, his national effort to find a cure for a disease which had afflicted him with paralysis. Marian and Frank escorted Mrs. Roosevelt to the money-raising ball, only to find at the door that Frank had no money, not a cent, not even for admission.

Mrs. Roosevelt paid.

Mrs. Roosevelt was highly controversial, especially in the South. She had proposed changing the racial and economic balances. She and Frank became soulmates. She was tough enough to take the criticism hurled at her, and so was he. She did very much like Frank Graham's manner, dealing with controversy by avoiding inflaming it any further; she was intrigued by this, but she was by nature more caustic. While visiting Duke University with Frank, she asked an official where the beautiful black hornblende gneiss rock had been quarried, the stone used to make all Duke's campus buildings.

It was not expected that she would interest herself in such working class matters. The officials didn't know.

Don't know where your own stone comes from, she replied, admonishing them.

Someone thought to ask if she knew Doris Duke, the young heiress.

Indeed I do, she's on two of my committees, Mrs. Roosevelt replied. It's amazing what that young lady doesn't know. She is deprived.

While Frank left friendship in his wake, Mrs. Roosevelt left consternation, but the two made an effective working team.

The Roosevelt New Deal had many new programs, every one known by its initials. Among them the PWA, the Public Works Administration, was used by Frank for building funds. One of the buildings Frank constructed on PWA money was the Woollen gymnasium, named after Business Manager Charlie Woollen. Many other buildings were remodeled on PWA funds.

The PWA was used to hire unemployed people, most of them unskilled, and put them onto useful labor at a living wage, to help get the families and the economy functioning again. Frank had workmen build walkways on campus, build miles of rock walls, and in many other ways enhance the place.

The NYA, the National Youth Administration, was used to help students stay in school by paying them for useful community work. For instance, a professor might have a student do research for him, making the minimum wage, 35 cents an hour.

Secretary of Labor Frances Perkins, PWA Administrator Harry Hopkins, Eleanor Roosevelt and occasionally perhaps the President himself set their minds to finding ways to help Frank Graham. Realizing they could not lure him to Washington, which they had tried to do, they decided to support him where he was.

Indeed, he was becoming the New Deal's man in the South. In addition, as a member of the select Association of American Universities, the University of North Carolina afforded its president a favored position to influence the presidents of the AAU's other twenty-some member institutions. Soon Frank was considered to be a main voice for academic freedom in the entire country.

Meanwhile, he was strengthening each year his ties to the so-called "do-good" organizations. His memberships increased to two hundred.

His first-name acquaintances were in the thousands. Arnold King accompanied him to Atlantic City for a week-long conference of the Association of School Administrators. Frank made a speech, made friends with all the people in the U.S. Office of Education. Charmed people, Arnold says, you couldn't understand it unless you saw it.

Bob Madry, Director of the University News Bureau, told about taking Frank down to Scotland Neck, North Carolina, to address a farmers' meeting. Frank got out in front, took off his coat, rolled up his sleeves, and started in on a familiar theme of his, American pioneer history. Frank told the farmers how their ancestors had gone from ocean to ocean, told how important farmers were, and so forth. He walked up and down, spoke in that easy tone he had. Hypnotic effect.

Bob Madry said he heard a farmer say to another one, Man, can't he talk?

He sure can, came the reply, and I don't need to understand a damned word he's saying.

From one of Frank's talks on the American pioneer:
    No American pioneer who ever stood with axe and rifle along the fringe of the unconquered wilderness ever faced an adventure more thrilling than that which calls us today as we stand with books, ideas, and inquiring minds along the frontier of the vast possibilities of our yet unmastered civilization.

His interest in the American pioneer movement doubtless was given focus at Columbia University; while getting his Master's degree there Frank studied with historian Charles Beard, who had focused on that as the central movement in the building of the United States.

At trustees meetings some of the trustees were openly critical. Frank was in hot water about half the time. Dave Clark, editor of the *Southern Textile Bulletin,* was one consistent adversary. Frank's call for fairer wages and better working conditions really terrorized Clark. Many textile executives liked Frank, among them, J. Spencer Love of Burlington Mills, but Clark led a group of enemies.

Their criticism was that he was simply too liberal for the South. He tolerated Communists, or so they said, and identified himself with labor organizers. He was pro-Negro. The zeal with which he has pursued these causes was not Southern. He was moving too fast. He was seeking to change minds and hearts in ways the Christian church had been trying for twenty centuries. One trustee was heard to say, I wish Frank would quit prodding God Almighty.

Also, he had moved the engineering school to State College.

Fiery complaints would rain down on him at trustees meetings. Some trustees would try to get him fired, but Frank was doing such an effective job representing the University and education generally, not only locally and regionally, but nationally, that no board of trustees would think of turning him loose. Frank had become the sort of force that many could complain about but nobody could stop.

Frank's defense of every professor's rights of freedom of speech and in publication was generally accepted in Chapel Hill, and at State and the Woman's College, but not everyone felt obligated to make extremist professors welcome.

Dr. Erickson was a far-left, perhaps a Communist, faculty member, and he became disgruntled at the lack of attention given him and his projects by the press, including the student newspaper. He called on the young editor and laid out his claim for attention, to which the young man replied, If you don't like the way I run this paper, you can kiss my ass.

Erickson went at once to South Building and reported the rude incident to Bob House.

Bob House considered the problem. Well, Dr. Erickson, I suppose you've come to me for advice, he said. He thought the problem over for a while, then said, If I were you, I wouldn't do it.

Frank had bouts with the bronchial disease which had become an annual menace. The attacks occurred often enough to cause distress in South Building and among the faculty, as well as with his family. His cousin, Edward Kidder Graham, had died during his presidency from a similar illness, influenza.

At each attack, everybody awaited Frank's recovery. His doctor, Otho Ross of Charlotte, a trustee, had told him over and again that he must not exhaust himself. Others had reminded him to sleep, to eat -- they had to remind him. He's like a child, Marian's sister Eliza said, very like a little boy.

Remind him to wear his hat outdoors; how many times had he been reminded, then somebody had to go find it? He sure could lose his hat, friends recall.

Nobody at the time knew quite what to do about the disease Frank had. He had suffered similar attacks since youth. They were not painful, but were suffocating. Frank's labored breathing could be heard all over the house. Now and then, Marian would have to escape to the outdoors.

23. Dr. Frank, almost lost behind the podium, presides over ceremony honoring President Franklin Delano Roosevelt with an honorary degree at Chapel Hill. *Southern Historical Collection, UNC Library*

CHAPTER SIX

FRANKLIN ROOSEVELT had become President of the United States early in 1933, and in his first hundred days had sent fifteen major bills to Congress, all of which were passed into law. In those one hundred days, the President appointed Frank a commissioner, making him vice-chairman of the Consumers Advisory Board, which was, as time permitted, to recommend a nationwide organization of local consumer councils, to work alongside the emerging labor unions to represent the mass of citizens.

One of Frank's major addresses was delivered to the Board and its guests and aides -- among them leaders of the New Deal. The day following his White House appointment, in Constitution Hall in Washington he asked for national economic planning to meet the needs caused by new atrocities of corporate industrial power, which, he said, unconscionably and irresistibly encroached on the freedom and security of the individual in his working life and the equality of opportunity for millions of people.

Later, in October, 1934, Roosevelt through Secretary Perkins asked him to become chairman of the Advisory Council on Economic Security and Frank accepted at once, seizing the opportunity to discuss advisability of the Federal Government establishing programs of unemployment insurance, social security, and relief for those suffering economic loss due to sickness.

At the White House on November 13, 1934, Frank was made chairman of the Council, and next day spoke to 150 delegates of the National Conference on Economic Security, invited by Roosevelt to assemble from all sections of the country. In this address, Frank set firmly his position on several social issues, recommending advancing the security for a citizen's labor, sickness and old age.

The views Frank expressed were controversial, could indeed arouse anger in 1934, and Frank's Council was by no means in agreement, even in its final recommendations. Before the Senate Finance Committee, February 2 of the following year, Frank represented the majority opinions of his Council and responded to questions, many of them from Senators antagonistic to his opinions.

An array of legislation had been recommended -- old-age social security, aid to dependent children, health and disability insurance, unemployment compensation, maternity benefits, vocational rehabilitation, better federal public health programs... Frank closed his testimony with an *extemporare* statement of his personal views --

I would just like to say this and then I am through. I think this committee has one of the greatest opportunities of any committee of the United States Senate, that any committee has ever had. With all of us doing the best we can with what we have, we can work out of this present situation. As I think of it now there are, in one sense, three large periods in American history. Here was a great wilderness, and the Americans with their axes and rifles, subdued that wilderness with initiative, enterprise, courage, daring, and social vision.

Then, with scientific knowledge and mechanical devices, we have mastered this great physical continent.

I think today we face, in a sense, a great wilderness, a great wilderness of unemployment, insecurity, desolation and fear. I believe the American people focused today in your councils and deliberative bodies can, in this generation, with inventive capacity and daring, enterprise and social vision, work out social problems and build a cleaner, a nobler, and a more beautiful America. That is my faith.

In his published papers, Roosevelt acknowledges that out of the Council came the Social Security Act of 1935.*

Also passed were provisions establishing unemployment compensation, various forms of aid to needy dependent children, to the health of mothers, to the needy blind, and to public health, along with the National Old Age Insurance Plan, which was at this stage conditional upon the states passing cooperative legislation. The Act passed the Senate and House August 14, 1935, and was signed by Roosevelt, who said it was "the cornerstone in a structure which is being built but is by no means complete."

Frank could have accepted a job in Washington, or for that matter at another university, but he stayed where he was. He agreed with his friend, Bob House, that they had signed on for life.

One example of his influence in Washington, used on behalf of the University, concerns a Japanese student, Jikasu Fukusato, who, because he had been unable to meet payments to the University, had had his visa cancelled. He was in custody for early deportation.

*The Published Papers and Addresses of Franklin D. Roosevelt, vol. 3, item 175, p. 455. New York: Random House, 1938.

By the time Frank heard about this from Vermont Royster, the student had been in a Raleigh prison for about a week. Even though office hours were over for the day, Frank went to work at once telephoning officials, trying to get the student released, calling officials in North Carolina; Norfolk, Virginia; Washington, D.C.; New York City. Each echelon of officials declared itself powerless. He did find out that matters pertaining to a person being in this country, either to work or study, fell under the Department of Labor, so he telephoned Frances Perkins, head of that Department, and asked her to intercede. She said this was a Federal legal case, no one could solve it without court action.

Frank asked if the President could do so.

Mrs. Perkins said he -- she supposed the President could and she was to meet with him tomorrow and would ask him.

I will phone him tonight, Frank told her.

Mrs. Perkins was uncomfortable with that.

Then have the student paroled to my personal care, Frank told her.

Mrs. Perkins' order to do so went out that evening, down the long chain of command. Meanwhile, Frank and Marian drove to Raleigh and were present at the prison, arriving as the student was released. They took him home and kept him there as their guest for many months.

Frank walked into a virtual hornet's nest of troubles now and again. He even took on athletics for a second time, this time not merely firing a coach, but trying to return athletics to a suitable, defensible place in university life. Fearing that football had got out of hand, he caused a committee of the National Association of State Universities to advance a plan, called the Graham plan, which would forbid athletes to receive financial aid from sources other than the institution and would require that athletes be successful in their scholastic work.

This was 1936. Four months of outrage ensued, and the plan began to lose supporters -- one university president after another. The plan was modified drastically, until little of the restrictions remained. Frank, in the wake of defeat, proposed another idea, that coaches should not be paid more than full professors. That was not accepted, either.

On the other hand, Frank made a hit with people who attended his meetings and heard his speeches. He left friends in every place he visited. And now and again he gave cause for suspicion. In 1934, for instance, a student -- in this case an alumnus -- was arrested, Alton Lawrence, the secretary of the North Carolina Socialist Party, along with thirty others during a strike. He was charged with trespass during a textile strike in High Point. Actually, it was a national strike, with over 600,000 workers out, some 70,000 of them in North Carolina, and anger was everywhere, every day.

At the time, early September, 1934, Frank and Marian were at Pawley's Island, South Carolina, on vacation. Frank heard or read about Alton's arrest. Alton was only twenty-two, a recent graduate. Frank sent him a telegram in care of the jail.

JUST HEARD OF YOUR ARREST.
GLADLY GO ON YOUR BOND.
CONFIDENT YOU HAVE COMMITTED
NO CRIME.

The fact of such a telegram found space on the front pages of newspapers in North Carolina and added to the criticism of Frank. Even some of his friends were perplexed, that he would get into this cauldron at this time, when he might have helped with the young man's bail unobtrusively.

Without public anguish and discussion there will be less progress, seemed to be Dr. Frank's attitude.

In September 1936, Roosevelt appointed Frank to a committee to study vocational education, and several months later expanded its consideration to include the relationship in education of the Federal Government to the states, which historically had maintained education as a sole responsibility. Frank had early on come to realize poor states had more children to educate and less to do it with, and the best hope was Federal participation. The specter of Federal control had to be assuaged, which in 100 speeches in seventeen states he did. In its report, the Committee recommended federal aid to public schools, to library service for rural areas, and to teacher and adult education. All came to no avail. The House Committee on Education would have nothing to do with it.

June, 1939, the President appointed Dr. Frank chairman of the Advisory Committee on Economic Conditions in the South, Frank to lead twenty-one other Southerners. The President told them he wanted a picture of the economic South "in order that we may do something about it." Further, he wrote, "It is my conviction that the South presents right now the Nation's No. 1 economic problem -- the Nation's problem, not merely the South's."

It's probable that the President intended to appoint a similar committee for each region of the country, but he never did so, and reaction to this first announcement was mixed, the pride of Southerners being ruffled by his bluntly stated appraisal.

Howard Odum had published a landmark study, *Southern Regions,* and in that and in other sociological papers were the needed statistics.

The report was soon assembled. It described the rich natural resources, abundant rainfall, timber and minerals, and dealt with abuses and neglect of them. The richest state in the region was poorer in income than any outside it. In the South lived twenty-eight percent of the citizenry, yet federal income taxes paid in recent years were less than twelve percent of the total. The South had only eleven percent of the bank deposits. The South had one-third of the nation's children, many growing up in poverty. Health care facilities were woefully inadequate. Due to rigged freight rates, the South was forced to pay more for shipping manufactured goods from the region than had been paid on those shipped in. Due to high tariffs, the South was required to buy expensive manufactured products, while selling its raw farm produce in unprotected world markets.

The sixty-four page report laid bare all these distresses. Critics wondered why the racial imbalance was not dealt with. Almost thirty percent of Southerners were black, and the blacks impoverishment was worse than the average; by combining these figures with those for whites, the report made the plight of the whites appear worse and the blacks' problems less bad. Some critics also felt that the report did not lay sufficient blame on the North for the South's subjugation after the Civil War and exploitation from the North.

It was in fact a politician's report, avoiding controversy, seeking solid, substantial, middle ground. Indeed, Roosevelt came into the South two weeks after receiving the Committee report, and used it in his Southern campaign for his second term as President. To have introduced race and the Civil War into that Southern campaign was, of course, not to be recommended. It was a Howard Odum type of report. For some time, he had been issuing, through academic journals and books, such information, often using the University of North Carolina Press. Of late, he had been advocating starting an association of selected Southern liberals, to act through studies, publications, and discreet action.

Frank Graham had been giving support to many Southern organizations at work, among them the Carolina Conference for Social Service, the Southern Policy Committee (which had prepared papers on the South), the Southern Tenant Farmers Union, and labor unions. A new organization was being formed at the time he was meeting in Washington with his Committee on Economic Conditions; in July 1938, a small group of Southerners were meeting in Birmingham, Alabama, to plan the Southern Conference for Human Welfare. In September, one hundred representatives from seven Southern states met, elected officers, and announced a Southwide meeting to be convened in November in Birmingham. Frank had not been engaged in any of these meetings, but he was asked by the new officers to give the keynote address in November. He accepted. Also he agreed to chair the Thomas Jefferson Award Committee, which was to choose a Southerner who had done the most to promote human and social welfare in line with the philosophy of Thomas Jefferson.

The award went to Justice Hugo Black, a native of Alabama, who had been appointed to the United State Supreme Court the year before. Frank chose the words from Jefferson to appear on the medal:

Equal and exact justice to all men of whatever state or persuasion.

That was the theme of Frank's address, delivered in the Birmingham Municipal Auditorium before an integrated audience, white and black, men and women, made up of pastors, labor leaders, politicians, League of Women Voters leaders, columnists, editors and the like.

Just before Frank was to speak, a Negro choir sang. The words and tones of a spiritual lingered in his mind, and in the great auditorium, as Frank took his place. He said,

In the overtones of that song in the South our coloured peoples are on the march into the promised land. This is their home. White and black have joined hands here to go forward by way of interracial cooperation toward the Kingdom of God.

Frank spoke for the helpless minorities and the underprivileged majorities. He dealt with the unequal treatment under law of the Negroes. Correcting this inequality, he said, was the main test of the genuineness of democracy and of Christianity. He sought equality of opportunity for all the children. He sought new rights for the laborers. He discussed concerns for farmers and businessmen. He wanted a new South to emerge from the present wounded and suffering one, orderly evolving, a South trusting to education and religion and the democratic traditions of the nation.

With all the marks that have been placed against us in the South let us prove at this Southern Conference for Human Welfare that we stand for the more helpless minorities and the underprivileged. Let us demonstrate, in our stumbling and defective way that we wish to go the Jesus way, the slow way of education and revelation of the inner life. Let us show that this conference stands for the Sermon on the Mount, the American Bill of Rights and American democracy.

Frank spoke, the sentences rolling forth as if from a new Bible, one which featured Christianity and American democrary, two matching pillars. He held the vast throng -- and for quite a long while, too -- his message well reasoned, and appealing.

Next morning the local police arrived, "Bull" Connor, the police commissioner, in charge, telling the officers of the Conference they were breaking the law, that Birmingham required racial segregation. The officers met and agreed that the laws ought to be obeyed.

The blacks moved to occupy the left side of the auditorium. Mrs. Roosevelt took her seat among them, which must have given "Bull" Connor cause for reflection. When the police dared insist that she move, she moved to a seat just across an aisle.

Work sessions remained integrated, and produced a number of excellent resolutions dealing with Southern problems, from human rights to freight rates to criticism of the Dies House Un-American Activities Committee, which supposedly was keeping tabs on Communists and their penetration of organizations -- such as this one.

Frank Graham, who left the conference the second day in order to attend a meeting of educators in Richmond, read in newspaper reports of the conference. The press account stated that the session had condemned all forms of segregation and was controlled by Communists. He wrote a friend, L. A. Crowell, Jr.:

> The resolutions that were adopted were nothing more than what the Conference for Social Service in North Carolina has stood for for a long time. This Conference has long stood for equal facilities for Negroes and for justice to them with regard to their legal rights.

Frank had been elected Chairman of the new organization, this in spite of his having refused the title before leaving Birmingham, and withdrawing his name from consideration.

On November 26 Congressman Martin Dies, chairman of the House Un-American Activities Committee, announced that he had ordered staff members to go to Alabama to "investigate the whole thing."

What they would find, if they were interested in Frank Graham, was that Frank was not an officer and was not even present when resolutions were proposed. Further, that the resolutions that were passed were moderate. None dealt with equality of races, segregation in the schools, railroads or buses. Resolutions were passed in favor of more equal justice and opportunity for the Negro, for suffrage qualification to be based on educational qualifications rather than the poll tax, for readjustments of freight rates on a basis fair to the industries, agriculture and business interests of the South, for federal aid to the states for the public schools, for social legislation for the welfare of workers and farmers as basic groups of our people.

Even so, the two heatedly emotional issues of the South, race and Communism, were now more directly focused on Frank than ever before, as were the two hot charges, nigger-lover and Communist sympathizer.

Barry Bingham, publisher of the Louisville *Courier-Journal,* and Mark Ethridge, editor, were two of the newspapermen at the Birmingham session. Ethridge wrote Frank his concerns that the racial charges had handicapped, here at the start, the good the SCHW hoped for. Frank replied December 20, 1938:

My Dear Mark Etheridge:

Please pardon my delay in answering your good letter. I am just now free to catch up with my non-university work.

The unfilled vacancy made by the death of our able University Controller in September, the large PWA building program in our three institutions, and preparations for the coming session of the legislature, on top of the regular daily routine, made it most inadvisable for me to take on any additional work this year. Furthermore, I thought that Mrs. Charlton should be elected Chairman, in view of all of her preliminary work, fine spirit, and general ability. When a member of the Executive Committee suggested that I be considered for Chairman as I was about to leave Birmingham for the Richmond Educational Meeting, I requested that my name not be considered. It had not occurred to me that I would be considered, yet I simply wished to make clear my disqualifications and inability to take on any more work, in case such a suggestion were made.

However, when the attacks were made on the conference and misrepresentations were made with regard to what I take to be its purpose and spirit, I called Mrs. Charlton on long distance telephone to say that if it meant anything to her and the conference, I certainly would not decline the chairmanship. She showed such sincere appreciation that I was glad that I could at least do that much. I also felt sure that you, Barry Bingham, and many other just as truly Southern and just as understanding and clear-headed, would stick.

There was much about the conference that was impressive to me. We should have the historical understanding and the social insight to know that with freedom and democracy inevitably go mistakes of judgment, tactics, and even action. The only way to have a mistake-proof meeting is to make the biggest mistake of all in not having the meeting free and democratic. Of course, the safest thing to do, as some people interpret safety, is to take the cue from our vested interests and privileged groups and not have the meeting at all. If we are to promote research with sincerity, we should at least by example teach our young people that they should take research findings seriously, for further consideration and even action. We should be deeply glad that our young people care enough about research findings to pay their own expenses to go to a distant meeting and work seriously for human betterment in the South. The fact that somebody may have said something unwise, or that youth doesn't know all the tactics of expediency, should not cause us to desert the little ship, however storm-tossed it may appear on the surface to be. This is the very time they need our understanding and any little wisdom that we may have to share with them. We also need their idealism and enthusiasm and insight much more than we are disposed to admit.

It gives me a lift for my small part to know and work with such men as you, Barry Bingham, and such fine women as we saw in action in Birmingham, and other of like mind and heart, and uncounted others who appreciate the South and can take it on the chin if necessary for the region and the people they love the most.

With high and warm regards, I am

> Faithfully, your friend
> Frank P. Graham, President

Ethridge subsequently helped Howard Odum begin a Southern organization of quieter nature, to bring together research about the South and make it more public than University researchers could achieve. Ethridge called a January, 1939, meeting, inviting twenty-five white Southerners to plan such a program, which would, he wrote, have an enduring structural relation in the whole South. Unable to attend because of University business, Frank sent a paper he had written on federal aid to education.

Frank had become the leader in the South of the academic crowd and the liberal crowd. He responded to the South's challenge magnificently, while remaining active as President of the three-campus university.

Woollen died and was replaced by Billy Carmichael, a North Carolinian from a Durham tobacco family who had worked as an executive in advertising, then later in the financial market in New York City. Most Chapel Hill decisions were now made by Bob House or Billy Carmichael. Frank's meetings with them and faculty members were scattered and usually were unscheduled; House or Carmichael

might stick his head in the office doorway for a word or two, or meet
Frank on the paths of the campus, day or night. Or come to the house.
These meetings might last the length of a question and a reply, or might
go on interminably, which occurred one night when Marian and a niece
watched them go back and forth across the street between their two
houses. Frank walked Bob home, then Bob walked Frank home, then
Frank walked Bob home, this continuing for an hour as the need to talk
and the pleasure of conferring were satisfied.

Back and forth across the street: the two leaders of the University
meeting in closed session.

Oh my goodness! Marian exclaimed.

What's the matter? her alarmed niece asked.

Frank doesn't have on his hat, Marian replied.

Frances Perkins returned to campus. Eleanor Roosevelt returned.
Marian was heard to say, Look at those two big women after my little
man...

Professor of Law Albert Coates was having problems of his own
with Frank, who would not include Albert's Institute of Government in
the University budget, which meant Albert had to fight for money on
his own. The Institute was involved in improving the performance of
state, county and city employees.

Howard Odum in Social Welfare, was trying to start a Department
of Social Science Administrators, to train government workers, and that,
too, was being denied university funding.

Albert Coates and Howard Odum were two stars of the Chapel Hill
faculty, and they were on a collision course with Frank and maybe with
each other.

Other problems abounded.

Louis Round Wilson was to be offered the vice-presidency of the
University by Frank. Wilson was in Chicago waiting for word, which
was due to follow the trustee's meeting. To his astonishment, instead of
an offer he received Frank's telegram stating to him he hadn't brought
it up.

There was a continuous pull and tug among professors, and
between departments. Frank was riding three bucking horses. The
system had struggles, jealousies built into it. Every new curriculum,
every new course, every increase or decrease of the budget shook the
temple pillars and walls. And what was Frank doing about faculty
salaries? Four thousand five hundred dollars for a full professor -- did
he seem to be satisfied with salaries?

There were lighter problems.

Luther C. Bruce recalls that President Graham was disturbed because alumni were writing him that fraternities had bars for serving alcoholic beverages -- beer predominantly. Frank asked the Dean of Students about this, and the dean asked L. C. to investigate.

I was a Phi Gam, L. C. says, and we didn't have a built-in bar. We had a rolling bar. Kappa Sig had a tremendous bar with secret entrances. There were bars in most all the frat houses. I got the warning and began attending meetings at fraternity houses. I told them Dr. Graham was going to drop in during final exam week, and I think it would be very appropriate if we dismantled our bars; it's a plain case of the better part of valor. Admittedly we in the University have no jurisdiction, I told them, you can do what you want to in your own house, but my advice is to get rid of those bars. About a week before finals, I phoned Dean Bradshaw and told him I believed it to be perfectly safe for Dr. Graham to look for bars. So at 2:00 o'clock in the morning, the first day of finals, Dr. Graham and Dean Bradshaw came around to each fraternity house and didn't find a single bar. They did find one fraternity man, drunk and sleeping in a fireplace.

Efforts went ahead to try to get President Franklin Roosevelt, himself, to come to Chapel Hill to speak. At the time, 1937 and 1938, Alex Heard as a student held several elected offices, including chairman of the Carolina Political Union. He enlisted Frank to help the Union in this effort. Alex drafted an invitational telegram. He put Frank Graham's name first, his own name second.

When Frank saw the draft of the telegram, he immediately suggested that the names be switched. Alex Heard switched them, as directed. When the answer came it was addressed to him personally.

He showed it to Frank who said, You see, that's why I wanted the names switched.

Frank's own communiqués from the President came in telephone calls from the White House. One from Roosevelt suggested Frank consider being his vice-presidential running mate, an invitation Frank rejected and for years kept secret. Also Frank had visits from Harry Hopkins, the President's most trusted advisor, intellectual of the New Deal, asking Frank about several matters.

Admittedly, faculty salaries fell during the depression years, the 1930s, but thanks to Frank's pull in Washington, the campus improved and jobs were available for local artisans. Under a North Carolina law passed in 1935, state institutions were enabled to participate in the program of the Federal Emergency Administration of Public Works. Through the sale of revenue bonds, the state supplied matching money for PWA grants.

Buildings erected with aid of PWA grants, beside Woollen Gymnasium, were three dormitories for women -- Alderman, McIver and Kenan -- two men's dormitories -- Whitehead and Lewis -- Lenoir Dining Hall, additions to the Carolina Inn, now owned by the University, additions to the Public Health and Medical Building, the Clinical Annex and the Infirmary. All that was completed by 1940. In 1940, Wilson Hall was completed. Of the money spent during this six-year period, 35.4 percent was self-liquidating bonds making the cost to the state a small sum. In all, thirteen new buildings had risen.

Frank served as chairman of the Conference for Southern Welfare for only twenty months, until June, 1940. He sought to identify Communists within the organization, and found, as usual, their vows of secrecy made the task devilishly difficult.

There had been five, perhaps six Communists at the Birmingham Conference; the best he could tell none was in authority. Opal Lee, or Howard Lee as he was sometimes known, might be another, Frank learned, but not before appointing him executive secretary of the Southern Conference. That error was a matter needing attention, Frank decided, and took to himself the arranging of the second big conference, which was to be in April, 1940, in Chattanooga. In January, three months ahead of the meeting, Representative Dies released a statement that the Conference was being planned by Communists.

The Editor of the University of North Carolina Press, W. T. Couch, attended this meeting and, responding to Frank's urging, proposed a resolution denouncing Russia for its aggression against Finland. The two realized this would cause the American Communists to come out of hiding, because publicly they would have to be in opposition. Of course, this was only a single resolution among many, but it did influence the Conference. The handful of Communists who supported a resolution condemning German aggression against the Soviet Union, sought to monopolize debate and kill the measure. Frank as Chairman ruled against them, deciding it was appropriate for this Southern Conference to take a stand on non-Southern matters. As the debate carried on into conference rooms, Frank heard himself called a tool of Wall Street, a lackey of the mill barons, a pseudo-liberal.

The resolution finally was passed, quite similar in form to Couch's original resolution.

We deplore the rise of dictators anywhere, the oppression of

24. Frank Graham, Eleanor Roosevelt and Josephus Daniels, editor of the *Raleigh News and Observer*. *Photograph by Hugh Morton*

civil liberties, the persecution of minorities, aggression against small and weak nations, the violation of human rights, and democratic liberties of the people by all Fascist, Nazi, Communist, and imperialist powers alike which resort to force and aggression instead of the processes of law, freedom, democracy, and international cooperation.

At the Conference an address by Eleanor Roosevelt was the other highlight. Her quavering voice went out to the multitude.

The battles had been costly to Frank. He was unable to find other eminent Southerners who would join. Advice came from all sides to let the Conference lie fallow, at least for a time. Graham reluctantly consented to leave the chairmanship and was willing to accept John B. Thompson as the Chairman replacing him. Thompson, although a pastor, lacked Frank's compassion and diplomacy; the organization became more confrontational and strident.

Frank was urged by friends to join them in leaving it. Barry Bingham, publisher in Louisville, Kentucky, wrote Frank:

You are a man who has a great responsibility and a great work to perform in the South. That work is too important to be jeopardized by your running unnecessary risks with public opinion. I feel you have performed a real public service in keeping the Conference afloat so far, and I know at what sacrifice you have performed that task.

Frank would not even consider resigning, and by so doing desert fellow Southerners working to create a more democratic South.

Marian thought Frank was happiest when the legislature was in session and he was running back and forth to Raleigh on behalf of the University. Bill Friday recalls driving him to Raleigh to meet with the legislators; usually Frank would curl up on the back seat of the car and go to sleep, awakening on the outskirts of Raleigh to ask to stop for a Coca-Cola and a banana. One Coca-Cola would have him energized by the time he reached the General Assembly, ready to go to work lobbying.

Often as not Frank would seek out his most active opponent, grasp both upper arms, holding him by his forearms, finally, an arm around him, steering him in the direction Frank wanted him to go. A large group of legislators might gather over to the side, waiting for Frank to release the victim at which time they would pounce on him and welcome the dazed fellow back into the fellowship of legislative mortals. This came to be known as "the treatment."

Whenever asked to speak in legislative committee meetings, Dr. Frank would rise to his feet. Josephus Daniels, elder statesman of the Democratic party, had given Frank that advice: stand whenever you speak of the University. Even when asked a question about the University, he would stand. He would speak simply, in friendly tones. He had a grasp of every number, every statistic, every detail, every remark by any legislator. He would speak directly to the ones present, all of whom he knew, and if he was allowed time enough to graduate to high plains of university descriptions, a sort of light appeared to illuminate him, and emanate from him, so great and awesome was his regard for the institution.

He never talked disparagingly about any member, no matter how ignorant or obstructionist, never went home and confided to Marian that so-and-so was a deplorable choice by the voters of his district, or that this one or that one should never be listened to. Even politicians who had placed themselves over and against him believed that when Frank asked to talk to them, or rose to speak, he was their personal friend.

Marian heard about Gladys and Albert Coates' plan to build their own house. They had lived hand to mouth until now, but the University had decided to include the Institute of Government in its budget. They bought a lot and hired an architect. Albert kept asking to see the sketch of the outside of the house, and the architects kept replying that the outside would be determined by function on the inside, that once the inside was set, the outside sketch would be provided.

Finally, the inside agreed to, Marian understood the architect showed the sketch of the outside.

I'll not build it, I'll not live in it, Albert Coates declared. And I've heard enough about the inside function determining the appearance. Two women have the same function, but one is pretty and the other is ugly as sin. Now you get me a house I'd be proud to live in.

Of course, the architects had to make changes, to make it look like something other than a tenant shack, as Albert called the first sketch.

CHAPTER SEVEN

FRANK WOULD NOT THINK to build Marian a house at all, Marian decided, which she regretted, although he had been heard to say every man owed it to his wife to build her a home. Of course, she had the president's house on campus. A great house, but it was quite public, and still was furnished with furniture cast-off from the dorms. She did have the cottage at Nags Head. That was, had been since 1911, her summer home; all year long she and Frank would talk about the trip next summer. By July the tuned-up excitement was almost unbearable. She and Hubert and Alice Neal would go on ahead. The cottage had to be swept out, storm damage needed to be repaired. This might amount to a screen door torn off a hinge, or roofing gone from the northeast corner. Usually there was debris to dispose of.

Once the house was ready, Hubert would return to Chapel Hill for Frank; either that, or Frank would get someone to drive him as far as the Kysers' in Rocky Mount, or a friend's home in Smithfield or Greenville or wherever, and Hubert would pick him up there.

Other members of the Drane family were welcome, too, and expected: Marian's sister Eliza, her daughter Elizabeth and granddaughters and other children; Jacqueline Nash was one of Brent Drane's daughters. Strong and athletic, Frank usually had a baseball, and used it as entrée into the youngsters' world.

Marian was serene, was certainly as happy here as anywhere else her family ever saw her. Marian didn't criticize Frank to others -- nor often to Frank, either, for that matter. Kemp Battle would come up from his cottage and say to her, Marian, knowing Frank as you do, make him listen; he joins too many outfits, he gives of himself too much, he sides with too damn many underdogs...

Marian absorbed the criticisms but did not nag Frank, nor did she appear to resent Frank's preoccupation and busy schedule. She enjoyed making his complicated life work smoother.

Once "Unkie" had finished his work about mid-morning, he would appear in shorts and a baseball cap and be ready for the beach. He gathered the children, simply all the children from up and down the beach. One of his nieces said, years later:

> We knew in our hearts that he wasn't grown up. Like us, he needed to be taken care of, fed and even deserved on occasions to be scolded. "Unkie" had a wonderful quality of sheer gaiety. He enjoyed being with us, splashing into the surf, playing in the sand, playing catch with the baseball, or any other ball, building huts out of scrap lumber thrown up on the beach. Once we built a sidewalk out of scrap lumber. "Unkie" was oblivious to food. Had to be reminded to eat. One favorite was blackstrap molasses. He added brewer's yeast to it. Aunt Marian commented that one could put most anything in blackstrap molasses and not affect the taste of it. "Unkie" couldn't cook. Marian did some of the cooking. Whenever she was there, my mother did more. If Alice Neal was at the beach, had not returned to Chapel Hill, she also did some of the cooking. Then, too, there was the Arlington Hotel only two doors away, and often the family went there for the evening meal, "Unkie" wearing slacks and a crisp white shirt that Marian or Hubert Robinson -- if he were still there -- had washed and ironed for him. There was no hot water. Nobody complained about that. There was the ocean to bathe in. On leaving for Chapel Hill, "Unkie" once asked niece Rebecca, Which is my toothbrush, Rebecca?

> "Unkie", I don't know. Which have you been using?

On some afternoons the troop would climb the sand dunes at Kill Devil Hills, or go into a laurel woods and play Indians.

At night "Unkie" and Marian would take Elizabeth and maybe other nieces to the motion picture house, The Pioneer in Manteo. They would see one of the Hollywood favorites. "Unkie" would eat all of Elizabeth's popcorn, and he would want to go back the next night.

Or the children played set-back, the card game.

Or "Kangaroo" Chinese checkers, the cut-throat version.

Or "Unkie" would settle in with Mr. Kemp and Mr. Frank and the Graham-Battle-Winslow conversation would begin, mostly stories from the past, often their school days. One story they had trouble with had to do with the cemetery in Chapel Hill and several women of the night -- whatever they were. Some of the students would pay them. Other students attacked one night to chase away the women, and there was gunfire and some of the women were arrested.

Mind-boggling for Elizabeth to figure out that story.

She recalls "Unkie" talked on occasion about his own family. He would talk for an hour about his Scot ancestors. He revered his mother. Also, he revered his cousin, Edward Kidder Graham, the one who had been his teacher, the best teacher he ever had, he said. "EK" had been president of the University at the time of World War I.

These evenings there was moderate drinking by the men, except "Unkie." Marian would take a glass of sherry. She claimed her father, "who was more divine than I am," never tasted a glass of sherry he didn't like.

Frank would sometimes chide her saying, Marian thinks I'm not a Christian because I'm a Presbyterian.

Niece Jacqueline Drane loved both Marian and Frank, but, looking back, acknowledges the family was aware of the stark differences between them: Marian was such a private person -- being the wife of a university president did not come naturally to her at all -- whereas Frank was a public person without thinking whether he was or not. Jacqueline says, Even as a child I would rather be like Marian than anybody I'd ever known, and I was with her every summer at Grandfather's cottage at Nags Head.

Eliza, the older of Marian's two sisters, was the one most critical of Frank, and for that matter of Marian, who was amenable to whatever Frank wanted, she felt; Marian fed him, paid his phone bills, put him to bed and nursed him to sleep, and he was as likely as not to go hurrying off with a stranger, leaving her stranded at the doorway. He took her very life for granted, Eliza felt. She also talked with Marian about Marian's estate, her and Frank's savings, their retirement funds. It was a brief conversation, indeed. There was none. No house, either. Where is the money Papa left you?

It was gone. No savings, except as Marian set aside for furniture she expected to buy.

For use where, pray tell? For that big barn in Chapel Hill which is nothing more than a student dormitory and meeting place?

And no children; too late now for her. To go childless into old age, that was her prospect.

I go with Frank, that was Marian's view.

Eliza became ill. Frank had a theory that she needed more ozone. He induced the children to help him place boards all the way from the house to the beach, making a walkway, so they could push her chair close to the water's edge, where he said the "ozones" were most abundant.

The nieces never knew whether "Unkie" believed this, about ozones, but the walkway was laid and Eliza was taken as close to the surf as he could get her.

She looked funny, sitting there, they thought.

One summer a Coca-Cola clock was washed ashore. Great

excitement. The troop carried their treasure to the house and with eager fingers dried it, removed its pendulum, its hands and dial. They sponged dry its works.

Reassembled, it was set on the buffet and was carefully wound by "Unkie" himself. At last the moment came. The troop selected him to perform the test. He set the hands to the correct time, moved the pendulum to the left, counted three and released it.

Tick tock, tick tock.

A never to be forgotten triumph.

That night, off to see the play, *The Lost Colony* -- an annual feast. The play was performed only a few miles away, at Manteo, with a cast of over a hundred, and many musicians besides. It used three stages in the outdoor theatre Paul Green himself had designed. Behind the stages were the waters of the sound, with the strip of beach peninsula beyond. The audience faced east, so the setting sun was to their back as the play began. The magic of theatre placed them in Elizabethan England in company with Sir Walter Raleigh, dreamer of establishing English colonies in the New World, and a band of colonists who are willing to set sail, braving dangers known and unknown. Among them is a beautiful young lady, Eleanor, wife of Ananias Dare.

Under lights, the sun having set, the magic of theatre takes the audience -- Marian, children, Frank, and all the others -- to Roanoke, to this very site, where Indians meet them. Here Fort Raleigh is built, the Indians helping. Here are Indian dances, here the death of Ananias and the birth of Virginia Dare. Other Indians attack. The ships do not return from England, must be off fighting the Spanish. Despair as the band of colonists prepares to leave Fort Raleigh and accept the safety offered by a friendly band of Indians.

> Now down the trackless hollow years
> That swallowed them but not their song
> We send response --
> O lusty singer, dreamer, pioneer,
> Lord of the wilderness, the unafraid,
> Tamer of darkness, fire and flood
> Of the soaring spirit winged aloft
> On the plumes of agony and death --
> Hear us, O hear!
> The dream still lives,
> It lives, it lives,
> And shall not die!

The music, the swirling colonial dances, the Indian dances, the symphony of the performance was overwhelming; the tragedy, yet the hope, the will to begin life in the New World. The play always left

AUDIENCE WITNESSING THE BAPTISM OF VIRGINIA
DARE—A SCENE IN PAUL GREEN'S THE LOST
COLONY, PLAYING ITS FOURTH SUMMER SEASON
FROM JUNE 29TH THRU LABOR DAY, SEPTEMBER
2ND, 1940. MORE THAN 250,000 HAVE SEEN IT
DURING PAST THREE SUMMERS.

Dear..

   Have just seen "THE LOST COLONY"—a
marvelous depiction of the birth of American
civilization. It is truly a beautiful and magnificent spectacle—Every American should
see it. The Roanoke Island Historical Association, of Manteo, N. C., will gladly send
you descriptive literature upon request.

POST CARD

PLACE
STAMP
HERE

OLD FORT B RALEIGH
AUG
1
1940
ROANOKE ISLAND, N. C.

BECKSELL POST CARD COMPANY, NORFOLK

John!
Sorry I mis-understood.—
Here they are.
This is a picture of
uncle Frank at the
Lost Colony. Can you
find him?
Cheers, Bon voyage,
and Thanks
for your grand work!
E:

25. Both sides of a post card featuring the Lost Colony drama at Manteo, on
Roanoke Island. Note that sitting in the last row *(below)* is, unmistakably,
Dr. Frank. *Courtesy of Elizabeth Matheson*

Frank and Marian in tears, and usually the children, too, no matter how many times they had seen it.

Each time, the family would go backstage. Frank would meet the members of the cast, identifying each, relating each performance to performances in past years, and the children would go as close as they dared to the dressing rooms where performers entered as Indians and left as townspeople from Manteo, or summer residents of Nags Head and Kitty Hawk, or students and faculty from the Carolina Playmakers.

Sometimes at Nags Head Frank would talk about the Graham family in Scotland. He might preface this by recalling that Marian had some Scots blood in her veins, too, was descendant of Governor Gabriel Johnson, the foremost Scots governor of North Carolina, through the line of his daughter Penelope. Frank's ancestors came from Montrose. Historically the Scots Grahams were administrators for the Dukes of Montrose. They became landed, owned from Gartmore, located about twenty-five miles north of Glasgow, all the way to Loch Lomond.

Robert Cunningham Graham was the greatest of recent Grahams. A greatly loved man, warm hearted, he was a founder of the Labor Party, a supporter of public education, a philanthropist so generous he lost the estate, Gartmore House and lands, and for a while was penniless. A huge monument to him stands in the village of Gartmore, which in Gaelic means "the big field."

Alice Neal's daughter recalls Alice taking her family to the beach cottage for three or four days, a private vacation. Back then blacks were not owners of property at Nags Head, and this was a special treat, which Frank and Marian provided.

Frank said one reason he chose a black for his driver was to seek overnight quarters for him in white-only establishments, convincing managers to allow Frank's servant to stay nearby. This sometimes was allowed, and in that way helped prepare the way for racial integration, which Frank believed inevitable.

Frank, Dudley Carroll, first Dean of the Business School, and others in Chapel Hill were often called on by the American Friends Service Committee in New York to help place persons fleeing Nazi Germany -- Jew and Gentile.

One fugitive was a coffee-shop, candy-kitchen proprietor named Edward Danziger, and Danziger made his way to Chapel Hill and with his wife opened a shop on the main street.

Danziger wrote about one New Year's incident:

With all the students gone home for the holiday, Chapel Hill had become very, very quiet. So Emily made plans for a

"Sylvester" celebration, a New Year's party. She suggested that we invite all those who were refugees like ourselves. There were several in Chapel Hill and a few more in Durham and Raleigh. We closed the store and arranged all the chairs in the back room in a kind of semicircle. We served franks and rye bread and a Vienna punch and had a good time.

It was already after 10:00 p.m. when suddenly someone knocked at the door. We thought maybe it was a customer who wanted to buy something he had previously forgotten, so I unlocked the door. But how great was my surprise to find Dr. Frank P. Graham, the president of the University at the door. "Good evening, Mr. President," I said. "What can I do for you?"

"I am not coming as a customer," Dr. Graham said. "I know that in your country New Year's Eve is a great celebration, and seeing light in here, I wanted to tell you how happy we are in Chapel Hill that you are here and to wish you a very successful and happy New Year." After that he wanted to leave, but I insisted that he come in. I said, "We have a few friends here, all people like ourselves, to celebrate the New Year. Please come and say a few words to all of us." He consented and talked for a few minutes to us, talking about freedom and democracy and the responsibility a free man has toward his family, his country, and the world. He wished us all success and happiness, and after shaking hands, he left.

We were very much impressed and discussed this happening for quite some time. Here were we, a bunch of refugees, foreigners with almost no knowledge of English, kicked out of our own country without money or any other belongings, complete strangers, the most unimportant people in the world, and here came the president of this great university and took time out to visit us, to wish us luck, to talk to us, to welcome us. We compared his attitude with the way a university president in Vienna or Berlin or Paris or Heidelberg would have acted -- and we concluded that even in the "good old days," the days of Kaiser Franz Josef or Wilhelm, no high-ranking civil servant, let alone a university president, would have wasted his time to speak to a non-academic group of nobodies like us. And we understood that somehow this country was different from the old country.

Graduating senior Sophia Cody was working in the Chemistry Department when her chair collapsed and she fell, cracking a vertebra. She was confined to the infirmary the day of her graduation ceremony.

About 9:30 p.m., during a storm, three men, dripping rainwater, visited her room and gave her the diploma.

They were Frank Graham and following him, Bob House and Governor Clyde Hoey.

26. Dr. Frank on the beach at Nags Head. *Photograph courtesy of UNC Alumni Publications*

CHAPTER EIGHT

SUNDAY NIGHTS the Grahams always tried to be at home. If the porch light was on, students knew they were invited to drop by between seven and ten. Frank would manage to return from journeys in time for these sessions, even if he had to ride the train all Saturday night. Alex Heard recalls he went by at seven one Sunday and found nobody home; he left a note, and next day he received from Marian an invitation to dinner, with an apology. She and Frank had thought, since the University was in spring recess, no one would come by.

Thomas Winfield Blackwell, Jr., recalls as a freshman he was walking across campus and was apprehended by a short, friendly man.

Blackwell? There are Blackwells in Winston-Salem. Are you from there? the man said.

Yes, sir. I am.

What are you taking here?

Everything they tell me to take. It all looks hard to me.

Would you like to come to tea at my house?

Winfield told him he had never been to tea, but yes, sir, I would. I really would.

Come next Sunday at 7 o'clock.

Where's your house?

You go diagonally through there till you get to Franklin Street, walk east past the Episcopal Church to the white house on the right.

Winfield went. Frank came to the door. There were eighteen young people inside. Dr. Graham greeted me by name, Winfield recalls, took me around the circle and introduced me to each one. He told me, this is Mayne Albright. He's from Raleigh. Winfield Blackwell is from Winston-Salem.

He took me all the way around. I met his wife that night. I remember a boy was named Julian Outlaw. He's from Hyde County, Dr. Graham told me, except they call it Hoid County down there. He introduced me to each one of them. There was L. H. Fountain of Tarboro, who later was in the North Carolina General Assembly with me. Still later he was a Congressman for about twenty years.

Every time after that, Dr. Frank knew me, asked about my family. Now, your father was not from Forsyth County, was he? Dr. Frank would say.

No, he was from Rockingham.

Now let's see, on your mother's side --

She was a Crist.

That's Moravian, isn't it? No, let's see, that's Welsh, isn't it?

Yes. Lived out on the Yadkin River. Yes, came from Wales.

My people came from Scotland. It's a dour place, Winfield. Some of them are dour people. Scotland, Scottish people. Harsh, rocky. Hard to make a living there, and therefore Scotland has turned out a lot of strong men.

Yes, sir.

Frank held him in tow while talking, telling him, North Carolina before the Revolution was the state Scots came to. You know why? The Governor appointed by King George was a Scot, and he decreed that Scots could have land free and live tax free. In they came. Even Flora MacDonald came. They settled both sides of the Cape Fear River from Wilmington upstream to Fayetteville. Strong, dour people, Winfield...

World War II pretty much changed everybody's plans, and those of organizations and institutions. The dangerous warnings had been issuing from Europe and Japan for some many months, but surprising, even so, was the German invasion of Poland, September 1, 1939. Great Britain and France on September 3 declared war.

Those two democracies weren't prepared for any such war. Soon Belgium, the Netherlands and France were overrun. In the United States two out of three people polled by Gallup believed the United States should stay out, even if England fell. Supplies were shipped, however, and the United States began the manufacture of planes and ships, munitions and guns.

This is our war, Frank Graham proclaimed. In 1939 he led the Board of Trustees into offering the full facilities of the University, its three campuses, to the effort to prepare and arm.

June 1, 1939, following a meeting at the Roosevelt White House, at which the President had spoken, Frank wrote Eleanor Roosevelt:

When I think of Hitler I almost despair; then I think of our democratically elected leader of the peoples of the world and I have faith and hope again. There has never been such a team as you two in human history.

In the letter Frank expressed his hope for a postwar United Nations.

I know the President could voice for the world the deep aspirations of people everywhere for a new international order through a more democratic league of peoples based on principles of justice, freedom, democracy and international law backed up by an international police force.

The United States accepted the title "arsenal of democracy" but manufacturing was hampered by strikes, even facing threats to world democracy. On March 20, 1941, President Roosevelt appointed Frank one of eleven members of the National Defense Mediation Board, later called, for most of its existence, the War Labor Board.

Coming as a surprise to Frank, the announcement sent him rushing to adjust his work at home and find a room to live in during his Washington stints. The thrust was to get war materials manufactured and delivered overseas without interruption, and as soon as possible.

The eleven members came from labor, management and the public. The three public members were likely to be the swing vote, and Frank was one of these. At the beginning he knew, as he admitted, next to nothing about labor union mediation, but he began to learn March 24, at the organizational meeting. At the time Bethlehem Steel was out on strike, Allis-Chalmers was tied up by strike-breaking troubles, Ford was closed down. Three hundred sixteen strikes, then in effect, were crippling industry.

Whenever representatives of labor and management met before any one of the Board's three panels, distrust and resentment dominated. Graham went out to meet informally with the people, find out where they were from, ask about their families, their schools and churches, find out what their fears were. In off-the-record meetings he would come to know them; even workers and managers who had been involved in strike actions for months, came to trust him. He began to develop a set of possible solutions, among them the maintenance-of-membership clause, which relieved the unions of most of their fear of losing status during the emergency. By this, a laborer was free to join or not join a union, but once a worker voluntarily joined he or she was required to remain for the life of the contract. The device worked time and again, in major strikes and small.

November, 1941, labor's own most belligerent leader came to Washington: John L. Lewis, President of the United Mine Workers Union. Lewis had a hold on steel mills and railroads and power plants -- American efforts to supply England. His bushy eyebrows, scowling expression, and mellow, baritone voice were well known, as was his arrogant manner. His complaint was not impressive. Having a closed

shop in most coal mines, he wanted a closed shop in the others, in
which he had already a ninety-five percent membership. He came
before Frank Graham and his colleagues with this need and his threats.
Frank did try to find out about his family and his church and all, and
did seek to be considerate. After the vote, which was against Lewis'
claim, on leaving one treacherous twelve-hour session, John L. Lewis
issued a tribute to Frank which became well known. To an aide he was
heard to say:

Who locked me in with that sweet little son-of-a-bitch?

Also, Wayne Morse, then dean of the University of Oregon law
school, reported he entered the lobby of the building where the Board
met, incidentally following Mr. Lewis and a harried associate, and
crossing the lobby Lewis told the man: Now be careful of that little
SOB, Graham; he'll lean across the table, stick his little chin out, and
ask you for your shirt and make you think you owe it to him.

On December 7, 1941, two years, three months and a few days after
Nazi Germany had invaded Poland, the Japanese, long allied in their
peacetime efforts with Germany, attacked the United States Pacific fleet
at Pearl Harbor, Hawaii. This was early on a Sunday morning.

The Japanese fleet had sailed on a far-northern, infrequently
traveled route, had maintained radio silence, and surprised the Navy.
There was no declaration of war involving the United States, not with
Japan or any other nation. Most of our country's security had for
months been internal security against sabotage. There were 157,905
civilians of Japanese ancestry in Hawaii, perhaps a few of whom were
helping Japan's consulate officers supply detailed reports to the
Japanese war machine.

At 7:55 a.m., the first bomb hit a seaplane ramp. Twenty-four
sailors on the battleship Nevada had taken places to display the
morning colors at 8 a.m. At 7:58 they saw planes approaching low in
the sky and heard other explosions. At 8 a.m. they began playing the
Star Spangled Banner. Japanese plane dropped torpedoes nearby and
passed low over the Nevada. The musicians completed the national
anthem in its entirety, as around them their part of America experienced
calamity, our defenses ineffective, the ships of our outmoded fleet lined
up for slaughter of their sailors, and sinking.

News of the attack shocked America. That evening in Washington,
while President Franklin Roosevelt met with his cabinet, many people
gathered on the street, spontaneously singing "God Bless America." A

sense of fear, mingled with fury, had gripped the nation. Confusion gave birth to insecurity. The nation was atremble, not from lack of bravery or even confidence, but from the shifting of all plans.

That very evening a mass of students came to Marian and Frank's house. At first Dr. Graham would meet everyone at the door, ask about his or her stay at the University, ask a few words about his or her family, referring to their previous conversations, welcoming each, introducing...

Tonight, however, there was no way to introduce everybody. The press of people was too great -- townspeople, faculty, students, all looking for understanding, stability, direction. It seemed the whole world had been blown apart, and consequently each person had personal problems to resolve.

About 9 o'clock Frank took a seat on the arm of a sofa. All the chairs and much of the floor overflowed with students. He sought to put into perspective the overwhelming event, examining the history of the Japanese and Nazi situation which had brought them into alliance and our country into another world war.

At 10:00 p.m. all the students left except graduate student Sophia Cody, who stayed to help Marian clean up -- every crumb and drink was gone. Frank asked her about his plan to dismiss classes, to call a meeting of all students next morning at eleven o'clock and try to calm the waters. He worked until very late on his message, which Miss Cody thought was just right.

Douglass Hunt was present that next day in Gerrard Hall. He cannot remember any of the arresting quotations from Frank. He says, I recall that I thought at the time what a sane, long-headed judgment he had about the between-war period and the test that lay ahead for the Free World.

At 12:29 p.m. that day, Roosevelt entered the House Chamber at the Capitol and received a standing ovation. His speech lasted only six minutes. Within an hour, with only one dissenting vote, he led the nation into World War II.

Frank was spending two or three days a week in North Carolina, serving the three-campus university, and most of his time each week in Washington. Marian wanted to rent an apartment there and be with him; he did not encourage this. The travel back and forth was tiring, particularly on the wartime, crowded trains, and his time in Washington was taken up sixteen hours a day with conferences. Instead, he rented a room for himself in a small boarding hotel.

Traveling home on Friday night often required his standing most of the way to Richmond, sometimes beyond. Of course, he entered into conversations with people he met. One night, riding back to Washington he began talking in the smoking room with a man who admitted to being quite discouraged. He had been all over the South, he said, trying to find an institution willing to cooperate with the U. S. Department of Agriculture in a new field. I've given up.

Frank, instantly interested, asked what field it was.

Agricultural statistics, the man said, and discussed the new field.

Frank liked what the man told him. I know of an institution I'm sure will cooperate, he assured the official. It's a great place to start this thing. That's the State College in Raleigh.

The man went on describing the wonders of the new field, telling Frank how statistical studies, the quick use of numbers -- it will all lead to computers, he told Frank, someday we'll have electronic computers to help us. Even Texas with all its money turned me down, he said. And you mentioned North Carolina State. I was there, I talked to everybody. I didn't make a dent at State.

Dr. Frank told the man he was making a dent right now.

There, in the smoking room, was born the multi-million dollar program in agricultural statistics which gave North Carolina State a leadership position in the nation.

Some months later, as the war neared its end, Frank was working in Washington on a crucial case for the War Labor Board involving reams of statistics, sheaf after sheaf, box after box of them, all in regard to a far-reaching labor decision. He later told about it:

> I was in between columns of statistics from management and labor as tall as this building. And to get some help and light, I went over to the man that President Roosevelt had put in charge of all federal statistics during the war. Name was Dr. Deming. And while I was there, a vice-admiral called him up and said -- I couldn't keep from hearing, he was talking so loud, and then I began to listen with great eagerness -- and he says, I want one of those higher mathematical statisticians that will help me shorten the period of approving a piece of ordinance I have, that I've got to have before this war's over. And the war was in a very critical stage.

Dr. Denning said, Well, they're very few and far between, in this country and the world, and I don't have one available right now.

And the admiral blew his top.

When the telephone conversation was over, Frank asked why isn't some university training the young people who are in such demand in agriculture, industry, education, business, the war itself. And Denning said, You're asking me and you're president of a university?

Frank took the question to the Rockefeller Foundation, where he knew Albert Russell Mann. This type of proposal was new to Rockefeller, but Mann knew about the work begun at North Carolina State, and he promised to be helpful with funding once Dr. Graham had promise of some North Carolina money.

On his return the next weekend to Chapel Hill, Frank approached key members of the General Assembly. No help at all. There was, however, a large foundation in the state, the Z. Smith Reynolds Foundation, and its chairman was R. J. Reynolds' son, Dick, who had attended North Carolina State. Frank found out Dick was in Hawaii, taking part in the big San Francisco-to-Honolulu boat race.

Before telephoning Reynolds, carefully Frank and Marian counted the time zones, discussing whether they were to add or subtract ten hours.

The result was an error, and proved embarrassing, in that Frank woke Dick Reynolds up in the middle of the night. Dick was angry and said so. This must be damned important, Dr. Graham, for you to call me at three a.m.

Frank thought quickly. It is, he assured Reynolds. I couldn't wait.

Frank told his story. At the end of it, Dick sleepily asked how much money Frank wanted.

Frank told him.

All right, go ahead, go ahead, Reynolds said.

How did you do in the race, Dick? Frank asked.

I won, he said.

His boat, the Blitzen, named after his wife, was a 57-foot yawl, which he piloted himself. Goodnight, Dr. Frank, he said, and went back to sleep.

With promises of money from Reynolds and Rockefeller foundations, Frank moved on, seeking a director. Gertrude Cox was by now at work in the Agricultural Statistics office at North Carolina State; she had been recruited from Ames, Iowa, and was organizing the program in Agricultural Statistics. She told Frank about Dr. Harold Hotelling of Columbia University.

Frank and Hotelling arranged to meet in a hotel room in New York City. Frank explained his vision of a teaching department and an institute of statistics.

Hotelling had for a year or more been trying to persuade Columbia University to follow just this course. My university doesn't see it, he said. No university in America is doing what you plan to do.

Frank invited him to move to Chapel Hill.

Yes, of course he would come to Chapel Hill and would bring his staff with him, he said.

Arnold King recalls Frank coming into his office in South Building. This was on his return from the 1946 New York trip. Frank said, Arnold, I have hired the entire statistics division of Columbia University, and I want you to go tell Archibald Henderson to move the math department out of one of the two wings of Phillips Hall, say the east wing. That's where I mean to put them.

Arnold took a slow walk to Phillips Hall. He approached the matter through the great Dr. Henderson's assistant, and used the Bob House approach: You might not know this, and I might not know this, but Frank Graham yesterday hired the statistics division of Columbia University...

Frank next telephoned the trustees' executive committee, asked them to come to Chapel Hill for a session, to discuss an exciting new development. All came except one. Frank told the trustees about the importance of statistics, and to a man they argued against the new program. There was no precedent for this university, or any university, having such a department or institute. At the luncheon break, Frank hurriedly put in a call to the one trustee who had not been present and asked him to cancel everything at once and come to Chapel Hill. Emergency.

The trustee did so, even though he was out of breath on reaching Frank's office. He listened while Frank explained to him about the war effort and the nation's need in statistics, also the time lost historically while universities admit new, needed programs, and how Chapel Hill must not fail to grasp its chance in this new field, an open doorway into the future.

Statistics? The trustee told Frank he had never heard such foolishness in his life.

Frank in later years reflected on the momentary helplessness he felt, the sense of defeat, but he claimed to have met the challenge. He rose to his full 5'4", and told the trustee that his attitude would not do. In the afternoon session he must sell the other trustees on an Institute of Statistics and a Department of Mathematical Statistics.

The afternoon meeting began. Frank called on the new arrival. The poor chap gathered his resources and spoke about the universities being slow, in his opinion, in meeting modern challenges, unpardonably, dangerously slow in not joining the next move of progress in the on-going industrial revolution. The key to the future was the field of mathematical statistics, he told them. There was no question about it. And so forth. He sold his colleagues, and everybody agreed with him and Frank, at last.

Arnold King says Frank had agreed to pay Hotelling $12,000.00 a year. That was more than twice the salary of any other professor on campus. When questioned about this, Frank told Arnold we'll get to that when we have to.

Of course, within a year the secret was known everywhere. Frank was unruffled by complaints. His own salary was still $6,200.00. Arnold King says he was able to stifle the uproar by saying, Look here, if Harold is worth that, maybe there are others around here who are, too.

And, as a matter of history, that was the argument which helped bring a wave of salary increases in the University; the General Assembly could see the awkwardness of holding to a policy in which some professors made more than twice as much as others.

"Statistics" became a jewel in the University crown, at North Carolina State and Chapel Hill, and enhanced the reputation of the Consolidated University of North Carolina.

Other changes on the campus came about because of the war. The Navy established in Chapel Hill one of its three V-12 training programs, new buildings were constructed, freshmen were admitted from high school junior classes and put in three-year university courses of study for some majors, and the campuses saw an increase in racially integrated meetings.

It seemed that the war itself brought citizens closer together, even in the segregated South. For instance, Dr. Lucy Morgan, Chairman of the Department of Public Health, used every excuse to get white and black students together. Integration of the student body was illegal, but integrated educational meetings were legal, and Frank encouraged her to hold these meetings on campus. Whenever the students met on this campus, they would stay away from the windows and pull down the shades. The integrated sessions would take place monthly at alternating campuses, North Carolina College for Negroes in Durham and the University at Chapel Hill.

During World War II, "The Lost Colony" shut down; one reason, the lights would be seen out at sea and might prove helpful to German submarines.

Germany surrendered May 8, 1945. Roosevelt, ill, met with Churchill and Stalin, and returned home to have Eleanor criticize the decision to give Russia control of Czechoslovakia, Hungary, Bulgaria, all of Poland. Frank was another who recognized that this gift to Stalin was a grave error; Communistic Totalitarianism had thrown its blanket of authoritarian government over the whole of Eastern Europe, he said.

Roosevelt passed away. His vice-president, Harry Truman, a feisty and honest fellow, a friend of Frank's since service on the National Defense Mediation Board, was sworn in as president.

Japan surrendered September 2, 1945, and later that year, as of December 31, Frank resigned his post in Washington with the War Labor Board.

Harry Truman had asked him to chair another commission, the President's Oil Board, to develop guidelines for moving the nation's industrial complex from a war footing to peacetime, and Frank consented, but he agreed to serve only for a few weeks, time enough to establish the procedures. He managed the assignment well, developing the Federal program for energy and setting the pattern Truman needed for other similar commissions.
At last he was able to go home to Marian, and to the University.

To help meet the demands of student veterans, war-surplus metal temporary buildings were moved to the three campuses and converted to married-student housing -- many students were married and others damn soon planned to be. The temporary classroom buildings were hauled in on trucks. The churches contributed their Sunday School rooms for use as dormitories. Extra office desks were put along hallways. Classes were scheduled from morning till night.
In Chapel Hill, the dining hall that had been in service when Frank was made president, Swain Hall, had been replaced in wartime by Lenoir Hall, a much larger student cafeteria. Swain Hall, itself, was turned over to the University Extension Division and a new venture, a dream of Professor Earl Wynn, to bring in surplus army radio and motion picture equipment and begin making documentaries, taking the resources of the University to the people of the state. Frank and Billy Carmichael supported this plan, and also the curriculum to teach students to use the communication mediums. Trucks began to roll from the military's warehouses, loaded with equipment. The old dining hall became studios.

In the post-war adjustment process the budget was shot through with instant decisions, emergency agreements. Of course, the administration was besieged with requests for money, for construction of office and teaching space, for more books for the library.

Townspeople opened their doors to the returning veterans. One of many was Mrs. C. C. Pickard. She and her twenty-year-old son Jimmy had a six-room house at 121 North Street, two blocks from the campus, and she put two single beds in each of three spare rooms and rented them to male students for ten dollars a month each, utilities furnished. One freshman asked if that rental included breakfast, and she slammed the door in his face.

In July, 1947, Marian went to Nags Head, took Hubert and Alice to help sweep out and open up the house, but Frank didn't get away from the office until well into August. He came in time to take her and the nieces to *The Lost Colony* and talk over the political situation with Battle and Winslow.

The upheaval brought to the society by the war effort had changed the world; in America, minorities and women had made progress toward more equal opportunity, and colonies of the old empires aspired to independence. President Truman and General George C. Marshall, who became the Secretary of State, had work for Frank and needed him. President Truman in 1946-1947 was putting together a civil rights commission to appraise what was needed to help the Negro citizens. He wanted Frank, as the South's most prominent liberal, to serve on it. Then, too, there was a civil war in Indonesia, where the rebels were trying to throw off Dutch rule. Could he go out there? General Marshall said the United Nations wants to have one American on a three-person commission, and Frank was the one.

Marian had hoped for greater calm. She had hoped Frank could put the University in order, and their home, too, which had served as a Red Cross center in the war years, yes, and that they could return to an ordered life together.

Not yet.

Maybe -- she began to wonder -- if ever.

President Truman on October 1, 1947, formally appointed Frank to the three-man ''Indonesia'' committee, and the University Board of Trustees reluctantly granted Frank an indefinite leave.

While Frank was off in Indonesia, Marian spent time in the garden, preparing for next spring's planting. She managed to catch up with

Professor Coker, and he gave her advice on what shrubs might be planted now. She wanted to paint the big drawing room, the one most used during the war, but the University painters were busy doing over the temporary housing units, and the room was too large, the ceiling too high for her to do it herself.

Hubert didn't want to do it, either.

Hubert didn't know what to do with himself while Frank was away. He would go to South Building as if expecting to find him there. Of course, he knew Frank was in Indonesia, Frank and University Law Professor Henry Brandis, who had been chosen as Frank's assistant. Marian knew they were trying to start a new United States, and to set the pattern for dissolving colonialism there and throughout the world. She suspected Frank would like to have the Dutch, after three centuries of rule, give up Bali and the Spice Islands, Borneo, Sumatra, and Java with its thousand people for every square mile of land, he would want them to give up the rice and sugar and tobacco and coffee and tea and rubber and tin...

She knew something about Indonesia now, Frank before he left having read about one hundred books. She had read to him much of the time, in order to help save his sight.

She certainly knew how far Indonesia was from her home, she knew this from the cards he had sent her and the letter he had written her and those mailed to his office, which Billie Curtis, his secretary had shared. Frank had gone first to Washington to talk to Secretary of State Marshall, then had gone to Lake Success in New York State to talk with UN Secretary-General Trygve Lie.

Then the journey:

To San Francisco, three thousand miles away.

To Pearl Harbor, two thousand more miles away.

To Canton Island -- she was not sure how many more miles away.

To New Caledonia, another two thousand miles.

To Sydney, another fifteen hundred miles.

To Darwin, an added twenty-four hundred miles.

To Batavia, eighteen hundred miles.

Hubert, lost without work to do, read every newspaper in the library for news about the war in Indonesia. Seventy-seven million people: that's how many were waiting for the decision about a change in colonial government.

Dr. Graham will treat them fairly, Hubert predicted.

Driving with Hubert to Fowler's food store, or walking across campus to visit Maxine Swalin -- she and Ben Swalin had the North

Carolina Symphony offices in a "temporary" building near the lower quad -- or walking to the Carolina Inn to meet friends for lunch, Marian was astonished at the changes. Not only were there new buildings and walks, but there were three or four times as many students, and an even higher percentage of men to women; almost all the veterans were men.

Another difference was the age of the students, and their attitude. You could sense the no-nonsense, don't-waste-time commitment that Bob House had told her about recently at dinner. He and Hattie had invited her to dinner more than once since Frank had left for Indonesia.

In Indonesia, Frank was ill.

The report terrified her. Bob House came rushing across the street late at night with the news.

She decided to go to Frank at once. Bob must call General Marshall or President Truman.

Bob didn't know the number, or how to phone them at night. He wondered if the Secretary of State would be listed with telephone information.

Over eight thousand miles away, Frank was ill.

She telephoned Eliza, told her.

Eliza was concerned, comforting. She would pray for him.

What to do?

Eight thousand miles away.

The *Durham Herald* newspaper reported on November 1, 1947, that the U.N. Security Council had passed yet another resolution, had called for a cease-fire in Indonesia, but reports later in the month said the Dutch were advancing, attacking, and there were stories of atrocities on the Dutch and rebel sides.

Bob House brought her all the news as he was able to receive it, much of it from Professor Brandis.

Frank's health was returning. That was the good news.

Even yet, late in November, he and the two other officials on the committee could not persuade the rebels to meet on ground the Dutch held, and the Dutch would not meet on rebel-held ground, either. Frank, meanwhile, was meeting the men and women on both sides, was getting to know them and know about their families and hopes and fears.

It was Frank who solved the problem of finding a neutral meeting place. He telephoned Secretary Marshall, requesting a ship be provided, one both sides might meet aboard.

One without guns.

Can you imagine Frank saying that to General Marshall?, Marian

27.   Dr. Graham and President Sukarno of Indonesia, in Karachi, 1958.   *Southern Historical Collection, UNC Library*

asked one of her nieces, who was staying with her.

Secretary Marshall sent Frank the U.S. Naval transport ship Renville. There had been danger from the illness, now there was danger from sitting in the middle of an open deck, with on one side a table of Dutchmen prepared to defend three hundred years of ownership, and on the other a table full of rebels led by General Sukarno. The two groups would not meet at the same table, and the U.N. team couldn't practice favoritism by sitting with either, so there were three tables.

A telephone call from Frank to Marian reported that on January 12 word had reached him that the Dutch in the Hague had accepted six principles Frank and Henry Brandis had composed. He was confident Sukarno and his followers would accept them, too, since they were guideposts for establishing a United States of Indonesia. Frank told her a call he made to General Marshall had, he felt, been helpful in bringing about the Dutch government's agreement.

A month later, Frank returned to the United States; he had delayed his return in order to talk personally with Indonesian and Dutch leaders. His two fellow-members agreed he should make the report to the Security Council, so he flew into Washington, conferred with President Truman at the White House and with Secretary Marshall, then flew to New York State where he was present for the Security Council debate. That debate lasted two weeks.

Frank presenting his report reviewed the history of Indonesia, the culture of the people, their struggles under colonial rule, their struggle for independence, and gave the six principles agreed to by all parties. He praised the Dutch, praised the Indonesian people, sought to soothe those who were angry and to begin the healing of the wounds.

He spoke for an hour and a half. His speech concluded with praise for both sides in the wrenching struggle.

Frank and his associates won the vote in the U.N. and a time of peace was established, a United States of Indonesia was struggling to its place in the world. A beginning -- at least that had been achieved, and peace restored, and the U.N. had been made a party to further developments, at the request of both sides.

President Truman said Frank and the other two men --
...have had a profound influence in putting into practice the ideal of world law and order.
The effectiveness of United Nations machinery as demonstrated by our work has given new hope to those who have faith that by such democratic processes this ideal can be realized.

Others also were laudatory. Ali Sastroamidjojo of Indonesia, speaking before the U.N. at Lake Success, said the Committee has already achieved the first significant success in the history of the United Nations.

Secretary Marshall termed Frank's work there a miracle of diplomacy.

CHAPTER NINE

OVER THE YEARS Frank selected a corps of young male assistants. All were alert, able, educated. None was an academic by type. All were alumni of Chapel Hill or North Carolina State.

Dean of Students Francis F. Bradshaw was one. He served Frank for several years, before pulling up stakes, leaving his wife and children and taking up with another woman and her children in New York City, where he became a successful consultant in industrial psychology. His departure was a severe personal blow to Frank.

Fred Weaver was one. He was a history major, sympathetic to Frank's ideals, respectful of his administration. Once Fred revealed he wanted to go away and get his doctorate, Frank asked that Fred drive him to Greensboro, to the Woman's College campus; on the way there and back, Frank laid on arguments for Fred's changing his plans.
Dean of Students? Frank offered that.
No, still no.
Fran Weaver, Fred's wife, recalls his telling her that, as the two drove into Chapel Hill and reached the president's house, Frank turned to him. I haven't mentioned duty have I? he said.
Fred Weaver became Dean of Students.

Alex Heard, class of 1938, was one. A political scientist, he stayed for several years as Dean of the Graduate School.
Bill Friday stayed. He had graduated from North Carolina State and the Chapel Hill Law School. Fred Weaver had reminded Bill that his wife, Ida, as part of her scholarship in Public Health, had contracted to work four years for the state, and she could conveniently do that here in Chapel Hill. Fred advised him to start his law practice later, to stay here and be Assistant Dean of Students. Bill Friday stayed.
Over the years other law students looked to Dr. Frank as a model or patron, among them Henry Brandis, Terry Sanford, John Sanders, Bill Aycock, Jimmy Wallace, Joel Fleishman, and Douglass Hunt.
Hunt recalls his first meeting with a sixteen-year-old, a freshman, Allard Lowenstein, who was to become an attorney and another of Dr. Frank's favorites.

Hunt says, Lowenstein in 1945 had been at the university only a few weeks when he came to Hunt with information that dormitory rooms were being assigned by the University so as to house many, if not most, of the Jewish students in a single building, in violation of university policy. The policy allowed for an expression of preference as to both room and roommate, and most rooms were assigned to students in the order in which applications were received. When Hunt presented the matter to President Graham, he at first expressed doubt, but asked for information.

Al provided the names and room numbers, evidence that few Jewish students were assigned anywhere else. Then at Doctor Graham's request Doug Hunt talked with the University business office, to Claude Teague, and learned that his interpretation of the policy was that students who would like each other and be congenial were to be assigned as roommates and grouped together in dormitories. They had concluded that Jews would like each other.

On receiving this information, Dr. Graham sent Hunt back to Teague's office to discuss the matter further, and while Hunt was there came to Teague's office, himself. Dr. Graham had a habit of writing with this finger, writing on his open palm whenever he sought emphasis, and he wrote on his palm now as he recited word for word the University policy. He did so quietly, but firmly, taking into account the sensibilities of a long-standing officer of the University. The university's established policy was to be followed.

Al Lowenstein was active in student government -- most of Frank's favorites had been -- and his excellence in public speaking and debate put him in the top rank. He and James C. Wallace, also an outstanding debater, were involved in Raleigh sessions of the North Carolina Student Legislature. In December, 1945, many colleges and universities sent all white delegations, and they passed a motion 110 to 48 inviting students from Negro colleges to send delegates in 1946. The motion was made by Buddy Glenn of Cleveland County, a student at Chapel Hill.

This, among other actions on the first day of the session, received headlines statewide.

Thad Eure, Secretary of State, asked to come to speak. He was a Democratic Party warhorse, a powerful politician, an ultra-conservative. He was invited, and he did appear before a special session, there to set the students straight. He was a forceful, old-fashioned speaker. As he spoke, delegates applauded loudly his homilies, and gave silence to his eloquent proclamations. I am fearful that you may be jeopardizing the beautiful picture toward which we are moving, he told students, referring to race relations being maintained on a continuing, segregated status.

Some students hissed.

Eure warned that students were endangering the state's appropriation to their institution. Jimmy Wallace replied, to the effect, that if silence instead of progress were the price of the University's appropriation, then to hell with the appropriation.

By the time Eure finished his speech, he was profusely perspiring. He entertained questions from the floor. A female student from New Jersey said, to the effect, wouldn't it be wonderful if I could go back home and say North Carolina is addressing the race problem?

That's what I mean, if the Yankees would leave us be, Eure replied, misunderstanding her point.

Finally he retreated behind the dais to get a drink of water. At once a delegate, Fran Privitte, moved that the chairman thank him for his remarks and the legislature adjourn *sine die*. This motion carried unanimously. When Eure returned to do further battle, Speaker Bob Morrison said in his deep voice, I'm instructed by this house and senate, Mr. Eure, to thank you for your speech and to tell you we are adjourned *sine die*.

Over the weekend state newspapers played the story of the abrupt dismissal and of Jimmy Wallace's retort. Many trustees and alumni phoned Frank, insisting on a reprimand of the students. Doug Hunt recalls sitting at Dr. Frank's dining room table with him and Jimmy Wallace, discussing the matter with him and other students.

Dr. Frank borrowed a mechanical pencil from Hunt, one with soft lead in it. Whenever he wrote he gouged, Doug Hunt says, and the lead kept breaking; also, Hubert Robinson kept appearing from the kitchen until Jimmy Wallace realized that his foot was ringing the buzzer.

Dr. Graham issued his statement. It was conciliatory but was uncompromising. Since rumors suggested that the students creating the motion for integration were Communists or Northerners, or both, he addressed that issue. The UNC students were from North Carolina, he wrote, and the motion would have passed without their votes. The students, he wrote, in large majority are serious minded and studious, with a high sense of sobriety, with a fine sense of decency, and a responsible sense of freedom.

When interviewed about his opinion, Frank said the move toward integration was in line with the efforts of Southerners, both young and adult, to bring the South into step. He referred to the long, sometimes slow, but always sure march of human progress.

28. Dr. Graham in his office, posing patiently while student Hugh Morton sought to balance the indoor light with that outdoors so as to include the Old Well in the shot. *Photo by Hugh Morton*

CHAPTER TEN

THERE WAS A welcome-home party for Frank, February 14, 1948, on his return from Indonesia. He came into the staff meeting the next morning, rubbing his hands together, eager to get going on university business. He had been gone so long, and the university business had been in a state of daily change; Bob House simply told him the University was going ahead very well... tell us about what you've been doing, Frank.

Frank did, reporting on Indonesia. Years later, looking back, Frank said,

> You know, there was a good deal of wavering inside the State Department. A few people weren't so keen for self-determination at this time, and Josephus Daniels was the only person that said a word to me about any advice, put his arm around me and said, Frank, you're going to Indonesia. Now, I know what you've stood for in North Carolina. You've stood for freedom and self-determination here, of educational institutions, of peoples and tenant farmers, workers and so on... And I believe you're going to stand there for the people of Indonesia.
>
> I did try to do that, because there was a move on to set up a United States of Indonesia, of really Dutch puppet states, and call it the United States of Indonesia. It would be like forming the United States of America under the Tories. Lock George Washington up and some others, and then put the Tories in charge of the several states and call it the United States of America. Well, that was the Dutch program in Indonesia. Now, whatever else I didn't do, or did do, and I failed to do many things, that's one thing I got in the way of, and my country either had to repudiate me or back me up.

Marian fixed one of Frank's favorite meals. The two of them ate in the dining room with candles lit. They had his traditional New Year's Day food, since he had not had a chance to get it in Asia -- black-eyed peas and smoked ham hocks; these were sure to bring him good luck for the year. He ate them with hot cornbread and cold buttermilk.

She mentioned several of the local happenings, but his comments were about his journey. He praised Secretary George Marshall, whom he believed to be one of the smartest men he had ever met. Interestingly, at the start of each news conference, Marshall accepted scores of questions from the reporters, then answered all of them at once. Working in his office, he would finish a task before going to another; should a telephone call interrupt, he would have the caller wait until he had fully completed the work at hand. General Marshall, Frank said, was in favor of ending colonial rule in Indonesia, thus overruling most of his staff of advisors, and Frank's telephone call to him at a critical point might have produced action on his part, spelling the difference in favor of democracy. Frank said he had insisted on talking to Marshall himself, which he was sure had cost the government a great deal of money, since he had to keep the telephone line open from Jakarta until Marshall finished a letter he was writing.

After the Indonesian success, Frank was a national figure and enjoyed having the notoriety. Mail poured into South Building from all over the South, the nation, even from other countries. People were forever and a day trying to get his attention for one cause or another, but his secretary, Billie Curtis, who knew his memberships and past correspondence, helped him keep order in the office.

He began turning down more of the invitations. He couldn't do all he was asked to do, and the warnings of his friends, Kemp Battle, Billy Carmichael and others, made him more selective.

An organization that sought his support and was turned down, publicized Frank's having wished them well and expressing sincere interest in their work. He had done nothing of the sort. They based this claim on the complimentary close of his rejection letters, *with best wishes, sincerely yours.*

By now Frank was recognized everywhere he went in North Carolina, by storekeepers, laborers, bankers, Indian chiefs. Once, Paul Green and Billy Carmichael were driving with Frank to Manteo to open a new season of *The Lost Colony*, they were in Carmichael's car when he was pulled over for speeding. The highway patrolman was aloof and unbending, until he saw the small man in the front seat. He greeted Dr. Frank, tore up the ticket, and suggested his friend drive more slowly.

There then ensued a ten-minute delay while Frank talked to the officer about his birthplace and family and his training at the Institute of Government.

Frank could not expect to walk a street in downtown Charlotte, Greensboro, Winston-Salem, Wilmington or Asheville without meeting an acquaintance. He was reckless about crossing streets, too. Ruth

Julian recalls his seeing her and her husband, Ira, on the other side of a busy thoroughfare; he came to greet them, calling to them, oblivious of the traffic, and scared them and several drivers of automobiles.

Hubert Robinson found that Frank now would not make a car trip anywhere in the state without stopping so many places he could scarcely ever reach the destination. The plan was to visit here and there, run in and say a few words of greeting and hurry back to the car, that's all; however, people never wanted him to leave, and he didn't want to leave, either.

One gain to the University because of Frank's notoriety was in finding donors. He could arrange to meet people with money. Sometimes he or Billy Carmichael would invite them to a special event on campus. Football games were a favorite. Charlie Justice was all-America halfback in 1948 and 1949 and his brilliant performance on the field made the seven home games special. Frank would invite prospects to the president's box, and to come to his house after the game for tea. Tea was not the drink everybody wanted after a big game, but tea, along with an invitation to give money to the University, was what they got. He was excellent at working the distaff side of families, too. He would take hold of a woman's arms or put his around her waist, and talk with her about opportunities to help young people at Chapel Hill, State and the Woman's College.

The alumnus with the most money in the 1940s was John Motley Morehead, the elderly Chairman of the Board of Union Carbide. Soon after graduating at Chapel Hill, in his father's laboratories at Spray, North Carolina, he had invented a calcium carbide. There and at Chapel Hill he perfected the process for its manufacture. His memories of Chapel Hill in the old days were enriched by years of reflection, and Frank was pleased to reminisce with him.

Mr. Morehead was the eleventh member of his family to graduate there, and his grandfather was twice governor of the state. He and his cousin, R. F. Patterson, had previously given the ten-bell carillon bell tower to the University, which among its tunes played the Scotch-Presbyterian hymn, *How Tedious and Tasteless the Hours When Jesus No Longer I See*, which was the favorite of Morehead's grandmother.

Yes, and mine, too, Frank was able to assure him.

Mr. Morehead chose at this time to give the University a planetarium. There were only five Zeiss projectors in the United States, none on a campus. He would buy the instrument, as well as a walk-in model Copernican Orrery, and build the building.

126

29.   Edward Kidder Graham, cousin of Frank P. Graham, served as University librarian and professor of English before becoming president of the University in 1915; he was the messianic "Hunter Griswold McCoy" of Thomas Wolfe's novel, *The Web and the Rock*.   *North Carolina Collection, UNC Library*

Frank accepted, of course, and made the rounds with him to choose the site, steering him to far reaches of the campus, to the south of Kenan Stadium where a large parking lot for planetarium visitors would not devour space needed for new dormitories. No, these wooded areas were not part of the Chapel Hill Mr. Morehead remembered. The site he preferred was on Franklin Street, beside the older campus buildings, and no argument could persuade him to put his gift in the woods half a mile away.

He mentioned he might later want to give something more to the University, an argument which attracted Frank's attention. No, he was not interested in faculty salaries and fellowships. He had been a student here, not a faculty member. No, he was not interested in the Woman's College or State.

Frank suggested scholarships.

Yes, he might be willing to leave twenty million dollars for scholarships.

Done. Yes, Uncle Mott, put the planetarium on the old campus, put it wherever you want it.

Marian knew Frank considered Edward Kidder Graham to have been the great teacher. She knew that, and she decided to read Frank what Thomas Wolfe had written about EKG. At once she was sorry to have done so, because tears welled up in Frank's eyes. For days after, she noticed he would open the copy of Wolfe's novel, *The Web and the Rock*, and read the opinion Wolfe expressed in youthful, vitriolic style, his pen, as Gerald Johnson said in reference to this novel, dipped in nitric acid instead of ink:

> Monk had heard the president of the college, the late Hunter Griswold McCoy, described by Alsop not only as "the second greatest man since Jesus Christ," but as a thinker and philosopher of the first water, a speaker of the most eloquent persuasion, and the master of a literary style which, along with that of Woodrow Wilson, by which he was undoubtedly strongly influenced, was unsurpassed in the whole range of English literature. Now, having, as most boys of that age do have, a very active and questioning mind, he began to feel distinctly uncomfortable when Alsop said these things, to squirm uneasily in his chair, to keep silence, or to mumble respectful agreements, while all the time he asked himself rather desperately what was wrong with him. Because, the truth of the matter was that "the second greatest man since Jesus Christ" bored him passionately, even at the tender age of seventeen.
>
> And as for that triumphant style which Alsop assured him

was practically unsurpassed in the whole field of English
letters, he made repeated attempts to read it and digest it -- it
had been fittingly embalmed in a volume which bore the title
of *Democracy and Leadership* -- and he simply could not get
through it. As for the famous Chapel talks, which were
considered masterpieces of simple eloquence and gems of
philosophy, he hated them. He would rather have taken a
bitter laxative than sit through one of them; but sit through
them he did, hundreds of times, and endure them, until he
came to have a positive dislike for Hunter Griswold McCoy.
His pale, pure face, somewhat pale and emaciated, a subtle
air he conveyed always of bearing some deep, secret sorrow,
and of suffering in some subtle, complicated way for
humanity, began to afflict Monk with a sensation that was
akin to, and in fact was scarcely distinguishable from the less
acute stages of nausea...

If the wine of life was here, he squeezed the grape
desperately, and it shattered in his fingers like a rusty post.
"Democracy and leadership," "education for the good life,"
"service, "ideals," all the rest of it -- did not mean a damn
thing to him.

Saddened, Frank would lay her copy of the novel aside.

Marian never told Frank that he was in the novel, too. Young Wolfe
had written that the only person more insufferable than Edward Kidder
Graham was his young cousin.

Frank was never one to duck a fight. Fred Weaver used to tell about
Dr. Frank phoning him at home one evening, asking if he would do
something for him. Frank said a reporter had telephoned, investigating a
rumor that at the student-sponsored concert that night at Memorial Hall,
blacks and whites were to be seated together.

Fred made the visit to Memorial Hall and phoned Frank at home, to
say it was all right, nothing to it, the blacks were being seated off to
themselves up in the balcony.

Dr. Frank asked Fred if he would do something more.

Yes, of course, Fred responded.

I want you to go ask the students in charge to seat the people where
they want to sit, Frank said, and call this reporter and tell him that at
Chapel Hill in public meetings we do not any longer distinguish.

30. Frank and Marian Graham. *North Carolina Collection, UNC Library*

CHAPTER ELEVEN

ONE OF FRANK'S MISSIONS was fairly to represent the Woman's College in Greensboro and State College in Raleigh as members of the Consolidated University. Also, he sought excellent faculty members for the other two campuses, as well as for Chapel Hill. Frank would discuss his travails and successes with Marian, with friends, with strangers on the trains, with students, as in this case:

There was a great director of the experiment station at State College. Well, we had two blows at one time. One was -- Washington took him away from the State College, R.Y. Winters, a native of Charleston and a great spirit. Well, the budgets for agricultural research had been very small, at best. And then when further slashes came, of course, that meant on a matching basis that federal funds went down, too.

And we lost our soils, the chief of our soils program. And soils is basic to a land-grant college, to a school of agriculture. So we decided that since the board of trustees by resolutions definitely put this responsibility on me -- I wasn't an imperialist out grabbing power -- they put it on me and made no mistake about where they concentrated that responsibility, so I thought, now let's make a beginning in the fundamentals -- that is, in the science of soils -- and build around that with the great groundwork, and tradition, and men that are already there.

Let's never forget that. So I went down to Washington and asked them to give me the names of a half a dozen of the real able soils men of the United States. I don't care where they are, let me have them. And they gave me, oh, about a half a dozen names. And I went around, exploring and checking on these men.

And I found each one of them was a good man, but not a one of them was a top man. And it shocked me to learn, later, that they didn't give me the half a dozen top men in the United States because they just seemed to take it for granted that a preeminent man couldn't even be approached about coming to a southern land-grant college or university. And that shocked me. And in checking on these half dozen that they gave me, I found out who the four or five best men in soils in the country were.

One of them was in Wisconsin, one of them was at DuPont, and one of them was at Ohio State. And one was at Cornell; I almost forgot that -- Bradley of Cornell. Well, Bradley was very much attracted because of the challenge, but he said, I'm getting on. I don't think I should leave Cornell. If I were younger, he said, I would come. But I've got a young man here, though, that's on the way. He's one of the State College's own boys from Rockingham County -- Reidsville, I believe -- named Cummings. So when you get your chief man, don't forget Cummings.

And I went to see Parker over at DuPont. He was from Alabama, a top student at Auburn in Alabama and also a top student in PhD work at Wisconsin. He was very much attracted, but somehow or other the word got around in the state that I was about to bring an agent of the fertilizer trust to State College. He felt that was such a handicap, he asked me to withdraw his name. Then that left -- well, I went to see the Wisconsin man, and by the way, he became Dean of the School of Agriculture at Wisconsin. He was so deeply rooted there and had such an opportunity before him, he said that much as he'd like to come -- but I'm saying that all of these top men were not looking down on southern institutions as beneath their greatest effort.

And that left Salter of Ohio, who was the top soils man in that part of the world. And he visited with me at my home in Chapel Hill. And I might say my wife, Marian, helped tremendously with him in interpreting our state and our three institutions to him. And he was much impressed by the opportunities at State College and what was there. He laid down one condition, and it wasn't salary. He knew our salaries were below the average. He said, I'll come if I may bring my -- he didn't say he was his protégé, but he was his protégé, Dr. L. D. Baver.

We didn't have quite that much money, but we said, All right, you bring Baver.

And Salter and Baver came, and they were two of the top men in the country. And this idea that southern institutions are second-rate by nature or geography or something is a myth. And there's just as much striving for excellence here -- with the money we have -- as there is anywhere. Sometimes I think more, on a comparative basis with the available funds.

You've got to challenge them with opportunity and also with decent salaries. You can't -- did you know that the three-fold University of North Carolina, with the lowest salary scale, is now at the top in the South in many ways? Including the southwest. And State College is now recognized as a university, on the basis of a severe test projected by students of higher education at the University of Chicago. And they put Texas and North Carolina as the two top in the southern states.

Frank's often-repeated contention was that universities had been slow in accepting their role as practical servants of the people, a charge which irritated many of the faculty.

He once in a recorded conversation expressed his views:

As you go through centuries you'll find that the colleges and universities, with all their great values in transmitting the great heritage of the Greco-Roman civilization and the Judaic-Christian heritage, were always about a half century behind in catching up with the needs of the people.

You remember in Renaissance times, the universities were ultra-scholastic as a heritage from the medieval period. And then with the coming of science and modern languages, the universities were a little bit slow admitting the sciences and the modern European languages to a basis of equal status with Latin and Greek. But the modern languages and science broke into the universities.

And then science and the old classics got somewhat exclusive and didn't want to admit the social sciences, even in the times of the social dynamics of an industrial age. Then the classics, and the sciences and social sciences felt a little exclusive about letting in agriculture and engineering, but through the Morrill Act, they got in. And the great land-grant college idea has become one of the basic parts of higher education in America.

The fine arts were never given space in Frank's progress report, and his success in the arts was not anywhere near as spectacular as in social and political sciences, mathematics and health fields. Indeed, it was disappointing.

On assuming the presidency, he inherited practical, lively programs in drama and in music.

The first professor and director of music had been hired in 1919 during his famous cousin's administration. He was Paul John Weaver. At first, following the death in 1919 of President E. K. Graham, he had difficulty finding quarters, many of the other faculty members resenting a new curriculum, and he met students under a tree. He found space in

Old West, then New West, then Person Hall. Within ten years he was offering the bachelor degree, had a faculty of five, and had one of the most talented and highly trained glee clubs in the country, which performed in 1927 in New York City, England and France.

Graduates of the University who forged careers in music included composer Hunter Johnson, a student from 1924 to 1926; Norman Cordon, 1922-24, the first American-trained singer to go to the Met; John Scott Trotter, choral conductor, student in 1926; band leaders Hal Kemp, who graduated in 1926, and Kay Kyser, class of 1928. Pulitzer Prize winner Lamar Stringfield had begun the North Carolina Symphony within the Music Department, and Paul Green was working with the composers-in-residence on new works. That was the situation when Frank assumed the presidency in 1930.

In drama, Frederick Koch had also been hired in the administration of Edward Kidder Graham. The teaching of playwriting and production of student plays was by many professors resented; however, Koch established a teaching and production company, the Carolina Playmakers, which attracted some of the best students in the University.

Paul Green saw his first play there -- his own. Thomas Wolfe discovered dramatic writing there. Betty Smith and other writers migrated there; she wrote *A Tree Grows in Brooklyn* while a member of the Playmakers. Nationally known in drama and music, the University was vigorous and practical in these two mighty art forms when Frank became president.

In his administration the blows began to fall. He found that the then chairman of music was not all he claimed, in terms of degrees. Frank fired him. He then had a faculty committee to select a new chairman; chosen by the members was a person of sterling academic qualifications, the President of the American Musicological Society, Glen Haydon. Quite soon the performance side of the Music Department began to suffer. One unhappy professor, looking back, says Haydon was interested in books about music more than in music.

The art department was started by Frank, himself, but here, too, he showed none of the charisma shown in some other subjects. Carlyle Sitterson says Frank was walking across campus, following a snowstorm, and came upon Arnold Borden, who was creating a very attractive snowman and began telling Dr. Frank about this sculpture. Frank decided to start an art department. He hired to head the department a painter who had recently done a sculpture for Mildred Graves of St. Francis of Assisi. He had no training in art, and the faculty members revolted.

An art historian was hired when Frank received a phone call from the American Friends Service Committee in New York, reporting that Dr. Clemens D. Sommer and his family, fugitives from Nazi Germany, had arrived in New York City. Frank said to send them to Chapel Hill. Sommer began his work for the University before World War II and reported having the same conversation with Frank every time he saw him, Frank asking when he was going to begin painting pictures?

In none of the arts was Frank successful in maintaining or building a successful training program for young artists; the programs became heavy with lore and learning, lacked life, they lacked the sounds and sights and feelings of the arts themselves.

Niece Elizabeth Matheson recalls being told by Frank that he was responsible for getting Josef Albers, another German fugitive, to Black Mountain College. Frank was proud of that. Influenced by Albers, that small, impoverished school in the mountains of North Carolina became for several years the most important training center of visual artists in the country. Albers taught the Bauhaus principles of abstract design and composition. Albers' slogan at Black Mountain College was this: God save us from spectators and humanists. Not a prayer that would have placed him in good standing with Chapel Hill's faculty, or many others.

Meanwhile, on more practical, applied fronts, new opportunities were developing, among them prospects of an educational television station license. And Ben Swalin and his wife Maxine had revived the North Carolina Symphony, operating it well outside the Music Department. Major changes were taking place in medicine. Kay Kyser had been persuaded to lead a statewide drive for a massive good health program.

After playing many roles in the Met and the lead in "Street Scene" on Broadway, Norman Cordon returned to Chapel Hill, he and his family, and Victor Bryant, trustee, helped him start the Institute of Opera in the Extension Division, which was meant to scout out talented singers.

Walter Golde, Cordon's voice coach, also moved to town. Almost at once Cordon discovered an excellent singer, Donna Patton, who had been Montana's runner-up for Miss America. She was in Chapel Hill now on an opera scholarship.

Also, Victor Bryant was discovered. A successful attorney, he often had claimed he would give up all he had if he could only sing well. He took lessons from Goldie and Norman, then he rented the Communication Center's recording studio for one evening. Donna Patton joined him. Goldie and Norman were present, along with Mack Preslar, the recording engineer, and the singers recorded a duet by Sigmund Romberg, which was described later as being unsuccessful.

Marian, as the President's wife, continued to receive reports and gossip daily. Some were intended to be passed on to Frank, as she knew very well, and sometimes they were.

She was surprised, in talking with Jack Merritt, the campus policeman, to find that Frank had more than once asked Merritt to accompany him to the Chapel Hill Cemetery, where Frank proceeded to ask about the people buried there, who they were, how they were related, what they had done for a living, what subjects they had taught in the University.

CHAPTER TWELVE

IT WAS NOT EASY being the South's leading white liberal in the 1920s and 1930s, and it became a harder bed in the 1940s and 1950s. In the earlier period, white liberals in the South had been few in number. If they obeyed the law, as Frank always had, they were tolerated as curiosities. Once the laws were being tested, however, once changing the segregation laws was at all possible, anger often erupted in the South.

For instance, in 1948 Bayard Rustin and two other black men and three white men came through the South, seeking a way to challenge segregated interstate busing, and he and his friends were dragged off a bus in, of all places, Chapel Hill, and were roughed up and threatened by white taxi drivers. The police rescued them and phoned Charlie Jones, pastor of the Chapel Hill Presbyterian Church, who was known to favor integration and to hold integrated church services. Jones took the six to his house, and he and his wife fed and reassured them, even while the taxi drivers threw rocks at the parsonage.

Frank telephoned Charlie Jones and invited him, his wife and guests to come to his house. Jones told him he was not getting help from the police, who had left and wouldn't return, and he thought he had better take his wife and guests out of town. He did so, then himself returned to his parsonage and braved out the storm.

As Frank and Marian recalled, Paul Green had once described the University of North Carolina as a great lighthouse casting its light afar, but dark at its own base. And so it appeared to be; rather dark at the base and growing darker.

Paul and Elizabeth had a similar experience when they had black author Richard Wright come to Chapel Hill while he and Paul were adapting his novel, *Native Son*, for Broadway. Paul was then living in a big house on Greenwood Road, at some distance from campus. He and Elizabeth were threatened, should they not evict "the nigger." Where to evict him Paul didn't know, for the Carolina Inn wouldn't, couldn't accept a black man as resident, and there was no "black" tourist court that Paul knew of. This rule of segregated residence had many fences girding it about, much custom and habit.

There was no place to send Richard Wright. Paul didn't intend to send him anywhere anyway, and he also rode out the storm.

The fury came from decades past, much of it from the degradation and guilt of slavery, the bloody Civil War and, in the South, the trauma of the reconstruction period. Some of it had to do with the color of black skin; some of it had to do with differences in the blacks' culture as it was perceived, their attitudes toward family, work, religion. The poor whites had most to lose by lifting of the bans which restricted the blacks, and were the ones most likely to be violent. The middle-class whites were the guardians of culture and were suspicious of admitting an alien culture.

The situation was dangerous, and was painful. In the South, lack of court and police protection for blacks was common, as was denial of their voting rights, repression of their freedom of speech, denial of adequate education or housing or hospital and other medical treatment, denial of a place to room while traveling, or to eat in a restaurant, or to use the toilet. A factory hiring both races must have four toilets, two for blacks, two for whites. They were required to have two drinking fountains.

President Truman's Committee on Civil Rights made its report on October 29, 1947. The commission members had met ten times, some of these while Frank was in Indonesia; Frank was not at the presentation. The committee recommended the elimination of segregation based on race, color, creed, or national origin, from American life.

The committee also recommended programs to help bring this about. Among them they asked that the separate-but-equal doctrine in education and public facilities be discredited, be labeled as yet another way to demean blacks, that the poll tax be eliminated, that the governmental machinery for protecting civil rights be strengthened.

The committee favored Federal compassion through grants-in-aid and a forced program of fair employment practices. Frank was not present at the meeting when use of Federal force was discussed, he opposed Federal coercion for civil rights or fair employment practices and wrote a minority statement for the final report:

> ...The best way ultimately to end segregation is to raise the educational level of the people in the states affected; and to inculcate both the teachings of religion regarding human brotherhood and the ideals of our democracy regarding freedom and equality as a more solid base for genuine and lasting acceptance by the peoples of the states.

The report was long, and the citizens most in need of studying it were not serious readers. Throughout North Carolina, even in the town of Chapel Hill and on the faculty, criticism of Frank became more shrill. The University, itself, felt threatened because of the President's representation of blacks.

President Truman's Civil Rights report had been released well before Senator McCarthy and his assistant, Roy Cohn, released their attack on Frank in a document sixteen pages long. A dozen organizations were listed as being Communist fronts, a dozen Frank had at one time or another joined. Chief among them was the Southern Conference on Human Welfare, which was described by the House Committee on Un-American Activities as being "perhaps the most obviously camouflaged Communist-front organization..."

> Frank P. Graham, head of the University of North Carolina, was the first chairman of the Southern Conference for Human Welfare and today remains as its honorary president. He is not a Communist and no doubt on occasion has had some differences with the Communist party. He is, however, one of those liberals who show a predilection for affiliation with various Communist-inspired front organizations.

These attacks encouraged defenders, and their efforts led to renewed attacks. The University rocked back and forth. One battery of charges had to do with Frank's having recently been made chairman of the Oak Ridge Institute of Nuclear Studies, a consortium sponsored by fourteen Southern universities to make atomic energy facilities available to the scientific staffs of Southern universities. At Oak Ridge, Tennessee, were the secrets of the atomic bomb, the most wanted, most valuable of America's secrets. Radio commentator, Fulton Lewis, Jr. claimed information that the Institute's own security team had recommended Frank Graham not be given clearance, only to be overruled by the Board itself. In six straight broadcasts on national radio, Lewis plunged ahead with dire warnings.

When this storm broke over President Truman, he made a personal defense of Frank to the press, spoke with feeling, and was indignant at the charges against him.

Eventually the fire and smoke of the exposure died down. There were a few speeches in the House and Senate, and they were reported in the state newspapers. Frank wrote a letter explaining his memberships, indicating pride and no apology, and sent it to Fulton Lewis, Jr., among others. His further response to the climate of fear was to make more and more talks to students, and he accepted invitations to speak to women's clubs, men's clubs, alumni gatherings, labor union meetings, farm meetings, where he stuck out his jaw, as Bob House told Marian, and laid out the truth about this country. He told students the advice coming out of the McCarthy charges was *don't take chances, don't join anything for fear of reprisal years later*; his advice to all citizens was *do take chances on making our country better than it is.*

Marian drove him to some of these speech-makings. So did Ida Friday, who recalls his getting in her car ready for a run to a nearby city where he was to speak and be interviewed. He had a sandwich in a box, the first food he had had that day. Along the way he said he believed, if she would excuse him, he would eat his lunch. He opened the box and a pair of pajamas popped out.

Ida bought him a sandwich. Frank, as usual, had no money on him.

He was often exhausted these days, Marian realized, and was certainly open to another attack of pneumonia. Her life had become even more different from the relaxed life in her father's rectory, where controversy was over such choices as Sunday's flowers and hymns, and personal matters in families of parishioners usually discussed calmly, sympathetically. Today her home was a seat of controversy, the telephone often ringing, most of the calls from supporters or critics. Marian didn't claim to know all of the callers, though Frank did. Jonathan Daniels told her on the telephone -- he was editor of the *News and Observer* -- that his father, Josephus, claimed to have built his home out of the rocks thrown at him, and Frank soon could do the same.

She didn't want to build her house that way.

She did want to build a house.

Jonathan continued talking about his father -- Frank had told her Jonathan was prone to do that -- and he said one Republican legislator once shouted in fury in the General Assembly that the state ought to move the capitol out of Raleigh, and leave only the prison, the insane asylum, and the *News and Observer*. Jonathan's father as editor of the *News and Observer* replied that the legislator had named the three institutions needed to keep North Carolina Republicans honest.

A reporter from the *News and Observer* came to the house to interview Frank, and Marian sat with him over a pot of tea, waiting for Frank to come home.

Tell me about your husband, he suggested.

I wouldn't know quite how, she admitted. She told the reporter she would not like to appear in his newspaper.

Al Lowenstein came by the house, hoping to talk with Frank. He told the reporter Dr. Frank had spoken to a dozen campus leaders late last night, about eleven o'clock. Students have schedules until about then, he said. They're likely to be free after eleven. Al Lowenstein said an organization of student leaders was being formed, the National Student Association.

Marian liked Dr. Billy MacNider, Dean of the Medical School, very much. One evening he came by the house to talk to Frank about the medical school and told them both a story about himself as a young doctor.

A farmer came to my office, he said, and asked me to come out to his house and treat his wife, who had cut her leg with an ax while chopping wood. Did she cut herself today? I asked him.

No, two weeks ago.

I went with him and found the lady had bandaged her leg with dirty rags, so I knew I would find gangrene. Not at all. Hers was a clean wound.

How did you treat this, I asked her.

With a bread poultice, she told me.

It was quite a mystery, but right then and there I had discovered penicillin and was too damn dumb to know it.

Walking through the arboretum, Marian stopped still, startled by newly penciled letters on the arbor post.

Ralph loves Nicky

Forever

How beautiful, she thought, life goes on.

Shouldn't write on school property, she thought.

Marian was shown a paper Frank had written about Thomas Wolfe, which she approved, although she did mention he or his secretary had misspelled *Wolfe*.

I recall Tom Wolf *[sic]* as one of the most vivid personalities who attended the University of North Carolina during my time.

He was one of the most popular students of his college generation -- a leader in his class, in the student government, and in the general life of the University. He was elected by his class to be a member of the Student Honor Council and by the student body to be Editor-in-Chief of the student newspaper, The Daily *[sic]* Tar Heel. He distinguished himself in Professor Koch's playmaking group, both as a writer of mountain folk-plays and as an actor in the mountaineer roles. He was considered, even as a student, to be one of the most brilliant writers who ever served as

Editor-in-Chief of the Tar Heel. Some of his editorials were reprinted in papers all over the State. He was the favorite after-dinner speaker at all sorts of banquets held by classes, societies and fraternity groups. He was early marked for distinction by Professor Edwin Greenlaw of the English Department and by Professor Horace Williams, head of the Department of Philosophy.

He was absent-minded and often had little sense of time. Sometimes he would start writing his theme for English class, due the next day, after his long bull sessions in a dormitory. In the torrential overflow of this ideas and style he would run out of the regulation paper required in the English course and then, after hours when all stores were closed, he would seize upon any kind of paper he could get his hand on to continue his essay, play, or short story. He would write on the back of wrapping paper, tissue paper, and any other thing that would keep the imprint of his flowing pen or pencil. Professor Greenlaw's impulsive indignation at such disorganized proce-dure would give way to enraptured appreciation of his genius.

I recall Tom's tender appreciation of his mother on the occasion of her attendance at his graduation exercises. He made engagements for her well in advance. I remember he gave me the opportunity and pleasure of taking her to the Senior Ball. She enjoyed very much seeing Tom enjoy himself.

The last time I saw him he came up to my room when I had flu. He and Corydon Spruill had a most enjoyable time talking of old days here, and his reminiscences were most vivid. He had his old gusto for conversation and zest for living which made him such a picturesque figure in his students days here.

Even after Frank's parents had died, Christmas was spent each year in Charlotte. Each year plans of his two maiden sisters revolved around Frank and Marian being present, and they were charming hosts. Marian detected, however, that within Scots still lingered a suspicion of anything which smacks of papist or regal celebration, even on occasion of the Christian festival. Presbyterian church services were few and were spare, were by her standards bare acknowledgement; she learned that in Scotland Christmas day was not even a public holiday, that its recognition came at regular services on the closest Sunday.

Frank's doctor, Charlotte physician Otho Ross, agreed with her about the meagerness of ceremony, even though he was also Presbyterian, but his contention was that public education was thought to be a moral equivalent in Scotland, that was where the faith of the

Scots lay, in the schools. He said in Scotland fifty-five per cent of students stay in school beyond sixteen, and the score is on the rise, while in England and America it was by recent statistics thirty-five per cent.

As if, Marian thought, that explained the lack of festivity at Jesus' birth.

The sisters did love Frank so much, that failing to spend Christmas with them would have been -- well, she felt it would have been un-Christian.

Out in the state, on his way to a Sunday afternoon appointment for a talk, Frank asked his two student companions to stop for a church service. He chose a Presbyterian church, of course. Afterward, and after Frank had met many of the people in attendance, the trio hurried through the rain to their car.

On the drive out of the parking lot, they saw an elderly lady leaving the church, vainly trying to open her umbrella.

Pull over, Frank said to the driver, Mac Nesbitt. He rolled down his window. Will you come with us? he asked the woman.

You little renegade, she snapped, slapping at him with her folded umbrella and hurrying on.

After a long while Frank broke the silence inside the car. Boys, he said, I'm asking you to never tell about this.

On March 6, 1949, North Carolina's junior United States senator, J. Melville Broughton, passed away. The task of filling the post by appointment fell to the State's governor, Kerr Scott.

Scott was a liberal Democrat, a plain spoken dairy farmer with grassroots support among working men and women. For his election he had pulled together a coalition of farmers, factory workers and elements of the black communities, and had launched a number of populist-type programs, including the largest rural road paving program ever undertaken in America. He had even championed legalization of wine-making by farmers, excusing it in this largely prohibitionist state by saying the people needed wine to use in their church communion services.

Into his hands, and his alone, fell the task of selecting a person to replace Broughton, to serve until the next statewide election, about twenty months. As one might expect, he received an avalanche of advice. He wrote names of prospects on the back of an envelope, and when that space was filled, he transferred the list to a piece of paper. To be on Kerr Scott's list was something of an honor, and he didn't mind adding to it, erasing from it, and showing it to intimates.

One of the intimates was Jonathan Daniels, editor of the *News and Observer.*

You don't have Frank's name on the list, Jonathan told him.

Kerr Scott mulled that over, transferred his cigar to the other side of his mouth. Do you think Frank would take it? he asked.

I don't know, Jonathan admitted.

Mrs. Scott knew there was a list. One evening Kerr Scott read the names to her, read them slowly, a name at a time, each time waiting for her opinion.

She said nothing until he reached Frank's name, and then she said simply, You can stop right there so far as I'm concerned, that's it.

The Governor was intrigued by the idea. It made sense politically. Should he choose any one of the three contenders who had the most political support, he would alienate supporters of the others. He asked Jonathan to sound out Frank.

Daniels had developed back trouble, a socket of his spine would occasionally slip out of place causing intense pain, and he rarely traveled far from his doctor; however, he risked driving to Chapel Hill. His meeting was with both Frank and Marian. The presentation appeared to stun them both. Prying Frank loose from the University would be traumatic, Daniels had realized all along, and he was not surprised by the immediacy of Frank's refusal, and by Marian's objection to Frank entering politics as a politician. Frank is simply not a politician, she told him, told them both.

Being a senator was an august assignment, and Frank would distinguish himself, Jonathan argued. Daniels was a persuasive spokesman, and did know Washington; Daniels had been Assistant Director, Office of Civilian Defense, Administrative Assistant to President Roosevelt and Press Secretary to Roosevelt and President Truman.

Frank said he must hesitate to accept any appointment which would require him to leave his post permanently. No, he would not accept.

Later, Governor Scott phoned Frank, asked him to reconsider. Frank told him no, he had thought it over and would not accept.

Scott sent Jonathan Daniels again to meet with him. Jonathan went down the list of issues being discussed in the Senate, among them America's actions in the Indonesia independence matter, the North Atlantic Treaty, the Marshall plan, the cold war, foreign aid, armament, disarmament. Frank would be helpful with all. Also, sitting in the White House was his friend Harry Truman, and in the State Department

32. Governor Kerr Scott, Frank Porter Graham and Jonathan Daniels.
Photograph by Ollie Atkins, courtesy of The Saturday Evening Post.

was another friend, Secretary George C. Marshall.

Frank and Marian wavered. The arguments were almost overwhelming.

However, when later Frank and Marian walked through their home together, and later visited the building site Kemp Battle had given them for a retirement home of their own, and walked through the campus, they decided not ever to leave Chapel Hill.

Frank phoned the Governor and told him his final decision was not to accept.

All along the Governor had been badgered by newspaper and radio reporters to announce his choice. He told them a dark horse entered his office about every hour, and there was no hurry to choose. Meanwhile, his mind became more set on Graham. Would Frank at least have a physical examination, to see if he was fit for the office.

Frank did so. He was.

The Governor and Jonathan came to Chapel Hill. At the Graham's house, the Governor told Frank nobody was tying him to anybody's coattail, he would be absolutely free to advocate civil rights bills, aid to education, whatever he pleased. The offer was, he said, not to be refused. He also promised not to leave the University in weak hands.

Back in Raleigh, the Governor invited to his office the head of State College, Harrelson, the Woman's College, Jackson, and Chapel Hill, House. He also invited Billy Carmichael and Jonathan Daniels. The six discussed the suggestion of Frank becoming a senator. The three university administrators were asked if they favored this appointment. Each admitted he had been hopeful Frank would not leave for other federal appointments, but not one raised an objection to his becoming a senator.

Governor Scott decided to make the announcement in Chapel Hill. O. Max Gardner had left a fund sufficient to give a prize each year to the member of the University faculty on any of the three campuses who had during the year made the largest contribution to the world. Making such a determination, especially for a given year, was a weighty matter, but for the first Gardner Award a professor at the Woman's College was selected, and the faculties of the three institutions were invited to join Governor Scott at dinner on March 22 to honor Louise B. Alexander and listen to her acceptance speech.

Ida Friday recalls the evening. Bill Friday knew something important might be revealed; Bob House had admitted as much to him but hadn't given any hints. The Governor and Mrs. Scott were present, as were the chancellors of the three campuses and hundreds of faculty. Bill and Ida didn't know from where the surprise was to come.

After dinner Governor Scott rose to speak and began congratulating Professor Alexander. He had an informal speaking style, conversational, rambling, hesitant. One might think Kerr Scott wasn't exactly aware of what he was thinking about. While I'm on my feet, he said, I want to make an announcement. The next senator from North Carolina will be Frank P. Graham.

Astonishment. Cautiously people asked each other what the Governor had said. Confusion. Disbelief. Belief. Cheers. A standing ovation.

Scott's few words had changed the lives of Frank and of Marian. She sat beside him at the head table, quiet as could be, watching the people gratefully as they thundered praise for Frank.

Indeed, the announcement affected the lives of everyone in the room. All tasks and assignments and responsibilities were altered. The University without Frank Graham? Who could imagine what that would mean?

Frank was called on. I said no, he told them, but the Governor is a stubborn Scotch Presbyterian. I found I would have to say yes.

The news went out over the press wires. Before reading about it, Harry Truman had been told the appointment was made. He couldn't have been more pleased.

On March 27th, a Sunday, a mere five days later, students, faculty and townspeople were invited to the president's house in the afternoon. More than fifteen hundred came. At twilight Frank was asked by a student to speak to the crowd.

> As I said to the Governor, this has been the most difficult decision of my life -- to leave this place, these institutions and these people which have been a part of my life for over forty years. I feel we will take with us your understanding, your thoughts and your prayers.
>
> Mrs. Graham and I thank you from the bottom of our hearts. Good-bye to all of you.

He and Marian joined in the singing of *Hark the Sound*, the college anthem. Many were weeping. It was, as everybody realized, the end of an era.

Among the townspeople, there generally was regret. Charlie Jones had been under attack at the Presbyterian Church, from members and

33. Saying Goodbye. Frank and Marian leave the President's home
and the University so that Frank can take the Senate seat in Washington.
Southern Historical Collection, UNC Library

from officers of the Presbytery, and Frank had been a reliable pillar to lean on. His daughter Mary remembers how, on Sundays as church let out, she and her sister would wait for their papa to finish talking with Dr. Graham in order that Sunday dinner could be served at home. There the two men stood, face to face, on the sidewalk, discussing the sermon, or Indonesia, or the student lunches, or the weekly, integrated dinner meetings, or whatever. Mary hid behind a bush, stomach grumbling, and waited, with her own prayer: that they would stop talking. Half an hour was the briefest of their conversations.

The Baptist pastor, Samuel Habel, might very well welcome Frank's leaving town. The First Baptist Church was divided as to whether to welcome blacks to the services, unless they agreed to sit in the balcony. The Assistant Pastor, J. C. Herrin, was working to bring integration about.

A few townspeople were displeased that a liberal who allowed Communists to attend the University would be a Senator. The faculty had a few Frank Graham detractors, too, among them some in the School of Medicine who felt that medicine had been held back, and they blamed Frank.

Then there were academicians who felt Frank and his financial administrator, Comptroller Billy Carmichael, had been diluting the University springs by neglecting the old-line departments, including Frank's department, history. They argued that the Extension Division was too much supported, as was the new Communication Center, as were the Institute of Government, the Department of Statistics, the School of Public Health, and increases within the medical faculty.

Admittedly, Frank's administration had been wary of humanists. Billy Carmichael had the habit of privately referring to them as *academaniacs*. Frank rarely sought out humanists for staff appointments, favoring lawyers and political scientists.

Many of the athletic people would not be unhappy to see Frank go. His efforts to "clean up" college sports in the University and in the Southern Association of Colleges and Schools had left them disgruntled, and wary of him.

Also, there were the low faculty salaries; Frank appeared not to care nearly enough about raising them. And his troublesome, public social stands, his idealism, causing him to see goals impractical now to reach.

On the whole, however, there was regret among faculty members that Frank and Marian were leaving. Not a few had accepted their own appointments because Frank Graham was here; others had stayed, even when offered higher salary elsewhere, because he was here.

The national reputation of the University at Chapel Hill had been enhanced and in part rested on the president's strong stands for freedom, openness -- a word he and Bob House often used -- and progress toward the goal of making the University the practical and timely servant of all the people of the state.

Carlyle Sitterson recalls standing nearby while Frank was packing up, preparing to vacate his office. Frank paused, stood at the window for a while looking out at the campus. Quietly, rather sadly, Frank said, I'm leaving here now, and I carry a lot of scars.

The University was quite willing to grant Frank a leave of absence, but Kerr Scott told the trustees this would make Frank appear to be a caretaker senator, appointed to fill out twenty months of the Broughton term and that only.

This has to be a permanent break with the University, he said.

And so it was.

Frank and Marian together visited the site, their building lot, met there with Hubert Robinson, discussed finding a workman to keep the lawn mowed, the bushes trimmed -- while we're away, Marian said.

Bob House was heard to say, wandering office to office in South Building, We love each other better and the place just seems to go better when he's around.

34.   Frank Porter Graham and Governor, then Senator, J. Melville Broughton, who died in office, Frank succeeding him.   *Photograph by Hugh Morton*

35. Frank and Marian during the Washington days. *Courtesy of the Division of Archives and History, NC Department of Cultural Resources.*

CHAPTER THIRTEEN

MARIAN WAS ADVISED by "Miss Mary" Scott to ask Hubert Humphrey to help her and Frank find a place to live in Washington, D.C. Miss Mary had heard only good about him, and Kerr liked him as much as she did.

Marian found that Senator Broughton's staff people had anticipated her need of an apartment and were able to advise her. Also, the other North Carolina Senator, Clyde Hoey, was willing to help.

Marian chose a small apartment in the Congressional Hotel. The sitting room window afforded a beautiful view of the United States Capitol about three blocks away, close enough for Frank to walk to work, which she would encourage him to do on dry, warm days.

There were a few staff people to be housed as well. Not many. Speculation in Chapel Hill as to whom Frank would take with him centered on favorite aides, among them Bill Friday. Ida Friday had more than a passing interest in Bill's possible selection; his going would toss their family into a career quandary -- her career as well as Bill's. It had been almost two weeks after Governor Scott's announcement that Frank mentioned the subject to Bill, came up to him on the South Building steps near the Old Well and said directly, Bill, I'm not taking you to Washington because you are needed here.

Frank gave the same message to others in places of responsibility on the Chapel Hill, Raleigh and Greensboro campuses. He selected to bring with him young people who had not as yet found a job, among them Allard Lowenstein, whose political views were Frank's own. He was as yet single, without a family to move to Washington, was a clean-living person and a hard worker. He seemed to have spent his college days doing classwork all day and at night attending student meetings he and others called. He was not a radical but did, like Frank, go where radicals were, was drawn to debate with them, was attracted to fire, as it were, going close but never being burned.

Even before Frank reached the Senate, on March 23rd, he was the topic of spirited debate on the Senate floor. The debate centered on the "Communism" issue. Senator John Bricker of Ohio invited the members to consider the new senator's controversial high-security clearance at the Atomic Energy Commission. Also, he had a statement about Frank that was from a Mr. Paul Couch, for eighteen years a member of the Communist Party. Mr. Couch admitted having respect for Dr. Graham and said he was not a Communist, but he claimed Frank had allowed himself to be used by them. He wrote,

> The majority of my associates in the party leadership regarded such people with secret contempt to be used until the revolution and then cast aside or liquidated.

North Carolina Senator Clyde Hoey rose to defend Frank, saying,

> That very criticism has been made in North Carolina, but there has never been any suggestion that he is not loyal and no one who knows him would hesitate to trust him.

Senator Wayne Morse, who knew Graham from service with the War Labor Board, said Frank was exceedingly high on his list of the twenty-five greatest living Americans. He said,

> The tribute that I now pay him, no man has the right to pay any human being, unless he knows the man so intimately that he can be sure that the characteristic of Dr. Graham I now state is a justifiable tribute. I say that Dr. Graham is one of the most Christ-like men I have ever met... I want to say I care not what board raises questions as to the loyalty of Frank Graham. Small though in stature he may be, he is a giant in loyalty.

Senator William Ezra Jenner, a cold-war isolationist, Republican of Indiana, told the senators it was common knowledge that Frank Graham was soft on Communism. When applause greeted this from the gallery, where sat many of Senator McCarthy's supporters, the vice-president reminded the gallery that demonstrations were not permitted in the Senate.

Senator Joseph McCarthy, riding the passions generated by the cold war, took the floor and attacked the Atomic Energy Commission for granting Frank access to national secrets.

Senator Claude Pepper of Florida rose to criticize these critics of

> ...a new senator who has not had the privilege of presenting his credentials to this body, and does not have the opportunity to castigate as false what may be said by those who would impugn his loyalty...

He said never before in his years as a senator had he witnessed such behavior.

In the wake of all this, on March 29th, twenty-three days after Senator Broughton died, one week after Governor Scott's announcement in Chapel Hill, Frank was to be sworn in. He had invited only his and Marian's relatives to be present, but five hundred friends made the journey on their own, enough comfortably to fill the galleries. This was said to be the largest attendance at the swearing in of a senator up to that date.

Marian and two nieces were present. Sitting in the seat reserved for the vice-president's special guest, Marian couldn't help wondering what her father would have thought, seeing Frank elevated to this -- this church-like entity, the world's outstanding body of legislators, the keepers of the inheritance of freedom and law, their room as near a temple as a secular body could ever have, with even the altar and banner and other symbols of august power. Her father would accept this honor as being worthy of meditation, dedication, affection, sacrifice, loyalty.

The Senators were in their places, even the publicity-seeking Joe McCarthy -- Marian couldn't help but single him out. Did he have with him his secret list of Communists in the State Department? Not long ago he had waved a piece of paper here on the Senate floor, but he had not let the list be read. Did he have Frank on a list? Would Frank come to know him, ask him about his family, grasp his arms, hold his hand in friendship, become a friend?

Dear Frank. Her little man. Right hand raised. Wearing his newest suit, the one she had had tailor-made in Durham a year -- or was it two Christmases ago? Her little man became a senator and was escorted by Senator Clyde Hoey to his own Senate desk.

Meanwhile, the Senate agenda was challenging. Frank had not left the Senate that first day before Senator Arthur Vandenberg, Chairman of the Committee on Foreign Relations, a Michigan Republican, asked his support of a bill dealing with the Indonesian question. The struggle for independence was yet in process, and the Dutch were having second thoughts about the independence movement. War threatened.

Frank met with Vandenberg the next day and Frank's knowledge of the subject, and even of the leaders involved, was helpful in judging what best might be done by the United States Senate. Frank could not support either of two bills introduced thus far; he felt they might anger the proud Dutch, or seem to desert the Indonesians. At the same time, as he explained to Vandenberg, defeating either of the bills might have the same result. An amendment was needed.

Frank had for the past several months been advising the State Department on the situation, and he turned to them now. He needed their influence to have Republican Senator Ralph Brewster of Maine, Chairman of the Special Committee on National Defense, introduce an amendment for his bill, in effect nullifying the bill should it give assistance to any state against which the United Nations was taking preventive or enforcement action.

Graham met with the Senators involved, and his last conversation with the State Department was at midnight the morning of the vote. The amendment was accepted, one uniquely bringing into alliance for the first time the United Nations and the United States.

Frank also had written a statement about the history of this dispute, and these sixty-four pages became the key text in the Senate for the floor fight. The bill passed.

Frank was not present. Senator Hoey reported that he was ill. Indeed, at that moment Frank lay in the hospital struggling to breathe. He was having his annual bout with "the old man himself."

After a week in the hospital, Marian helped him into the back seat of a used car she had bought and drove him to North Carolina.

Where to take him? Where was home? She took him to her sister's big house in Hillsborough, and she and other members of the family tended to him there.

All of April Frank was ill. He began to stir about in the house in early May. On May 1 he had Senator Hoey enter his statement supporting a Federal Aid to Education Bill, which passed in the Senate but failed in the House.

The second week in May, Marian drove him to their Washington apartment, and on May 12 he returned to the Senate. The six lost weeks weighed heavily on him. Still weak, he restricted himself to committee meetings and conferences. Yes, and the morning prayer service for senators, which he faithfully attended. A few times he went to the Senate dining room, usually on invitation of Senator Wayne Morse or Paul Douglas. On such occasions he would order two of his favorites, liverwurst and buttermilk.

As time allowed, he prepared his maiden speech in the Senate. It might not be heard by two senators, but he felt called upon to prepare it carefully. In it he listed thirteen measures for strengthening democracy in the United States, including a fairer minimum wage -- it was then 75 cents an hour; cooperative medical programs -- there were none to speak of; and faithful observance of the laws, without nullification by any state of the decision of the Supreme Court regarding equal suffrage and education in the States, as the supreme law of the land.

Frank spoke for a long time, even by Senate standards. When he began there were only a few senators attending, but as he continued many others came in from the cloak room and offices. Here there shone the same sort of radiance which had emanated from him in the General Assembly when he had risen to talk about the University.

When at last he was through, Senator Hoey asked for the floor.

> Mr. President, I have sat here for the last hour and, in my opinion, have heard one of the finest addresses it was ever my privilege to hear on the Senate floor. The man who has just addressed us has given us a pattern... for America in the great objective and offensive toward world peace.

Frank felt later that he had represented himself well. In the gallery sat Marian and Al Lowenstein.

In a short while, Frank knew every Senator. Most of them did not agree with his views on disarmament, or on having more open immigration policies, or on the Federal government funding the nation's public schools, or with his liberal views on civil rights. Few agreed with the entire agenda. However, almost all were Frank Graham's new friends.

His office was impressive, the furniture was provided by the Senate. In one corner stood the banner of the Marine Corps, a gift to him by alumni of his outfit in World War I. His day's schedule centered here from early morning, when he walked from his apartment, through sessions of letter writing, telephone calls and visits, until about noon, when he would gravitate to the Senate floor, to begin the second phase of his day's work.

His evenings, often as not, were spent with Marian, reading and planning, among the plans sketches of the room arrangement of the house they intended to build in Chapel Hill. Come time for sleep, the living room couches served as beds.

On Sunday they often attended Episcopal service together at the National Cathedral. He had not been in town long enough to join a Presbyterian Church, and Marian the first week had gone to the National Cathedral and met the vicar and the dean, and had volunteered her help in the book store, the offices, and the thrift shop activity. Marian liked thrift shops.

The Cathedral service was uncomfortably formal for Frank, but he was adjusting.

How many years had it been since he had gone with her to the first of her father's services? Eighteen years ago.

When there was less than a year remaining of his elected term, Frank was advised, he must plan his re-election campaign in North Carolina. The naiveté with which he accepted the challenge is shown in a statement quoted at the time:

> We won't have to worry about fund-raising; Marian and I
> have saved $10,000 toward building a house.

Idealism, trust, friendship were attitudes Frank and others of his staff had toward the approaching campaign. It would all go well, they were sure.

36, 37. The candidate on the road. Above, Frank works in his hotel room office. *Division of Archives and History, NC Department of Cultural Resources*. Below, Frank speaks to the constituents from the back of a convertible. *UNC News Bureau Files, North Carolina Collection, UNC Library*

38. The candidates for US Senate, 1950 (left to right), Bob Reynolds, Frank Graham, Willis Smith.   *Photograph courtesy the Asheville Citizen Times; Time, Inc.*

CHAPTER FOURTEEN

THE DEMOCRATIC PARTY nominee in North Carolina was virtually certain to win a statewide race with the Republican candidate.

In selecting a Democratic candidate, a primary was held. A runoff was possible if no candidate received a clear majority of the votes cast for the office. In the early 1950s, many poor whites and Negroes did not vote because of indifference or alienation, or because of intimidation and downright exclusion, this being most effective in those rural counties where blacks made up one-third to one-half of the population.

Most statewide campaigns in North Carolina were orderly. The Democratic Party machinery creaked along, nominating for Governor an Eastern North Carolina candidate for a term, then four years later someone from the Western half of the state. The United States senate term was longer -- six years. An incumbent could succeed himself and usually did. By giving the job to Frank Graham, Governor Scott had effectively given it to him for many years into the future, unless something unusual happened.

Frank knew this. He had accepted the Senate appointment as a lifetime commitment.

Kerr Scott told intimates at the time that Frank was the greatest humanitarian of our time, and the best known and most liked man in North Carolina; I don't see how anybody can beat him.

Also, in North Carolina Frank had an experienced team behind him. The Governor's political chiefs were the same men and women who had worked to elect him, county-by-county, with support into the back hollows, through villages, towns and cities.

Frank also has a loyal cadre among the intellectuals and his thousands of friends.

As of the first of the year, nineteen weeks before the primary, nobody had announced his intention to run against Frank. On January 31, 1950, a former senator, a "right disreputable" Robert Rice Reynolds of Asheville announced. His five chief planks were:

(1) to keep America out of war;

(2) to fingerprint and register all aliens;

(3) to stop all immigration for ten years;

(4) deport all alien criminals and undesirable aliens;

(5) abolish all isms *except* Americanism -- Nazism, Fascism, Communism.

His motto, harking back to fellow Ashevillian Thomas Wolfe's first novel, was "look homeward, Americans." Bob Reynolds was also known for having wed the Hope diamond. At least he had married the daughter of Evalyn Walsh McLean, who owned it, and owned much else. Previously a senator, his service had been colorful and embarrassing. In Asheville he had not distinguished himself since as an attorney. One performance -- and his flamboyant nature lent meaning to the word -- was defense of several young men who at the Asheville bus station offered a ride home, about fifteen miles, to a pretty young woman, and raped her. His defense was largely an interrogation of the young woman about her underwear, chiefly her "bloomers," his choice of words. The men were convicted by a jury of twelve mountain men.

Bob Reynolds was not going to win, but he would muddy the political waters.

Olla Ray Boyd, a hog farmer, formally announced. He wouldn't win either. Predictably he would poll a few hundred votes. A perennial candidate, he appeared to be an amusement more than a contender. His wife, however, favored him, telling the press,

He's not much of a husband and he won't be much of a governor, but don't think he won't get it if he goes *atter* it.

Rumors begin flying a month or so later that the conservatives, among them certain of the textile barons, were seeking somebody to run against Frank and were having a tough time. These seekers were opposed to Frank's stand on workmen's compensation, and Frank's habit of worrying about the workers' low wages. Textile workers in North Carolina made about half what textile workers made in New England.

The rumors became statements of fact when Willis Smith agreed to be the conservatives' man. He was a distinguished corporation lawyer with officers in Raleigh, and had been recently elected President of the American Bar Association. He was Chairman of the Duke University Board of Trustees. He had served in the State House of Representatives and in 1931 had been speaker. His main supporters, the political organization Kerr Scott had defeated two years before, still held big moneybags, as the politicians expressed wealth, and had knowledgeable, veteran chiefs. It was not as well endowed with younger workers. One

39. Frank and his campaign staff. *Division of Archives and History, NC Department of Cultural Resources*

of these, however, was the news director for a small Raleigh radio station WRAL, Jesse Helms. After meeting with Graham and Scott, he had planned to climb aboard Frank Graham's bandwagon as director of public relations until Willis Smith filed on February 25th.

So there were three serious contenders, forgetting Mrs. Boyd's husband for the moment, only one of whom had not run previously for public office anywhere, Frank Graham.

At once leaders of the political organizations looked for weakness in the opponents. Frank was vulnerable in that he had been a member of Harry Truman's Civil Rights Committee. Its most controversial stand was to call for integration in employment -- the Fair Employment Practices Act -- with federal government sanctions to enforce it. Frank had written the minority statement in the report which opposed the imposition of federal sanctions, but admittedly he had signed the full committee report. Another of Frank's vulnerabilities was all those pro-Communist charges.

Weakness in Willis Smith as a candidate? Well, nobody knew him, he had rarely taken a stand. It was apparent that some of the thirty-six companies he represented were among the lowest paying in America, and had the poorest labor policies. Perhaps that was worth exploiting.

The campaigning began with the Graham and the Smith political forces wanting the middle of the road, that being where most voters could originally be found. Both candidates' opening statements were reasonable. Willis Smith mentioned the civil rights and Communism worries, said they appeared to him to put Dr. Graham over to the left, well away from the middle of the road. Frank's early speeches were discussions of issues, among them European recovery, the farm program, federal assistance to the states for medical programs, aid to education, and voluntary approaches to civil rights. Nothing critical of Smith. Frank wrote his speeches himself, would not allow his staff to help, not even to the extent of making new speeches out of old ones. He spent hours writing when his staff would have preferred for him to be out in the field.

As the campaign developed, Frank revealed the serious political flaw of not replying directly to attacks. One need not call Willis Smith a liar to reply, he was told by Jonathan Daniels and other advisors. Frank did defend himself, at least modestly. He denied that he was a member of any subversive organization, or that he had ever been. This was germane, but it was all done rather academically.

Governor Scott was helpful in stating his own opinions in political jargon. Communist, he said, is no more than a cuss-word nowadays, it is used far too frequently; probably William Jennings Bryan would have been called a Communist had the word been common in his day.

Frank's speeches tended to make broad international sweeps, and long lists:

> In a world, in which more than 700,000,000 people are regimented within the prison walls of the Communist policy states, more than 700,000,000 stand with us for human freedom, and more than 700,000,000 have not yet chosen sides, the great responsibility of our day is for the people of our State and country to be strong in military, economic, democratic and moral power in order to (1) preserve our historic liberties; (2) provide for the common defense; (3) promote the general welfare; (4) balance the budget short of unbalancing the nation and the world by turning the earth over to a monstrous dictatorship; (5) stop Communism; (6) win people away from Communism for freedom; (7) prevent the third World War; and, under God, establish freedom, law and peace on earth.

His chief list was unwieldy itemization of his platform, with fifteen goals:

> 1. The preservation and strengthening of the American system of free competitive capitalism... as the best answer to Socialism, Communism and Fascism.
>
> 2. Responsible economy in government without wasteful sacrifice... working toward balancing the budget and eliminating deficit spending.
>
> 3. Intelligent reduction of Marshall Plan funds and other wise economies.
>
> 4. Federal aid to the states for education, with state and local control.
>
> 5. The recognition of agriculture as one of the main pillars of our economic society... for the continuance of the parity price support program for basic agricultural commodities under democratically imposed controls.
>
> 6. The conservation of soils, forests and water power.
>
> 7. The lawful freedom of the self-organization of workers and businessmen and . . . the establishment of equality of bargaining between responsible labor and management.
>
> 8. Reasonable minimum wages and social security against the hazards of old age and modern society.
>
> 9. A continuation of the improvement of race relations on the North Carolina pattern. I oppose the use of federal power in race relations, which would cause setbacks in the fine progress of relations between the races. I favor the more fundamental approach to the problem through the slower but the more enduring influence of education and religion... I favor local, federal, and state cooperation for the elimination

of the poll tax and prevention of the few remaining instances of lynchings.

10. Instead of socialized medicine or the Murray Dingell Bill, which I oppose, I favor the extension to the national level of the principles of the North Carolina Medical Care Program . . . based on private and public, lay and professional, state and federal cooperation to provide more hospital beds and to train more doctors, dentists, nurses and medical technicians without federal control.

11. The extension of rural electrification and rural telephones through private capital, where available, supplemented by farmers cooperatives on a sound, businesslike, self-liquidating basis.

12. A strong national defense through Selective Service, the strengthening of the National Guard, the ROTC naval and air power, military and naval research, and the National Science Foundation . . .

13. More adequate housing... for veterans and other people of low income and middle income groups.

14. The leadership of the United States in the United Nations for the strengthening of the United Nations toward international disarmament, international control and inspection of all atomic power, and the prevention of a third World War.

15. Local-state-federal cooperation in the development of our seaports, fisheries, soils, forests, water resources, natural gaslines, minerals, national parks, parkways, tourist facilities, diversified agriculture and diversified industries.

It was quite a platform, perhaps too long and involved. Another criticism his staff, practical politicians, found was that Frank could not be scheduled reliably. By contrast, if Willis Smith was to speak to a Rotary Club at noon, he was there at noon. Nobody was sure where Frank was at noon. Winfield Blackwell recalls at the height of the campaign Frank visited Mrs. Burton Craige in Winston-Salem, mother-in-law of Gordon Gray, the new President of the University. Dr. Frank was in there while his driver, who this time happened to be Marian, and Frank's coordinator were begging him to come away. Dr. Frank, we have to get on to Salisbury.

Frank would reply that he was talking to Mrs. Craige.

He talked to Mrs. Craige for hours.

Carlyle Sitterson's mother was in charge of the Democratic Women for Lenoir County. Sitterson says,

Now, my wife's father happened to be in the famous class of 1909 -- that was Frank Graham's class. Frank went down to Kinston to make a speech, and my wife, Nancy, went

down to help arrange a reception. I was talking a day or two
later to her father and asked how did Frank Graham do in his
speech. Her father said, He made a wonderful speech about
world peace and didn't win a single vote.

Another problem the campaign staff had to face was that Frank was
often away serving in the Senate. Even in May, the month of the
primary, he left the campaign trial, flew to Washington for a vote on
the European Recovery Program. Frank preferred trains to airplanes, but
this time he flew, and his vote saved the bill from Senator Taft's
amendment to strike half a billion dollars.

Next day he was back in North Carolina.

Three weeks to go until the vote. He was lined up for talks and
meetings right up to the deadline, every day, when a pneumonia attack
struck him and he was put to bed.

In addition to missing part of the campaigning, he was missing the
debate in the Senate on a civil rights bill. A filibuster was threatened;
some senators wanted to cast a vote for cloture to stop its occurrence.
Frank received reports by telephone. The senior North Carolina senator,
Clyde Hoey, had declared opposition to cloture, to limiting debate.
Frank was advised to let Hoey say as much on Frank's behalf when he
cast his own vote, to say that Frank Graham is unable to be present but
has asked me to say he would also vote against cloture if he were here.
It'll mean fifty thousand gained votes in the election Frank was told.

Workers in many of the State's one hundred counties sent word up
the line: Have Dr. Frank stand with the Southern senators, against
cloture. Frank was reminded he was for free speech, so let the Southern
senators talk, grant them freedom of expression, let them filibuster.

Frank lay in bed in the Sir Walter Hotel in Raleigh, trying to
breathe, and to decide; the element he didn't have was whether
adequate debate had been allowed.

Al Lowenstein flew to Washington. On his own, he tried to
persuade Senate friends of Frank's to contact him, urge him to do what
was politically expedient. Al was rebuffed. Senator Richard Russell of
Georgia told him, Young man, don't you tamper with Frank Graham's
conscience; that's what we in the Senate love about him.

Frank did not take any action in the matter.

Marian allowed his staff to visit him; not once did she interfere.
Frank decided not to allow a leaflet prepared by A. B. Upchurch of his
campaign to be mailed out, which revealed in thousands of printed
copies Willis Smith's representation of companies with poor labor
relations.

As the voting day approached, a series of advertisements appeared in newspapers reporting the Senator McCarthy charges, linking Frank one way or another with Earl Browder, head of the Communist Party, now serving time in prison, Paul Robeson, black Communist actor and singer, and Henry Wallace, left-wing Presidential candidate two years earlier. In that campaign Frank had supported Truman, not Wallace.

Frank's staff asked FBI director J. Edgar Hoover to release a statement, giving the conclusion reached by the FBI's two exhaustive studies, hundreds of pages of investigation done into Frank's background, including any possible links with subversive organizations. Hoover replied that, in spite of his feelings of friendship, he could not break his long-standing policy of not making public disclosures. The staff knew that the hundreds of pages on Frank in the FBI's files were added proof that he was not and had never been a Communist.

As to the race issue, Smith said that he sincerely believes Frank had signed the Civil Rights Committee Report without having read it.

On election day, in polling places across the state there was a record vote. Propped up on pillows in his hotel room, Frank followed the results. He held a lead from the first reports, a larger lead by nine o'clock. Reports of jubilation reached him from his headquarters. Aides came to congratulate him. They noted Frank, emaciated by weeks of illness, appeared even smaller than before, but was pleased.

He asked if liquor was being drunk in his headquarters and was glad to hear that there was none.

By morning the final vote was tabulated.

Frank Graham   303,605 votes
Willis Smith   250,222
Bob Reynolds   58,752
Others   5,900

The vote was the heaviest in the state's history. Frank was close to an absolute majority. A runoff was unlikely. As canny Kerr Scott had foreseen, he was unbeatable.

Joy welled up in tens of thousands of families in the state. Pride, too, in the size of the vote and of the victory. The "branchhead boys" had whipped the city tycoons. The common man had reasoned out the truth -- not the first time, either. A liberal had won in a Southern state at a time of two hot issues, civil rights and Communism. Frank had even carried Willis Smith's home county, and he had carried Chapel Hill and Orange County four to one.

There was pleasure in the White House, as well. The campaign had been closely watched there, and Vice-President Barkley twice had visited the state to try to steady the Democratic party and help Frank Graham. President Truman had been in contact with Jonathan Daniels, Gladys Tillet and other national party leaders. The northern press, noting the fall of Senator Pepper a month earlier in Florida in a smear campaign, considered this to be a new test of the anti-Truman strength in the South and country, with Frank credited with supporting Truman's Fair Deal programs, and Willis Smith opposing them.

Marian drove Frank to Nags Head. Her house was not prepared for springtime use, and they stayed with Fred and Emma Neal Morrison, friends for years. Marian tried to make Frank rest, to stay in bed, but he asked her to come with him to the water's edge. And please bring two beach chairs. So the two of them sat with their feet washed by the salt water. She put a blanket around Frank's shoulders and a hat on his head to save him from the springtime breeze. He told her all about ozone in the breakers.

Frank Winslow and his wife Nemie, Kemp Battle and his wife Maude Bunn came visiting, congratulating the Senator, celebrating his success.

40. Dr. Frank campaigning. *Division of Archives and History, N*
Department of Cultural Resources

41. Dr. Frank, hands outstretched to the voters.   *Photograph by Hugh Morton*

42. Candidate Graham leaving the polling booth.   *Division of Archiv*
and History, NC Department of Cultural Resources

CHAPTER FIFTEEN

JUST AFTER THE first primary, doctors told Marian that another bout with pneumonia would doubtless kill Frank. They told her exhaustion seemed to precede the attacks, to avoid exhaustion at all cost. Rest, see to it that he rests, sleeps well, eats well.

Defection from both the Reynolds and Smith political camps had begun early on election night, and continued during the following days. Their candidates had been trounced.

Among the Willis Smith camp, politicians and monied supporters knew from past experience that the Kerr Scott people were inheritors of the old North Carolina populist, agrarian movement, and were the devil's own when it came to compromise with big businessmen and conservatives. The Scott brand of politics had been spawned in the South in the days of Governor Charles Brantley Aycock, who believed in the betterment of the average man. The populists had programs for conservation of natural resources and development of human resources. They advocated higher returns for human labor, in factory and farm. This led in North Carolina to Governor Aycock; the state built a new school a day during his administration.

The populist movement in Georgia was led by Tom Watson, who started out working for similar goals but couldn't get elected until he struck on the race issue, which he rode relentlessly against blacks and other minorities. It was he who approved the lynching of an innocent Jewish manufacturer, Leo Frank. The Georgia movement became a hate-filled one.

Just now the race issue was simmering in all parts of the nation, with another Supreme Court decision due. What if the decision came this week or next, at the close of this session of the Court, Smith supporters wondered, and Willis Smith rode the race issue in North Carolina? Among members of Willis Smith's defeated team who favored a run-off was Tom Ellis. Hitting Graham with Browder and other Communists hadn't worked, the voters hadn't bought Frank Graham as a Communist. Now they would attack Frank Graham on the racial issue.

Reports reached the Frank Graham camp that the Smith people were looking for money and were polling their county managers. They still needed to convince Willis Smith to run. He was balking, even dictated a telegram stating that he would not run, and ordered it sent. His staff did not send it.

On June 6th, a week and a half after the first primary, the Supreme Court handed down a decision reaffirming equal facilities for blacks in post-graduate education and on railroads. Further, the decision pretty well abolished segregation in graduate schools, using University of Texas and the University of Oklahoma cases.

Smith lieutenants went to work, using among other forums Raleigh radio station WRAL, already known for its rousing right-wing orientation; the same day as the Supreme Court decision was announced, they began broadcasts, urging voters to convince Smith to call for a second primary run-off. Listeners were asked to come to a rally at Willis Smith's home tonight.

That night, a remote-van was parked in the Smith house driveway, Jesse Helms manning it, and announcement after announcement went out on the airway saying, Come hear Willis Smith, come hear Willis Smith.

Terry Sanford, head of the Young Democrats of North Carolina, was not present but recalls reports reaching him:

> As I recall it, they had a rally over there when they were deciding whether to call a second primary. He had a meeting where they were singing "Let's hang Frank Graham to a sour apple tree." And Jesse, as I recall, was there leading it. And a fellow named Daniel from Fuquay, who is dead now, he was an ally of Helms.

Elmer Oettinger was news editor of WPTF, a competitor station. He recalls reporting the facts and figures about the rally on his station. Next morning Jesse Helms came up to him on the street and claimed, angrily, that he had prevaricated this story, that the numbers given of people in the Smith driveway were way too low. You're not telling the truth, Helms told him. Oettinger said his figures came from two reputable reporters on the scene, people with no irons on the fire. May I simply suggest you don't have prevarication as an excuse, he told Helms. People had to pull us apart, Oettinger says.

Dr. Frank's own view of the Court decision had been expressed in briefs supplied to the Supreme Court by the Southern attorneys general; they had used his stated views to argue against the Supreme Court decision. The Graham campaign pointed this out in a news release, and a new statement from the candidate was issued:

> I still oppose as I have always opposed, the Federal
> government forcing non-segregation on states and regions...
> I reaffirm my oft-expressed faith in the North Carolina
> program of mutual understanding, respect and cooperation
> between the races, under which both races have made the
> greatest progress in the last several decades of any
> dissimilar groups in any one area in a like period in human
> history.

Willis Smith had this statement before him when he consented to lead a vitriolic, race-baiting type of campaign. An widely held and often expressed opinion reported that Smith's views on this matter were not markedly different from Graham's, or from those of most others in the state. In his announcement Smith said he had waited so long to call for a run-off because he believed that race would inevitably lead to the kind of campaign he did not want to take part in.

He told the press that his mind had changed when aides showed him the voting pattern during the first primary. In black precincts the vote had been almost exclusively for Graham. His aides termed this "block voting." And he saw block voting as a threat to the kind of democracy North Carolina has enjoyed over the years.

Therefore, under the banner of democracy, his aides led him to the field, to do battle with Frank Graham.

The vote was to come in just ten days' time.

Soon he issued a prepared statement explaining he had waited to call for a run-off until the Supreme Court decision, to see if his running would unnecessarily create ill will. His statement asserted, there have long been people who are constantly on the watch to stir up discord between the races for political reasons, as exemplified in the inflammatory report of Harry Truman's Civil Rights Committee, on which Frank Graham served.

Meanwhile, work of designing and printing and distributing campaign material, signed and unsigned, proceeded apace. One batch was signed by a "Know the Truth" committee:

> WHITE PEOPLE WAKE UP BEFORE IT IS TOO LATE,
> YOU MAY NOT HAVE ANOTHER CHANCE.

Some of the material was printed in batches of up to a hundred thousand copies. With less than a week remaining, the avalanche was released at local levels across the state, many from county headquarters of the Smith campaign. Some of the materials were attributable to the Smith campaign, others not. There were handbills saying that a vote for

Graham was a vote for mixing whites and Negroes in schools. There were circulars with pictures of Negro and white children playing together, of Negroes sitting idly on a porch while white people worked in the fields, and one broadside pictured a Negro soldier dancing with a white woman. On one, a woman had the superimposed face of Marian Graham.

In one county school buses were stopped and the children told they would, if Frank Graham is elected, be sitting beside "nigger kids" by next fall.

Reports reached Frank and Marian Graham that the picture of her dancing with a Negro had been superimposed by a Smith campaign staff member, rumored to be Jesse Helms working with a photographer, but there was no proof, and Frank did not want an announcement made that his wife had not or would not dance with blacks. He repeated over and over, I just don't want to campaign like that. Helms years later would deny knowing about or sanctioning scurrilous campaign material; however, Pou Bailey, later a Superior Court Judge, who worked in the Smith campaign, told one reporter Helms contributed to practically every ad that was run. He said, maybe Jesse didn't create those ads, but I'm pretty sure he saw all of them.

Willis Smith circulars urged workers to save their jobs. They appealed to white parents to save their children at home and in schools, and to farmers to save their farm labor. Of course, such tactics were acknowledged to be a disgrace. It was "Tom Watson" transferred to a state where, by common agreement, such tactics would not be used by the Democratic Party. Willis Smith denied that his headquarters was doing any of it; rather, local groups over which he had no control were doing it.

A supporter called out to Frank Graham at a rally: Is Willis Smith the biggest liar in North Carolina?

Frank paused to consider. I haven't said that, he replied. I wouldn't say that. No, I wouldn't say that. I'm not saying anything against any human being.

One attack on Frank was for having nominated a black to the United States Military Academy at West Point. This nomination became a major concern to voters as he and Marian and aides drove from one local meeting to another. Frank, as senator, had indeed put forth a nominee, a white, and he had included as alternates the names of two other students who on the examination had come in second and third. One was a black, Leroy Jones, the second alternate.

Frank, explaining to voters why he had bothered to send the third name, even after he had been advised not to, said,

> I did what I thought was the right thing. If that will keep me from going back to the United States Senate, I don't want to go. I don't want to conceal anything. I don't want to be expedient. I want to be honest.

Marian stayed beside him. Her husband was in the lions' den and the lions were chewing on him. When workers spit at him, she stood beside him, her little David in shirt sleeves, battling Goliath -- there he stood at a crossroads country store.

No, I do not stand for forced integration of the schools, he replied to a question. It would set this state back for years. It would lead to great bitterness. You would find support for schools languishing. The result would be worse for both races.

She listened as he told farmers the acceptance of one race by another was a matter of generations: These are things which, he said, must work out gradually through the teachings of Jesus.

The last campaign stop for Frank and Marian was in High Point. The date was June 24, 1950. Years ago it was here that a younger Frank Graham, as professor of history in the University, had come to the defense of the workers. Today there were no large crowds to greet him, few bothered to come to meet him on street corners or factory yards. Instead of crowds, there were protesters, among them children chanting: No school with niggers, no school with niggers.

Many of the workers would not shake his hand. Occasionally, he was cursed vilely. There were remarks about lynching. People furious at any loss of their standing, spewed out expletives. Al Lowenstein remembered that Dr. Frank was badly shaken. Did you hear what that man said? Frank asked him.

There was the customary "get out the vote" effort on election day, Saturday, June 25, 1950. Both candidates had highly motivated workers. Tens of thousands of volunteers canvassed the districts; no inconvenience was too great, every vote counted. There were charges of intimidation, especially made by blacks, and charges of some overzealous workers paying for votes. When Frank and Marian reported to their own polling precinct and took their places in line, poorly dressed blacks came to stand in line with them, and news pictures of the staged event were hurriedly sent out all over the state.

Election night the vote returns came in to the headquarters in the

Sir Walter Hotel in Raleigh. In the eastern counties, where the largest percentage of blacks lived but often did not vote, the counties were overwhelmingly for Smith. In the state as a whole, Smith led sixty-one counties of the one hundred. At 9:43 p.m. before final totals were in but as soon as the outcome was clear, Frank, requesting that Marian not accompany him, took Jeff Johnson and Bill and Mary Coker Joslin, three aides, and rode the elevator down from his sixth floor headquarters to shake hands with the victor. On seeing him, many of Smith's followers were hostile, but Frank approach Smith, offered his hand, smiled and said, I wish you every success.

Late that same night Bill Friday drove him and Marian to Hillsborough. None of them said a word on the way. At the door Frank turned to Friday and said, I'll see you tomorrow.

Marian put him to bed. Next morning he told her, and later told reporters, I'm so tired that I haven't been able to think, so I'll say nothing.

The final vote was 281,114 for Smith, 261,789 for Graham.

Dr. Leonard Fields was that night attending the national convention of the American Medical Association in Chicago. The chairman interrupted the night's session for a special announcement: Frank Graham has lost the North Carolina campaign. The doctors rose in mass and, except for a few, applauded. Leonard Fields kept his seat.

Didn't you hear, a doctor shouted at him over the din, they beat that federal medical man, Graham.

Yes, Fields told him, and it's the worst tragedy I can think of.

Chapel Hill was in shock. Bill Cochrane, then Assistant to Senator Hoey, recalls that on the night of the loss, his wife Shirley, who grew up in the town and also had attended the University, lay down on the living room floor and cried like a baby.

Next morning Bob House met his adult Sunday School class, as always. The lesson was based on one of the Old Testament stories; House seemed to have memory lapses as to which one. His mind was on his friend.

Down the street at the Presbyterian Church, Charlie Jones kept an eye on the door. Even at quarter past eleven, he was watching for Frank to arrive. The church was packed, except for one seat on the aisle near the back, where normally he sat.

Across the street at the Chapel of the Cross, David Yates, the rector, said goodbye to each and every parishioner at the door, missing only two names. When all were gone, he walked along Franklin Street to Marian's house, now occupied by the new President, Gordon Gray. Yates always thought of it as being Marian's. He paused for a moment's prayer.

The Grays had torn out her rose garden, which surprised him.

New day, Monday, the people in South Building were quiet, reflective. Conversations were sparse. President Gray came to his office about ten o'clock and shut the door. No doubt he was in there phoning trustees and editors, trying to measure what impact this would have on the Consolidated University, and on education in the state.

Many supporters dispatched messages to Frank. Judge Susie Sharp commented that Frank had shown the state that at least one person in politics would rather be right than senator. Someday the state may realize that yours was really the victory, she told him. At any rate, I would rather have lost with you.

John Sanders, a university student, wrote Frank about his disappointment,

> Not for you or for the cause which you champion, but for the people of North Carolina, who, lacking the confidence of their own conviction, voted against their own best interests and the best interests of the nation.

Where were Frank and Marian? Several of their friends in South Building tried to find them. Not in the Sir Walter Hotel. Bill Friday says they're in Hillsborough. Do they have a phone as yet at the Nags Head cottage?

Did Frank want to return to work in the University? Was there any administrative job here for him? Would the University dare hire him now?

Would he be willing to teach history again?

Not many years remaining before his retirement. How old is Frank? Is Frank sixty-four?

On Franklin Street business went on, but with intermittent flares of anger. Judge Luther J. Phipps, a deacon representing segregation at the Baptist church, and elsewhere, had supported Willis Smith. Several people scowled at him as he walked toward the bank. A faculty member stopped at the barber shop nearby. For years he as a customer had sat in the chair nearest the window. No, I won't sit in your chair this time, he told the barber. You voted for Willis Smith. I want to tell you something: you're a barber, but you live in a nice home in a nice part of town, you're a member of one of the men's clubs, you're respected, and you know who makes -- who's responsible in this state for making workers respected? Frank Graham. Your son goes to the University. You know who made our University the most respected in the South? Frank Graham. And you voted for Willis Smith. So I want you to know why I'm taking another chair this time.

Across the state there was anger. Even many who had voted for Willis Smith were apologetic. Hell, I never thought he'd win, some would say. Given more time, I would have voted for Graham.

Progressive state, North Carolina?

Well, it had appeared to be for a while.

Jonathan Daniels in his office at the *News and Observer* vented his rage, using carefully chosen words for Smith's organizers. Now they'll deny it, of course they'll deny it, he shouted, they won't have the guts to face their own demagoguery and brutality and evil.

Frank's sisters were in mourning. Marian's family was in mourning.

Niece Elizabeth Matheson recalls conversations concerning her Uncle Fred, an Episcopal minister in Monroe, North Carolina, the family wondering what he was thinking. He had been Jesse Helms' scoutmaster.

The type of campaign that had been led by Willis Smith was condemned by politicians within the state, and by the National Democratic Party. President Truman was furious. He had lost a supporter in the Senate, and had picked up Willis Smith, a well-heeled, conservative, segregationist Democrat. It boded ill for other progressive candidates, and for Truman, himself, politically.

And the black citizens, what might this mean for the admission of blacks into society?

For a day or so the big Hillsborough house was closed up. Reporters were turned away. Marian and Frank both made it clear that he did not want to discuss the campaign.

By Wednesday Frank was talking to Al Lowenstein and other workers. On Thursday he finished a statement thanking his supporters which he ordered printed on both sides of a card to save money. One reason for economy: During the campaign he had returned all large contributions, as a matter of principle.

Frank began worrying about the work he ought to be doing in Washington as a Senator. He told Marian a nomination of a black, William Hastie, for a judgeship was being held up by Senator James Eastland in the Judiciary Committee, and Graham ought to pry it loose.

And there were bills, floor debates, committee matters, stacks of mail in need of attention. Would she drive him the two hundred-fifty miles to Washington?

Douglass Hunt recalls Frank's arrival in the Senate office building the Monday following the defeat. Frank met Senator Olin Johnston of South Carolina in the elevator. Johnston had won re-election by warning of the dastardly things happening in the South that had to be opposed, including appointment of a black to West Point. In the elevator Frank said, Tough race down there.

Senator Johnston said, I had to reach down pretty low in the barrel, Frank.

Frank said, And when you reached the bottom of the barrel, you hit him with me, didn't you?

Johnston laughed uncomfortably and admitted that this was so.

Doug Hunt also recalls phoning Frank's office during the first day of Frank's return. He dialed CAPITAL 1234 and asked for Senator Graham.

The man answering exclaimed, My God, is that little bastard back already? Click.

A lady's voice then answered breezily, Senator Green of Rhode Island's office.

The first vote to come up in the Senate was over cloture, the device to shut off a filibuster. This vote was over the same issue which had occurred during the first primary, an affirmative vote would gag segregation senators.

When the clerk called the roll, Frank voted nay, opposing cloture.

Republican Senator Irving McNeill Ives, Republican of New York, was the first to reach Frank's desk. He wanted to know why Frank hadn't sent word when he was campaigning that he would vote nay. You would have won the election, he told him.

I wasn't here then, Frank told him.

He explained to a host of curious individuals that the purpose of the cloture rule is to end a filibuster. There is no filibuster, so I voted against the cloture rule this time.

Later Graham was one of five senators who voted against the McCarran Act, requiring registration of Communists and Communist-front organizations in America. It passed; Truman vetoed the measure. The House and Senate voted to override Truman's veto; Frank was one of ten senators who voted to sustain it. Repression is the way of frightened power, he said, freedom is the way of enlightened faith.

It sounded, his friends decided, very much like he was his old, own self again.

There were occasional signs of his hurt, however. Doug Hunt remembers having dinner with Marian, Frank and Al Lowenstein at the Congressional Hotel, in the Grahams' apartment. In the course of the conversation, he says, we talked about all manner of subjects. The defeat was mentioned, Mrs. Graham and Al were saying if we had only done so and so.

Dr. Graham in a real flash of anger said, Now, that's enough of that. We did the best we could.

It was the only time Hunt ever saw him angry.

Before leaving the Senate in September, 1950, Frank left three major statements for the record.

On the 21st he presented the case favoring statehood for Alaska and Hawaii. Alone among Southern Senators he favored their admission at once.

On September 22nd he left in the Senate a seventeen-thousand-word statement dealing with his membership in the scores of committees and organizations, only four of which had been listed by the Attorney General as Communist fronts, and that years after his membership. In two of these he had merely contributed money to hospitals in Spain and China which treated Republicans who had fought Japan. Another was sponsorship of a four-day youth conference of the Southern Negro Youth Congress. As to the remaining one, he had resigned when he came to believe that its claim of helping the foreign-born was not its chief concern.

On his final day in the Senate, September 23rd, he left a paper which he had titled "An American National and International Program." It was a comprehensive document, obviously having required hours of work over a long period of time, a well laid out, comprehensive collection of thoughts on America at home and abroad, its military preparedness, economic health, the welfare of its people, and world leadership.

In late September, soon after the Senate's autumn recess, Frank and Marian drove to Chapel Hill and moved in at 404 Pittsboro Street, a small rental house next to the home of Marian's sister-in-law, Florence Drane. Willis Smith was now running against the Republican candidate; he and other Democrats were facing the November election. Frank was asked to speak at Democratic Party rallies in the state's twelve congressional districts. He spoke at eight, supporting the Democratic Party candidates, including Willis Smith, and speaking laudatorily of Roosevelt's New Deal and Truman's legislative Fair Deal.

The night before the November vote, he and Marian and Al Lowenstein had dinner together. Lowenstein still rankled from the June defeat and volunteered the view that there's one man in this room who won't vote a straight Democratic ticket tomorrow.

There are two people in this room who won't vote a straight ticket, Marian said.

Frank said nothing, but next morning he walked to the voting booths in the town hall, alone, and voted.

He and Marian still had a small savings account, the money she had set aside someday to build a house on their lot. She had several nice pieces of furniture, some of them from her family.

She must have come soon to realize Frank didn't want to build their home here, where his political embarrassment would become an embarrassment to the University. Also, if he stayed there would be university issues brought to him that would be none of his business. Living in Chapel Hill was living in his own shadow.

President Truman proposed he appoint Frank head of the American Red Cross.

Frank declined.

The Civil Aeronautics Board? The Federal Trade Commission?

None of these offered a sufficient challenge.

Truman asked him to stand for considerations as Director of the National Science Foundation. Frank decided to do so, and, while waiting for that to develop, he turned down other offers, among them presidencies of several colleges and universities and, to his surprise, associate-editorship of a newspaper. Also, a law firm wanted him, and he rejected a position with the U.N. Point IV Program dealing with refugees and world relief.

Meanwhile, the savings were being spent. Once appointment of a non-scientist to the NSF came into question, he withdrew from that, leaving him and Marian with precious little money and fewer avenues for work.

November 27, 1950, Smith was sworn in as Senator; Helms became his administrative assistant in Washington. Smith was to serve in the Senate for only thirty months before death from coronary thrombosis.

Frank accepted work at the Department of Labor as Defense Manpower Coordinator, was one of President Truman's men, helping to keep American industry supplying the nation's armed forces fighting in Korea. At the Department of Labor Frank negotiated the settlement of a strike in Alaska which threatened the Korean War effort. Nights and days he sat in the meeting room, sometimes falling asleep in the chair. Once the session at long last was over, one of the dock workers approached, loomed over him. You know, Frank, he said, you're a sweet little son of a bitch.

Reminiscent of John L. Lewis. Frank would later boast of the remark, as Stuart Sechriest, Professor of Journalism, remembers.

During Frank's tenure at the Labor Department, he and Marian still had their little house in Chapel Hill. His nieces recall his returning to it from Alaska, still afire with enthusiasm for statehood for Alaska.

Working in Washington for the Labor Department, Frank would, week by week, travel back and forth, in order that Marian could have her home in Chapel Hill among friends; however, travelling would not be practical should Frank accept a post at the United Nations, which he was offered. There he was to negotiate the cultural and political disputes between India and Pakistan which threatened to break into a war. Frank would be an officer of the United Nations, the sole U.N. negotiator for India and Pakistan, reporting to the Secretary General.

Marian patiently argued against his accepting the challenge. His health was a consideration. She had brought to their house a collection of nice furniture, she was even yet decorating the rooms, hanging newly framed pictures in the bedrooms.

Frank accepted the offer. The immense challenge offered him release from the throes of recent defeat. Marian was heartbroken. She was, as her sister Katherine noted, a quiet person happy in her home -- she was that type of individual; during her years with Frank she had lived in an institution, a big house for guests and meetings, or she had lived in a utility apartment. There had been only a few months in her own cottage. Nothing gracious here, nothing of the quality she would prefer, but at least a home, and there was a garden and there were friends and family nearby.

Now came the time to say goodbye, yet again.

For Frank, it was an exciting opportunity. For at least three months he would be dealing with one of the world's problems, one which shook the pillars of great societies. Here was an opportunity for the U.N. to prove its worth, and for two peoples of two powerful countries, and of two religions, to come to the altar of world peace.

Eleanor Roosevelt in 1950 had suggested to President Truman that he send Frank to Asia, as a roving ambassador to the Near East and Asia "to talk philosophy and get a line on attitudes and reasons for those attitudes that we really do not understand too well."

This was another idea that did not work out for Frank. Truman appointed Eleanor Roosevelt.

43. Frank Graham meets with the press -- which had come to criticize, but stayed to listen; Karachi, June, 1951. *Southern Historical Collection, UNC Library*

CHAPTER SIXTEEN

WHEN FRANK TOOK the United Nations job the early summer of 1951, Marian rented for her and Frank a two-room apartment in the Commodore Hotel in New York City; soon they moved to a residential hotel, the Beaux Arts, on East 44th Street near the sparkling new U.N. building. Their nieces, Frances, Rebecca and Elizabeth II, occasionally visited them there.

The apartment was small. The kitchen was of the galley type, without counter space. Even the skillet had to be tiny, only large enough for one egg. The electric skillet was larger, and whenever she used it Marian would place it on the balcony.

Tonight you and I are having a wonderful Danish mushroom salad, Rebecca recalls her aunt telling her one afternoon. Frank will have slaw, because he can't tell the difference.

They had a good laugh, but it was true; that night Frank had slaw and buttermilk, and didn't care about the difference. Returning from a short trip, he had gone to sleep on the bus and had arrived home late for supper anyway.

Frank was happy as he undertook the work at the U.N. He had an immense challenge, that of seeking settlement of the dispute over Kashmir which had stirred up religious hatred between Moslems and Hindus, political hatred between Pakistanis and Indians, leading to arms buildup and fighting. Hundreds of people already lay dead and buried in this divided land.

Fred Weaver, Dean of Students at Chapel Hill, used to tell about his first visit to their New York apartment. Where are your things? he asked, looking about the bare rooms.

Frank said he and Marian had sold some of their furnishings in order to buy books about India and Pakistan.

Books were everywhere, books from the U.N. and the New York Public Library, as well as those Frank had bought. All were books Frank was reading.

Rather, that Marian and Frank were reading together. His eyes would not allow him to read many hours a day, so she would read aloud to him, helping him as he delved into decades of detailed history, into the souls of the Muslim and Hindu religions, into the topography, geography, economy, politics, mores of the countries and people, their superstitions, beliefs, family practices. All was stored in Frank's brain.

Niece Rebecca recalls he asked her to read to him from some major Indian holy writings. In spite of her best efforts, he fell asleep.

The previous U.N. officer to try to deal with the controversy over Kashmir had been unsuccessful. That had been Owen Dixon, Judge of the High Court of Australia. He had found on arriving in Asia that both sides had agreed to a plebiscite for the people of Kashmir, in order that they might choose to be part either of India or Pakistan, but over about a year and a half nothing had been done. Meanwhile, the powerful armies of India and Pakistan were preparing for war.

As Graham read Sir Owen's reports, his own excitement grew. Here were two nations at loggerheads. Neither Pakistan nor India would withdraw its forces from Kashmir until the other had done so. Also, there were the Azad Kashmir military forces.

Far more points of disagreements here than agreement, but Frank proceeded to draw up a list of matters India and Pakistan would certainly agree on, and these, he decided, would be the materials for the first discussions.

Frank and his staff arrived at Karachi, Pakistan, June 30, 1951, in the morning. Driving into the city, Frank became concerned about the poverty of the throngs of people. This city of 300,000 was serving as home for more than twice that many refugees from Bombay and Western India, Moslems in flight from the Hindus.

Except for William B. Aycock, a young law professor from Chapel Hill whom Frank had asked to be a personal aide, none of Frank's staff knew him. They assumed he was a gray-haired bureaucrat with the university, no doubt impractical and moving into a veritable lions' den. Skepticism was rife among them, as among their peers in New York and Geneva, and among the leaders of the warring nations, and was rife among members of the Pakistani press who came together to meet this new mediator. They were armed with loaded questions.

Frank met the press with his customary good nature, and with soft replies and kindness, and with knowledge of the situation and its history and of the culture and religions of the peoples, so that the reporters began to ask in order to learn. The press conference became a seminar, the astonished staff members watched in awe. The press, which had come to ridicule, stayed for hours.

Frank met that first afternoon with the Prime Minister, Liaquat Ali Khan, who no doubt was asked about his parents and other ancestors and where he was born, and might have heard a mention of the United Nations' hopes. From officials, as from reporters, Frank learned that Pakistanis suspected India was out to destroy their country, and were using Kashmir as a ploy.

On July 2 Frank and his staff landed at the Palam Airport at ten a.m., and the party drove into New Delhi, where Frank met with the press and in the afternoon with India's Prime Minister, Jawaharlal Nehru, at the President's home. Here, too, Frank found fear, bitterness, skepticism, and here, too, he met people with warmth and personal friendliness. Nehru later told his parliament Graham was in India for months before he ever even mentioned a United Nations resolution.

Before Fran and Dean of Students Fred Weaver married, but after the announcement of their engagement, she visited Marian in New York. This turned out to be the day Frank was returning from his first long visit to Pakistan and India and his report to the Security Council in Geneva. The U.N. was sending a limousine to take Marian to Idlewild Airport, and she invited Fran, who had never met Frank, to accompany her.

They waited a long while in the airport, but finally here came the U.N. delegation, Frank in the lead. Several reporters were present, and Frank talked with them, then greeted Marian, who left a spot of lipstick on his cheek, which he would not allow anyone to wipe off.

And this is the little lady I've traveled a long way to meet, he said to Fran.

They rode into the city together, Frank expressing pleasure over the partial success he had achieved; however, he told them about the poverty, the refugees, the war-wounded, the millions of children deprived of good health and education in this time of collapse and despair.

I gave them the money we were saving for a house, he told Marian, speaking simply, holding her hand.

She said nothing, not a word in reprimand.

Marian made the best of New York City. She visited art museums, enjoyed the theatre. One North Carolina friend who was a frequent companion was Frances Ferguson, whom she had known in Edenton. Frances' husband was with United Press International and often was given tickets to events; Frances and Marian would go to the opera and to concerts at Carnegie Hall. Movies, too. They went to many of those.

Marian used to make doll clothes for Frances' collection. Made a hat for her lady twelve-inch doll. Sometimes she would come up to the Fergusons' apartment and spend the day with Frances, sewing.

She recalls that Marian admitted to having been disappointed when Frank took the U.N. job. She also was not happy about their apartment at the Beaux Arts, either, nor were her sisters, who believed she should have better.

Marian did, indeed, love Frank, and even beyond love surprised Frances by admitting she liked to hear him snore -- he had a loud snore. I like to know he's sleeping soundly, Marian told her.

St. Bartholomew's Episcopal was her church, where she attended Sunday and weekday services and did volunteer work, including duties at Everybody's Thrift shop. Often she sent nieces gifts she purchased there, usually beautiful clothes. Rebecca says Aunt Marian had excellent taste, took a great interest in clothes and was an accomplished seamstress.

She enjoyed being visited by family and showing them New York. When she had left North Carolina, one acquaintance was heard to say, Poor Marian, as if she hasn't been through enough; now she has to go to New York and entertain Ralph Bunche. Well, there were no such entertainments. When Frank was away, she lived a quiet life, and when Frank was home, she had a quiet life with him, helping him with his books and papers and personal letters. If family or Al Lowenstein or other friends were nearby at mealtime, she would prepare a light supper, or would lead them to the restaurant downstairs.

She and Frank did seek to keep contact with Chapel Hill. Often Frank brought small gifts from India or Pakistan for friends there -- a brass trivet, an ivory letter opener.

In return, Gladys and Albert Coates gave him a copy of "Cyrano De Bergerac" and marked a passage which reminded them of him.

CYRANO
I carry my adornments on my soul.
I do not dress up like a popinjay;
But inwardly, I keep my daintiness.
I do not bear with me, by any chance,
An insult not yet washed away -- a conscience
Yellow with unpurged bile -- an honor frayed
To rags, a set of scruples badly worn.
I go caparisoned in gems unseen,
Trailing while plumes of freedom, garlanded
With my good name -- no figure of a man,

> But a soul clothed in shining armor, hung
> With deeds for decorations, twirling -- thus --
> A bristling wit, and swinging at my side
> Courage, and on the stones of this old town
> Making the sharp truth ring, like golden spurs!

On visits to North Carolina Frank met with dozens of friends, some of whom knew of his report in Geneva and New York of progress being made, and the requests by the Security Council that he continue -- the Russian delegate alone expressing annoyance.

Tom Lambeth, who sometimes drove Frank place to place, recalls sitting in the kitchen of Kerr and Mary Scott's home on Haw River; Frank was visiting with Miss Mary. An hour went by while the two reminisced about people they both knew, some of them having passed on, Frank recalling words of a poem Miss Mary had in part forgotten. At one point Frank told her, Now Miss Mary, I know you told the Governor to appoint me to the Senate.

No, I only said you'd be a good one, she replied. She mentioned Senate-nominee Willis Smith's coming through a receiving line in Raleigh, where she and Kerr were greeting the guests. On reaching her he extended his hand. She looked at his hand for a moment, then at his face, and said, Oh, I couldn't do that. And turned away from him.

You've always been a good friend, was Frank's response.

When Elizabeth Matheson finished college, she lived in New York in an apartment with friends, and visited Marian and Frank along with others from North Carolina, among them Al Lowenstein, who was now a student at Yale Law School and was in Students for Stevenson during Adlai Stevenson's 1952 campaign. Also, he was President of the National Student Association.

Al talked with Dr. Frank about his own projects, used him as chief advisor, two others being Eleanor Roosevelt who lived on Washington Square West, in Greenwich Village, and Norman Thomas, Socialist Leader.

Elizabeth recalls Al and Frank being upset with the South African rule over Southwest Africa. Al flew there and smuggled out, in the trunk of a car, a young male leader of the insurrection, and brought him to New York City to speak at the U.N. Al wrote a book about this, *Brutal Mandate, A Journey to Southwest Africa.*

She recalls conversations critical of the Franco dictatorship in Spain. Al and Frank criticized totalitarianism everywhere, and Al, an organizer, had contact with young people everywhere. Al flew to Spain on missions.

Occasionally there were receptions given by Al for Frank and Marian in New York, gatherings of friends. The receptions were treats without alcohol. Al would invite a hundred people to meet Frank Graham, say at 9 p.m. at Al's apartment, one so small the guests overflowed into the hallways and neighbors' living rooms. Meanwhile, Frank and Marian, standing throughout, greeted people by name and were greeted.

In his second landmark report to the Security Council, Frank was able to report further progress; of twelve points Frank had submitted to leaders for their consideration, India had by now agreed to eight, Pakistan to all twelve. Again the council voted overwhelmingly to continue Frank's negotiating, the debate marred only by Jakob Malik of Russia, who declared Frank was a tool of the Pentagon and claimed that his effort was an Anglo-American plot to subvert Kashmir and create a base for aggression.

In February, 1952, Frank was conferring in Paris; in March he was in Asia; in April he made his third report in Geneva, in which he admitted negotiations were as yet hampered but recommended the two nations be encouraged to enter into direct negotiations under U.N. auspices. This was encouraged, and talks began in August in Geneva. The talks ended in September and Graham in October asked the Security Council for talks to be resumed, which they were. At the end of March Frank recommended that the U.N. withdraw from participating directly, so that the Prime Ministers of the two countries might discuss the issues and settle them.

The Prime Ministers agreed, and their talks turned out to be cordial. The two men were obviously determined to work matters out peacefully. It appeared as of August, 1953, that the problems were being solved, not only in regard to Kashmir, but overall relations between the two countries.

It was with this success in prospect that Frank returned to North Carolina to meet his friends, and it was in June, 1953, in Raleigh, that he attended the funeral of Senator Smith, who had died of a coronary.

Frank was present, seated on the back row of the Edenton Street Methodist Church, paying his respects in time-honored North Carolina and Scottish traditions. What did the little man on the back now think? Only kind thoughts. Might a spectator compare the two of them now: one of them but two years ago beaten, now a success on a world stage?

November 10, 1953, Nehru wrote a personal letter to Pakistan's Mohammed Ali, leader of Pakistan. He was worried about news of a possible military pact between Pakistan and the United States.

That same month the pact was announced.

On December 9, Nehru wrote an official, not a personal letter, stating such a pact would "affect the major questions we are considering and, more especially, Kashmir." He wrote Mohammed Ali about Kashmir. "In fact, it becomes rather absurd to talk of demilitarization, if Pakistan proceeds in the reverse direction with help of the United States."

In November Frank had received word that India would not, as a result of the military pact, settle the Kashmir problem, and that the ultimate solution would be a boundary along the lines of the present cease-fire lines.

Frank Graham was asked to stay on as U.N. Representative for India and Pakistan, in hopes that, in spite of the military build-up, peace could be saved. He agreed to do so and continued to be helpful. However, much of his duties now consisted of travels within the country, speaking to groups about the U.N.

At the start he had been asked by the U.N. speakers' bureau to make one talk only, to substitute for a scheduled speaker who was ill. On that occasion Frank wrote a speech on the train, met with the people, no doubt took them in hand, asked where each was from, spoke to the assembly for an hour about the United Nations, and left an enthusiastic audience of friends. Soon his secretary, Daisy Lippner, was scheduling talks often, and Frank was made chairman of the U.N. Speakers' Bureau.

He received fees for each speech, and he turned the money over to the U.N. Children's Fund.

Actually, Frank made more money at the United Nations than he had ever made previously, and he increased his gifts to charities, to co-workers, to political campaigns -- overcoming his own rules against partisan help while on the U.N. staff.

Down in North Carolina Terry Sanford was Kerr Scott's campaign manager while Scott, who could not succeed himself as governor, ran for the Senate. Terry says Frank gave him two three hundred-dollar checks at the beginning, and mailed in more checks later. Deciding Marian was not privy to this, and believing Frank had done enough, Sanford recalls tearing up four or five checks, and wasn't even worried about putting Frank's checkbook out of balance, because he suspected Frank had never balanced it in the first place.

In 1954, 1955, 1956, 1957 Frank updated his report on Kashmir and waited to be asked to deliver it.

Frank made speeches in his home state, too; he always accepted an invitation, it seems, if at all possible. On July 30, 1956, he was in Raleigh at a session sponsored by the American Institute of Cooperation, his subject being "the Plight of the Farmers in Our Country." In his speech he came out strongly for farm cooperatives, and in one spurt traced the spread of the cooperative movement from Toad Street, Rochdale in Lancashire, England, to the European continent, America, Asia, Africa, and the islands of the world. His talk ended, as most of his did these days, with a few words about the United Nations:

> While there is still time to turn the despair of the engulfing
> night of our generation into the hope of another morning for
> all the children of men, the peoples of the earth cannot lag in
> the organization of their strength and the cooperation of
> nations for universal enforceable disarmament and the
> control of thermonuclear power toward a more productive,
> freer and fairer life for all people on this earth as the
> God-given home of the family of man.

One outbreak of temper came in 1957. The Security Council requested that its president for that month, Gunnar Jarring of Sweden, examine with the Governments of India and Pakistan any additional proposals which, in his opinion, were likely to contribute toward the settlement of the dispute.

Frank heard of this entry of yet another mediator through gossip, that only, and sought out the one responsible for Jarring's appointment, Pierson Dixon, Britain's delegate. Frank's secretary, Daisy Lippner, was astonished on hearing the reports. Another staff person, witness to the attack, told her he had never seen Dr. Graham that way before; he really told Dixon off right.

Kerr Scott won the Senate seat left vacant by reason of Willis Smith's death. He considered his victory a vindication of Frank Graham's defeat, and twice sent an aide, Bill Staten, to bring him from Hillsborough to stand beside Scott on victory night. Frank would not come.

The day Scott was sworn in as Senator, Frank did attend. Joel Fleishman and Tom Lambeth were there, too, seated in the gallery with him and Miss Mary. Russell Long saw Dr. Frank come up into the gallery, grabbed him, led him down. All ex-senators have privileges of

Dearest Sibly,

The poems are wonderful — I take off my hat to you — but I take up my pen reluctantly — realizing sadly my literary shortcomings!

I know you haven't time to read a line — But we both want to thank you for sending you the poems — and to tell you of our pride and pleasure in reading them. We copied them to keep!

To my complete dismay, I today found a letter from you to Frank that I had brought upstairs in a shopping bag the middle of April — and lost — I have apologized profusely to Frank and now do the same to you. He would have

been so glad to send you
material on S.A. & S.W.A.
and Al's part in the Case
before the Trusteeship Council.
I am so sorry that my
forgetfulness and carelessness
deprived him of that pleasure,
and perhaps deprived you of
some help. Please forgive
me. We have a wonderful letter to
the Press written by a man who
was at the Winthrop meeting. I'll
bring it for you to read.
                    Will see you next weekend.
D.V. In the meantime Good
Luck.   Love,
                    Marian.
May 26th   I left today for Westtown to make
           a commencement address. Then on to Shaw U.
           in Raleigh for an Honorary Degree Monday!

44. Marian's letter to Elizabeth Matheson. The notation "D.V." is for "deo volente," or a gentle code for "God willing."   *Courtesy Elizabeth Matheson.*

the Senate floor, he told Frank, and your privilege is greater than anybody else's.

As they came out onto the Senate floor, other senators greeted him. Frank, you've been away too long, one said. That day's newspaper had reported a dispute between Russell Long and Stuart Symington. Soon Frank had Symington by the hand and pulled him over to Russell Long. There were the two senators, neither of whom wanted to initiate talk with the other, and would not have talked except for Frank.

Frank was faithful in his correspondence, including family correspondence. All his letters showed thought and concern.

Niece Elizabeth he wrote from Nags Head:

> ...I have a suggestion about the novel. You say you don't have the creative ability but you do... the suggestion I have concerns gathering material during these next few years, and writing down impressions, scenes, conversations and characterizations as they come and <u>when</u> they come at the most unexpected times. Keep a pad and pencil nearby, bedside, etc. The plot will evolve. Hillsborough, Chapel Hill, Edenton, Nags Head are full of people, events, complications, tensions, scenes, etc. etc. all about you. All great creative work comes out of life about you, day to day, not some far off place in some distant time but here and now.
>
> You don't need to say much of anything about it to cause people to think you are queer or <u>unique</u> but just grind away, store up, record what you see and hear and think and imagine and in ten years you'll have a great story to tell which would astound you now to think you could tell. Someone said 10% inspiration + 90% perspiration = genius. You have not less than 10% God-given from your mother, father, grandmother and grandfather, plus Dr. Drane. The 90% is up to you.

Some of Frank's letters were written in doggerel.

116 East 56
NYC
March 12, 1955
Dear Elizabeth
  Congratulations on Geography! and History!
  But how about more difficult Math,
  too often object of students wrath
  It is of many proofs the best, and most reliable
as a test
  of youthful work and celebration. When you
reach its highest station
  we'll hold a family celebration.
  Marian and I are sending you membership
tickets, too,
  from Roanoke Island Association.
  In fitting historic commemoration
  of time and place of hopeful birth
  of England's first child on western earth...
  Since Marian has written to Elizabeth yesterday and to sisters today, I'll add no more but
simply send the love of both of us here
  to
all of you there.
  Affectionately, alphabetically and algebraically
yours in triple A's
  Frank G.

Another letter to grand-niece Elizabeth, this one from
  Marian:

  Dearest Libby,
  The poems are <u>wonderful</u>. I take my hat
off to you -- but I take up my <u>pen</u> reluctantly,
realizing sadly my literary shortcomings!
  I know you haven't time to read a line. But
we both want to thank you for sending us the
poems. And to tell you of our pride and
pleasure in reading them. I've copied them to
keep!
  To my complete dismay, I <u>today</u> found a
letter from you to Frank that I had brought
upstairs in a shopping bag the middle of April
and lost. I have apologized profusely to
Frank and now do the same to you. He
would have been so glad to send you material

on S.A. & S.W.A. and Al's part in the case before the Membership Council. I am so sorry that my forgetfulness and carelessness deprived him of that pleasure and perhaps deprived you of some help. Please forgive me.

We have a wonderful letter to the Press written by a man who was at the Winthrop meeting. I'll bring it for you to read.

Will see you next weekend -- D.V. In the meantime, <u>Good Luck</u>.

Love,
Marian

F. left today for Westtown to make a commencement address. Then on to Shaw U. in Raleigh for an Honorary Degree Monday!

May 26th

CHAPTER SEVENTEEN

AS AN EMPLOYEE of the U.N., Frank decided not to send money to the 1960 campaigns of Jack Kennedy for President and Terry Sanford for Governor of North Carolina. That might lead to an unfavorable news story.

Terry Sanford was running for Governor on an education platform -- some termed it a Frank Graham platform. Incidentally, at home Sanford had kept a green booklet since Frank's campaign in which he entered ideas for meeting racist attacks, should any occur. Some notes were rejoinders, replies to irritating or leading questions, some were tactics. For instance, Sanford refused to deal with the black leaders in Asheville and Wilmington before the first primary, in order to be able to avoid a charge of Negro bloc voting statewide -- even though he needed those votes.

Tom Lambeth, who would later serve as Sanford's Administrative Assistant, recalls Frank addressing the problem of making a contribution to the campaign. Tom says Frank would always do exactly right, but was capable of the end run. In this case he invited all of Terry's staff to come to lunch with him. He would pay for it, he suggested, and each one would then contribute the value of his lunch to the campaign.

This was done. Tom gathered together all the troops.

In 1960 civil rights demonstrators had been unable to find a North Carolina leader to come out for them, to represent their actions, to lend respectability. Jake Phelps of Duke University suggested they try Frank Graham; he never had ducked a fight, Jake said. Invite him to come down from New York, then send out a report on his talk to the Associated Press.

Frank received the request in New York and agreed at once. As soon as that was known, advice poured in to him from whites and blacks, almost all of it urging caution. The demonstrations were emotionally upsetting, socially unsettling; the mature black leaders were unsure of them, most white leaders, liberals as well as conservatives, were wary of them or downright opposed.

On the appointed evening Marian drove Frank to St. Joseph's AME

Church in Durham, where about one hundred fifty black and white young people were gathered. Frank was pleased to meet them. In his address and to the press, he said he had come here to measure with them the length and breadth of the American dream. He said,

> The Freedom Riders were not breaking the law. Now, they were breaking a local law, a statute of a town or state, but the Supreme Court of the United States has declared those local laws and statutes illegal, so they are fulfilling the law, rather than breaking the law. And this charge that you are breaking the law is not sound.
>
> Those people who sit down, wanting the same service for the same price, and for stores to sell to them, are trying, not to overthrow the republic, but to fulfill the promise of the republic, not to overturn rights of person and property, but to establish rights of person and property for all people, in accordance with the present law of the land.

He told them the echo of the American Revolution had gone out and had circled the earth and had come home again.

In an interview, in answer to a question from Anne Queen, Director of the University at Chapel Hill's YWCA, Dr. Graham, in reference to integration, said:

> I remember a very fine young colored woman, Pauli Murray, who applied for admission here -- this was before the Supreme Court decision -- and it was my responsibility to answer her. And I denied her admission, and she understood it. But I saw her later, and I think it was in New York, and she said, "This is a right ironical situation. You denied me admission to your university. That's my university, too, because my great-grandfather gave you one of your buildings."
>
> Now, before the Supreme Court decision, we obeyed the law, but during that time, we stood for a policy of openness and study... We had unsegregated seminars in the Alumni Building. That was before the Supreme Court decision, and that was not a violation of the law. We obeyed the law.
>
> We obeyed the law of the land before 1954, let's obey the law after 1954.

Marian's Nags Head house was damaged by the Ash Wednesday storm of 1961, and she and Frank gave the main part of the house to a neighbor, Carolista Fletcher, granddaughter of novelist Inglis Fletcher, who moved it across the road and set it on a big sand hill. The back wing Marian and Frank kept and used for guests, and they built a small cottage on the ocean front.

The family became even more important to the Grahams, and the annual treks to Nags Head were as dear to both of them as ever.

In one Nags Head summer letter to niece Elizabeth, Frank mentioned Marian's illness:

> Marian had a slight operation after a thorough check up in the Columbia University Hospital. All reports good. She is thriving in the clean air, eating seafood, etc., etc., etc... Our Marian's little cottage becomes more precious every day... the Battles are calling us to go out to dinner. Marian sends love with mine. We miss you, dear Libby.

He mentioned that his nephew, Bennett Perry, Jr., had a very charming lady friend from Richmond here for the weekend. She cooks and sews continuously. I hope she passes muster.

Marian told her family the new Nags Head cottage was, she realized, the only home she would ever have.

Also, she told Eliza she was ill. She would not discuss the illness further with her sister, nor would she discuss her will or estate. She simply said that there had never been much. Fortunately, medical insurance came with Frank's job.

Frank maintained contact with Alice Neal and Hubert Robinson. On more than one visit Alice received a sizeable sum of money from Frank, her daughters recall, with instructions to lay it by for her old age. Alice's daughters say he would drop by to see them and their mother, would ask if they were taking care of her.

As she went into her final illness, they recall, she asked them not to tell Mr. Frank once she passed on. He's too busy.

However, Kate must have told him, because on the day of her funeral, here he came from the airport, carrying his suitcases, and there was a welcome of tears, hugs and kisses, Alice says, and they went to the funeral service at St. Paul AME Church together. Then he returned at once to the Raleigh-Durham airport and flew out.

Alice was only 66 at her death.

Hubert Robinson was honored at his retirement from the University in 1961 by friends. Frank, who could not attend, sent a telegram of praise. (Hubert later was elected to the Chapel Hill Board of Aldermen.)

Several efforts were made to persuade Frank to return to North Carolina. Terry Sanford was one instigator.

WESTERN UNION

CLASS OF SERVICE
This is a full-rate Telegram or Cablegram unless its deferred character is indicated by a suitable symbol above or preceding the address.

W. P. MARSHALL, PRESIDENT

220

SYMBOLS
DL=Day Letter
NL=Night Letter
LT=Int'l Letter Telegram
VLT=Int'l Victory Ltr.

The filing time shown in the date line on telegrams and day letters is STANDARD TIME at point of origin. Time of receipt is STANDARD TIME at point of destination

RA06 BA059

B UDA063 LONG NL PD=UD NEW YORK NY 29=

1961 JUN 30 AM 8 54

:TONY JENZANO=

MOREHEAD PLANETARIUM CHAPEL HILL NCAR=

MY GRATEFUL APPRECIATION AND BEST WISHES TO MY DEAR
FRIEND HUBERT ROBINSON HE HAS SERVED ABLY AND LOYALLY FOR
31 YEARS. FOR 19 YEARS FEW PEOPLE WERE CLOSER TO US AS AN
EFFICIENT AND DEPENDABLE MEMBER OF OUR UNIVERSITY HOUSEHOLD.
FOR 12 YEARS HE HAS HELPED YOU TO MAKE THE MOREHEAD
PLANETARIUM A CENTER OF WELCOME AND A REVELATION OF THE
SUBLIMITY OF THE FIRMAMENT AND THE CONSTANCY OF THE PLANETS
AND STARS IN THEIR HEAVENLY COURSES. HIS OWN CONSTANCY AND
GOODNESS HAVE BEEN A FAITHFUL PART OF IT ALL, WHETHER
DRIVING A CAR, ATTENDING A HOME, KEEPING THE PLANATARIUM,
UPBUILDING A CHURCH, SERVING ON THE TOWN COUNCIL OR
ENRICHING THE ROBUST ESPRIT DE CORPS OF OUR COMMON
UNIVERSITY COMMUNITY. MY WIFE JOINS ME IN HIGH ESTEEM AND
WARM GOOD WISHES FOR MANY MORE USEFUL AND HAPPY YEARS TO
OUR DEAR FRIEND HUBERT, ONE OF GOD'S NOBLEMEN. SINCERELY=
        FRANK P GRAHAM.

THE COMPANY WILL APPRECIATE SUGGESTIONS FROM ITS PATRONS CONCERNING ITS SERVICE

45. Telegram from Dr. Frank to Tony Jenzano, director of the Morehead Planetarium (and employer of Hubert Robinson) on the occasion of Hubert's retirement. *Southern Historical Collection, UNC Library*

Preparing to run for governor, I was getting around the state, I was beginning to take an active part in many things, including the university. I would occasionally see Frank Graham. When Bill Friday became president -- we had a little group active in making Bill Friday president. I suppose the first officer that Bill had to pick was a new chancellor, and he put me on that committee and he said to me, Just get Bill Aycock's name on the list...

I got to know Spencer Love very well, I had met him two or three times, and he and I set out to get Frank Graham back to Chapel Hill. When I was in New York, two or three times, I went to see Dr. Frank. I went to Greensboro a couple of times to Spencer Love's office to talk to him about how we could get Dr. Frank back. I talked to Bill Friday about it and Bill Aycock.

But there was some barrier there that I never quite could discern adequately, to do something about what[ever] it was. I don't know, there was a reluctance. I just wanted Frank Graham back in North Carolina, back at Chapel Hill, back here as a presence. He was getting unconnected with the University. He had -- by that time, of course, he had been in the campaign, he probably felt rejected -- I don't know. But anyhow, for all practical purposes, he had -- the disconnection between him and North Carolina had occurred, and I thought to bring him back as some kind of professor or scholar-in-residence, to let him meet with students and teach students would have been great for the University, great for Bill Friday and for Bill Aycock.

And I never could tell whether the resistance was pressure in Chapel Hill not to have him back: he was politically controversial. Or whether here was just an absolute stubbornness on Frank Graham's part. Or whether we didn't put the right kind of pressure in the right kind of places, but Spencer Love and I certainly did devote our attention to it.

In 1962 Dr Frank made this statement about why he did not remain in Chapel Hill:

Well, I really didn't want to leave Chapel Hill, but I had been here nineteen years, and I think now that nineteen years is long enough for anybody to serve as president because you build up enmities in battles over hot issues. You have scars, and its just as well to move on and let some younger person come in and carry on. I think it was better, really, for the University, for me to... not pass away, but to pass on.

Tom Lambeth and Joel Fleishman raised money to buy Frank a new

car, a blue Ford, which they presented to him at the airport. What he
did with it they never learned. They raised much of the money from
Democrats who had not supported Frank in the campaign -- conscience
money, they called it.

Others offered to raise money to build him a house in Chapel Hill.
Spencer Love was one of them. Frank refused, politely but firmly.

He did arrange to talk with several of the leaders of the University
student body over the years: John Sanders, Dick Murphy, Banks Talley,
Henry Bowers, Eli Evans, Joel Fleishman, Tom Lambeth.

Terry Sanford as Governor continued to try to get Frank back into
the State to stay. The stains of political defeat had, after all, been
erased; even people who had worked for Willis Smith were denying
they had been involved. Since then liberals, including Terry, had been
elected. Kerr Scott had run for the Senate and won.

Governor Sanford's administration was in several ways a reflection
of Graham-type programs: the first statewide anti-poverty program in
America, which soon after became the prototype of President Lyndon
Johnson's War on Poverty; the Good Neighbor program, first in the
deep South, aimed at bringing about better relations between races,
announced to the press on the University campus; any number of
education projects, among them a summer residential school for
outstanding eleventh grade students named the North Carolina
Governor's School; a residential school for students needing remedial
work, the North Carolina Advancement School; a residential high
school and college for professional training of performing artists, the
North Carolina School of the Arts; and a private agency to initiate and
coordinate some of these and other educational programs, the Learning
Institute of North Carolina.

Frank Graham was suggested to head the Learning Institute. The
Board of Directors would be the State Superintendent of Public
Instruction, the President of the University of North Carolina, the
President of Duke University, and the executive director of the new
state anti-poverty program. State and private funding was in hand, with
much more likely from state and national foundations and the federal
government.

Frank was visiting in North Carolina at the time. All of Terry
Sanford's aides -- he had a small staff of five -- knew Dr. Frank. They
agreed this was a perfect challenge for him. At the United Nations he
had worked his magic, had done his work, was now being denied the
right to make his final report.

Frank was in Hillsborough. Niece Elizabeth remembers one of the Governor's aides calling on him there, to follow up, to try to persuade him.

Much expectancy, glowing prospects, but finally came the reply: not now.

And considering his health and age, seventy-seven, the meaning was clear enough: not ever.

46. Dr. Graham, a familiar figure at the microphone, late in life.
Southern Historical Collection, UNC Library

CHAPTER EIGHTEEN

FRANK HAD STAYED at the U.N. during three of its administrations, often requesting the chance to make his final report and leave, and he had been denied that right.

Even so, he was year after year persuaded to stay on by the chance that an interim solution would occur. Remaining the sole mediator for India and Pakistan, he had a final report to deliver.

He had submitted six reports, and at the cottage at Nags Head he worked on a seventh. Elizabeth Matheson recalls the women mandated quiet during the morning hours while "Unkie" went over the report. Year after year he continued the process of reading books and journals, corresponding, editing, discussing, arranging, persuading.

Daisy Lippner admitted he was often ill, that each winter he had pneumonia. Everybody on the U.N. staff was fearful Frank would die. He did insist on keeping his speaking commitments, in any case, whenever he could possibly do so. In winter she sometimes managed to put engagements off till spring.

One engagement she recalled his making was a talk at the Elk Hill Falls, Pennsylvania, Methodist Women's Club. He agreed to be there, and to her consternation, the time of the talk was the evening before President Kennedy's inauguration, to which Frank was invited -- was to sit on the main platform with senators and other ex-senators, and to be the house guest of Senator and Mrs. Paul Douglas. She and Frank discussed this conflict, Frank seeing no problem. He would make his talk in Elk Hill Falls and taken an overnight train to Washington.

That was the sort of trouble she had with him. Fortunately for them both, snow fell the day he was to leave, trains were tied up, and his talk at Elk Hill Falls had to be canceled. Off Frank went to Washington.

Next morning Senator Douglas phoned to ask where Frank was. No, he had not arrived at his home. Daisy Lippner alerted U.N. security.

Midmorning she was listening on her desk radio to Mr. Kennedy being sworn in, when Frank arrived in the office. He had carried his overnight bag from Penn Station, so he was tired, but also was elated. The most wonderful news, he told her. When he had got to Penn Station yesterday, he had found there was a train that could take him to Elk Hills Falls, Pennsylvania. He had been able to make his talk, but had had to miss the president's inauguration.

Douglass Hunt once ran into him at the Raleigh-Durham airport. Dr. Graham was holding to a metal post for support, he was so drained of strength. Jane Grills, on her start of an international trip, came upon him, worn and weary, in the Washington National Airport. She had known him while she was teaching in the UNC Department of Radio, Television and Motion Pictures after World War II. He remembered her, and bought her a cup of coffee. He was eager to give her a going-away present. A search through his pockets produced only a few cents, not enough to buy a gift, so he gave her his copy of the *New York Times*.

During these years, Chapel Hill friends often arranged to see Frank in New York, and he was the same friendly person, knowing everybody, remembering everything. The guards, the guides, the waiters in the dining room all were found of him. Being with him there was like being with him out on the sidewalk at the Old Well in Chapel Hill.

Among his friends at the U.N. was the office postman, who had wanted to buy a house and could not get a loan. Frank co-signed his note at the bank.

Another was a U.N. guard. Frank had helped him get members of his family admitted through the Immigration Department. At his wife's funeral a big limousine of the United Nations stopped in front of the Bronx Church and Dr. Graham popped out. He was the only United Nations official present.

Governor Sanford's aides were often invited to have lunch with Frank at the U.N. One joked with friends about the length of time required to go from Frank's office to the dining room -- a long wait for a hungry man. Frank even knew visitors in the hallway whom he had met in some town or other. One lady who had met him briefly ten years earlier was astounded to be stopped in the hallway by the little gray haired man calling her name, who recalled their previous, brief conversation.

Members of a committee to choose a new chancellor for the Chapel Hill campus visited him one morning to discuss their progress. Frank had not found a person on their list who would be ideal. Later one of Governor Sanford's aides came by. Was there a suggestion? Frank asked.

He liked the suggestion of Paul N. Ylvisaker for chancellor, the political scientist, author and anti-poverty activist. He told the Sanford aide that humanists, when put in charge of a department or school, were like a wet blanket thrown over it. I don't know just why, he said. At once he put in a phone call and listed Ylvisaker.

Another concern: a commission headed by Irving Carlyle was discussing admitting male students to the Woman's College. Frank had written him a letter -- it was over fifty pages long -- opposing this. Also, in the letter he opposed introducing liberal arts at North Carolina State. He continued to believe, as at the time of consolidation, that the Woman's College should model itself on Bryn Mawr and Smith and North Carolina State on MIT. Carlyle had not publicly released his letter, and Frank didn't feel free to release it himself. Therefore, he felt unable publicly to enter the debate.

As to his opinion on student sit-ins at the University of California at Berkeley and other campuses, he replied -- writing with a finger on the palm of his hand -- that universities should admit students on the basis of potential, judge them on the basis of improvement, and make students part of administrative procedures at all levels.

When he was eighty years old, *The New York Times* did an article about Frank for their October 15, 1966, issue. He was visiting in Chapel Hill when they located him.

The reporter found that Dr. Graham was saddened by the advocacy of violence by Stokely Carmichael, head of the Student Nonviolent Coordinating Committee. He said:

> Those Negro leaders decrying Martin Luther King and Roy Wilkins and looking down on them as out of date should really see they are standing on the shoulders of those they're looking down on. I hope the great body of nonviolent, law-abiding, decent Negroes will rally to the side of A. Phillip Randolph, Martin Luther King, Roy Wilkins, Whitney Young and James Farmer and get the nonviolent civil rights movement back on track.

47. John Motley Morehead, benefactor to the University, and Dr. Frank, at an annual UNC alumni meeting in New York City. Hugh Morton, president of the Alumni Association, stepped in front of the speakers' table and made what is probably the last picture of Mr. Morehead, who slipped on ice leaving the building, broke his hip and died of pneumonia three weeks later. *Photograph by Hugh Morton*

CHAPTER NINETEEN

MARIAN GRAHAM'S ILLNESS first showed up as a loss of hearing. She noticed the loss at her church's concerts. The diagnosis, once made, was a disease destroying the connective tissue of her body, *lupus erythematosus*.

Her doctors in New York did not know of a cure. They treated the symptoms.

The situation was quite beyond Frank. She had been part of his life, and he of hers, for over thirty years. From the beginning they had both thought that he would die first. Death held no fear for him, it was to be accepted; however, loneliness was never acceptable. He was unable to imagine life without Marian.

He felt guilty about having denied her luxuries she would have enjoyed. Denying himself, he realized, was a feature of his character, but going beyond that he had denied her, as well, had been unable to bring himself to buy her beautiful clothes -- he knew she loved them -- or beautiful furniture, he had not given her a home. How often had she talked of the lot in Chapel Hill, of building a house?

He had heard a niece ask her if the house wouldn't be too close to the women's dormitories, if the noise wouldn't keep them awake. Marian had replied, Oh, we'll both be too old by then to hear the noise.

In April, 1967, she was taken to Doctors' Hospital in New York. He haunted her room and walked the hallway outside. Niece Elizabeth sometimes was with him.

The doctors told them they didn't know what more to do.

A week went by. Marian held her own. Frank said to Elizabeth, perhaps we should take her to another hospital.

He did not.

She is not near death, he was told.

There was secrecy about her being ill. Marian didn't want any visitors.

Yes, we can take her to another hospital, he decided, but again did not, and left New York on yet another U.N. speaking engagement, which he was duty-bound to make, as Marian reminded him. He was on the road -- the long road of America -- when on April 27, 1967, word reached him that she was dead.

Bill Friday, president of the University, met the plane bringing Marian's body to North Carolina. Frank got off the plane, an old man, weary beyond thought, and came across the tarmac, his overcoat dragging. Bill put his arm around his shoulders, much as Frank used to slip an arm around him, and said Marian's sister was at the Hillsborough house waiting. I'm taking you home.

A throng of people came to the Chapel of the Cross for the funeral service. Among them was Sophia Cody, whose gowns had often been repaired by Marian when as a student she had no money. Women were present who had served with her on church committees and functions, and as "Gray Ladies" in World War II.

Before the service Frank sat in one of the side rooms and talked with her friends. At the cemetery, however, he would not leave the car. Tom Lambeth recalls approaching his open car window and at once Frank asked him to be sure and see after Marian's sister, Elizabeth Webb.

Afterward, at the home of Bob and Hattie House, Frank was weeping. He tried even so to speak to everyone who came there. Everyone else was weeping, too.

Hattie House said to Sophia Cody, It surely is difficult to console everyone when I have just lost my best friend.

Frank mourned for months, some say for the rest of his life.

From New York Frank wrote a letter about Marian, which he sent to their friends.

> She gave selflessly to me and to countless others the quiet blessing of a life whose inner resources came from the deep humility of her deep spiritual faith.
>
> People to her were individual persons and children of God and brothers of all. This sense of human brotherhood was deepened here in her work in the Union Settlement, Everybody's Thrift Shop, and the Woman's division of St. Bartholomew's Church, and more than a decade of our years at the United Nations.
>
> ...Her home and her heart were always open to all who came.

A niece recalls visiting him at the New York apartment, where he was living alone. She was with him when he appeared for the first time to notice the smallness of the skillet. How could a man use such a skillet?

Al Lowenstein came to lunch.

He would cook eggs for Al, Frank offered. One at a time.

Al was criticizing Richard Nixon while Frank cooked.

Frank said, Al, do you think eggs are what they used to be?

Frank Wilson's daughter Margaret recalls being on her honeymoon with her husband, Bob Wiley, at the St. Regis Hotel in New York. At 9:30 a.m. the desk called her room to say her Uncle Frank was in the lobby and would come up.

No, no, not yet, she shouted.

He came up half an hour later, explaining he had got out of bed at seven. He had read until his vision dimmed. This was a Sunday; he went to Marian's church, to take her place, and found her church didn't have a nine o'clock service. He had not known what to do, so he had come to see Margaret and her young husband.

Frank's doctors urged him to retire. He would not. The year Marian died he returned to North Carolina only to make three commencement speeches in late May and June.

Also, he made talks on occasion for the Alumni Office of the University. On one occasion he recognized everyone at a luncheon, and called each guest by name in the course of his talk. At a large gathering at the Commodore Hotel in New York City, attended by hundreds eager to hear him, he was handicapped by a score of speakers preceding his address, each briefly testifying to the need for donations to the University. Many pleas were not as brief as planned, and the clock had struck eleven before Frank was introduced. It's too late to keep you here longer, Frank told the audience, so I say goodnight.

Frank scheduled a speech in St. Louis, Missouri. Civic leader Homer Wadsworth was asked to introduce him. Wadsworth thought the matter over: nearby lived Harry Truman. He was ill and had declared in his colorful, declamatory manner that he would never make another damn public appearance. However...

Homer phoned the ex-president and told him Frank Graham was to be in St. Louis to speak --

I'll come, Harry said interrupting.

And will you --

I'll introduce him. That little son of a bitch likes heat in the kitchen all the time. And another thing, Mr. Wadsworth, I want him to come out a day early and stay with Bess and me. There are a lot of wrong-headed friends of mine who need to meet him.

All that was done as Harry Truman ordered. Truman made a glowing introduction, one Homer still remembers. He placed Frank among the great men of the generation.

Frank was prepared to make his speech when abruptly Harry, sitting at the head table, took hold of his arm. Hold up, hold on. Frank, he demanded.

Once again Harry got to his feet.

I've introduced many a person and often I've not cared to hear what they say, he said, but I want you to wait for me to go down front where Bess is, so I can sit with her, and I can hear what you say.

In New York City, on June 16, 1967, Frank suffered a heart attack, and while in the hospital admitted that his life since Marian's death had simply been unbearable, her death still cut to the core. That autumn from New York he wrote Chancellor Sitterson: I am writing you this little note to say that I am on my way home.

Marian's personal items had, in the main, been packed up by Elizabeth Matheson some time ago and taken away, but there was packing to do for his own few things, and final bills to pay. He mailed Marian's New York St. Bartholomew's church a farewell contribution.

No, he would not go to Nags Head. The cottage since Marian's death was church-owned, and his permanent use of it was not expected.

Hillsborough was a possibility.

Either there or Chapel Hill, where his sister Kate, now widowed, had a house.

He would go there. Dear Kate. Pure sunshine. Her place was near the campus, was not far from the new hospital complex that Reece Berryhill, Billy Carmichael and others had built.

And only a short walk to Marian's grave.

At his sister's house in Chapel Hill, Frank usually would read until two or three in the morning. Now and then he would rest his eyes. It seemed his vision was getting better as some of the other parts of his body deteriorated.

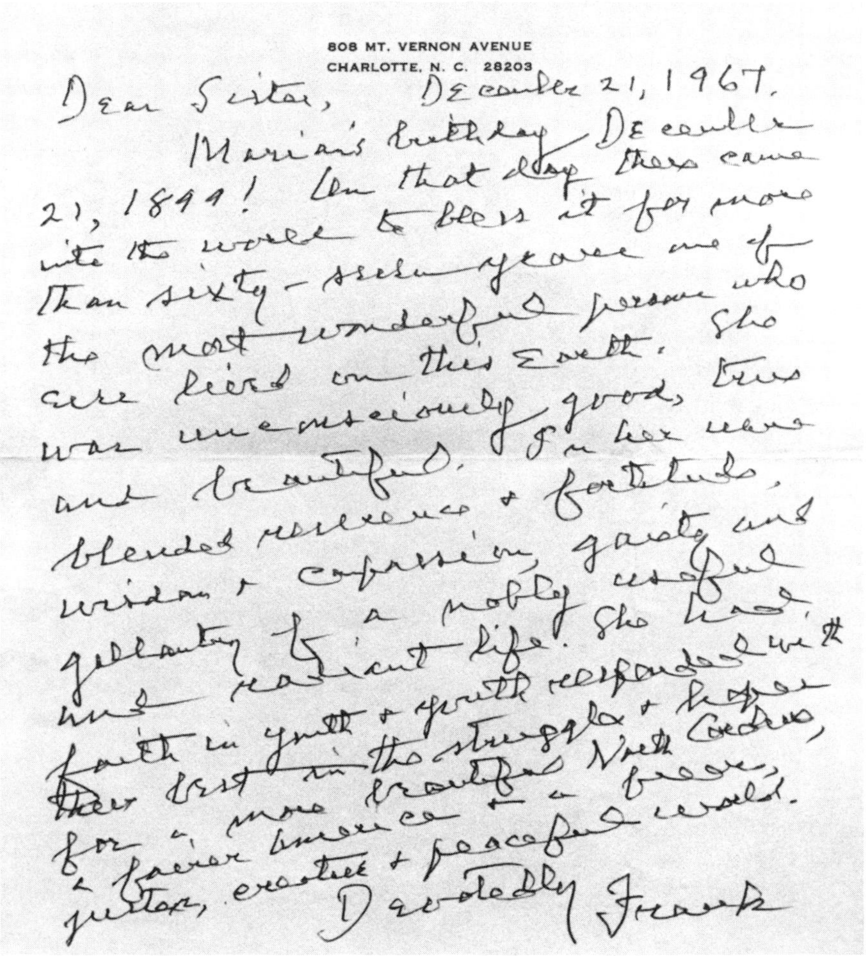
808 MT. VERNON AVENUE
CHARLOTTE, N. C. 28203

Dear Sister, December 21, 1967.

Marian's birthday December 21, 1899! On that day there came into the world to bless it for more than sixty-seven years one of the most wonderful persons who ever lived on this Earth. She was unconsciously good, true and beautiful. In her were blended reverence & fortitude, wisdom & compassion, gaiety and gallantry of a nobly useful and radiant life. She had faith in youth & youth responded with their best in the struggles & hopes for a more beautiful North Carolina, a fairer America & a freer, juster, creative & peaceful world.

Devotedly Frank

48. Letter to Eliza Drane Webb of Hillsborough, after Marian's death: *Dear Sister, Marian's birthday, December 21, 1899! On that day there came into the world to bless it for more than sixty-seven years one of the most wonderful persons who ever lived on this Earth. She was unconsciously good, true and beautiful. In her were blended reverence and fortitude, wisdom and compassion, gaiety and gallantry of a nobly useful and radiant life. She had faith in youth and youth responded with their best in the struggles and hopes for a more beautiful North Carolina, a fairer America and a freer, juster, creative and peaceful world. Devotedly, Frank.* *Letter courtesy of Elizabeth Matheson*

Doug Hunt asked if he might visit him, to introduce his wife to Frank. Frank's sister Kate told him he could come to see Frank at ten o'clock next morning. Kate said, I'll tell him not to read tonight, and he'll be up by nine.

He was, indeed, and for the visit dressed in a gray suit. Miss Kate left Hunt and his wife in her living room. Frank was in a mood to reminisce. He talked about Al Lowenstein and Jimmy Wallace during their student days, when he was the president around here, as he said. You might not believe it, but I didn't want to be president, I enjoyed teaching.

An hour later Doug and his wife were ready to go, and it was only then, when Frank got up from the chair, that his frailty was noticeable. He sort of sagged, Hunt said. Clinging to the Hunts, one on each side, he came down the steps, a long flight of steps, to the road.

Dr. Frank, you had better get back in the house, Hunt told him. Why don't you get in the car and we'll drive you up the hill?

Frank said, Ah no, I have to walk a mile first.

Doug didn't see how he could take such a walk. Frank learned far forward, needed support even now.

You have on a winter-weight suit, Dr. Frank, Hunt told him.

He must walk a mile, he insisted, and Hunt says as he drove off, in the rearview mirror he saw Frank standing in the dappled shade, waving goodbye.

Elizabeth Buford came to see him. Her grandfather was Frank's first cousin. They talked about their Scottish ancestors: that is, he talked and she listened, and on the afternoon of the first visit they took a walk. A slow, slow walk. He wore a loose fitting white cotton garment.

Is that Marian's? she asked.

Child, I don't know whose it is, but it's comfortable, he said. He mentioned having shingles, which by then was covering much of his body.

I have always admired you, she told him. I'm told you get angry about things, but never with people. I like that.

He told her, Not getting angry gives you great strength.

She told him the only time she had ever seen her grandfather weep was the night of Frank's election loss.

She asked if he still got pneumonia every year.

Oh yes, he said.

Grandfather did, too, she told him, and he lived into his nineties.

Terry Sanford came to see him with law professor Dick Phillips. They sat with Frank on the wall down below Kate's house, across the gravel road from Battle Park woods.

No, I never go into the woods, he told them.

In the course of the conversation, Terry Sanford mentioned the election defeat and suggested that Willis Smith's death in office, coming soon after his election, had been God's retribution.

Frank said, Willis Smith was a distinguished man.

On occasions Frank would have the services of a car and driver and would visit friends, among them Hubert Robinson. Robinson had cancer of the prostate and was kept at home now, cared for by his family, frailty and senility creeping up on him. He would tell Frank of his experiences in local politics and in turn would listen to Frank's stories of the old days, interrupting whenever the stories became strung out. We don't have much time, Mr. Frank, he would say, returning to a story of his own.

Frank would let him have his way. Each visit Frank would confer with the family members about his care and would leave them money. The two men were moving along toward the end of their lives. They would, Frank knew, end up in white and black burial grounds, segregation still ruling the burial of the dead as well as affecting the living.

He and Kate sometimes talked about their "baseball brother," Archibald "Moonlight" Graham*, the medical doctor who, to Frank's everlasting delight, had been a baseball player, on varsity teams in Chapel Hill and at the University of Maryland, then on a minor league team, and finally for a single inning with the New York Giants in 1905.

Neither Kate nor Frank had seen Archie in years but often talked glowingly about their brother's athletic prowess. Taller than me, Frank would say. Chances were, now that Archie was forced into retirement in Chisholm, Minnesota, he would come East, surprise them.

Kate was a retired school teacher, who said it was a disappointing day when she could not make her students laugh. She was about Frank's height, was cheerful always, and generous. She managed her brother lovingly and carefully. He was not allowed, for instance, to neglect meals, and he could take walks only on sunny days and if he stayed in the neighborhood. She had an apartment built for his use adjoining her house, where he could have privacy and his personal library. She stood by to welcome guests, her own and Frank's, and serve sherry, if desired.

The caller might be Professor Louis Round Wilson from the library, whom Kate and her late husband Shipp had known for as long as they had lived in Chapel Hill. Dr. Wilson reminded Frank that he was

* See Appendix G

already a faculty member when Frank arrived in 1905 as a freshman.

Bob House often would come by, he and Frank to talk for hours on end, and Bob would play his harmonica, Frank tapping his foot and singing folk songs and hymns.

Students came by. To a group of students Frank made the error of saying North Carolina had been the last state of the original thirteen to enter the Union. We insisted on a bill of rights and would not join otherwise, he told them.

Rhode Island was the last, Dr. Graham, a student corrected him.

Frank considered that. Yes, but I always thought we meant it more, he said.

Once the shingles disease came to affect his entire body, Frank wore fewer and fewer clothes, until he would wear only a robe. Even so, he would take his walks, and his walking along Gimghoul Road in a robe was a familiar sight.

The medical bills were expensive, and Miss Kate garnered many of them. Frank had a small pension from the state and one, also small, from the Federal Government. If he had kept his speaking fees from the U.N. he would be well-off. The federal pension was for his services in the Marines, on the War Labor Board and other Roosevelt and Truman commissions, and the months in the Senate; then, too, Bill Cochrane, who worked for Senator B. Everett Jordan, had got him appointed to a federal commission for a month or so.

My insurance can be used to pay you for these medical bills, Kate, he would tell her.

His insurance would help, that was true. A policy for $10,000.

Charlie Jones came by to see him. He had been ousted by the Judicial Commission of the Orange Presbytery and had been pastor of the Community Church for many years. He was thinking about leaving the Community Church, taking a job in the secular world. He thought he had been a pastor for too much of this life.

They talked about the integration of the restaurants in Chapel Hill, both decrying the state sending five young people off to prison on felony charges for civil disobedience. The University had done nothing to defend them or to get them out of prison, either.

College athletics appear to me to be as crooked as ever, Frank told one elderly coach who met him out walking.

The coach said there was one question he had always wanted to ask, Dr. Graham, Why did you give the star athlete, a great player, Monk MacDonald, an F when you were teaching?

Because there was no grade lower, Frank told him, with a smile.

Professor Guy Johnson came by to see him often. A leading sociologist of the South during the thirties, forties, fifties, even now in the sixties Johnson was writing about integration. On one visit he predicted the time was near when the South would be, as a section, untroubled by racial conflict while the North and West would be caught in considerable turmoil. He said riots, demonstrations and slogans such as "Black Power" and "Burn, baby, burn" will convince whites that the Negroes pose a threat to their security.

Frank told him he understood that the late Howard Odum -- he died in 1954 -- in his last and unpublished book indicated the Negro was not yet ready for full citizenship.

Johnson excused Odum, said he had been getting old. He had visited prisons and found voodoo charms on prisoners. Johnson had the Odum manuscript, he and his wife Guion on Odum's death took it to their home and put it away.

Frank admitted the civil rights movement was in jeopardy. Much that he had worked for was in jeopardy. Even the Democratic Party was in trouble. The tumultuous Chicago convention of 1968 had cast it in disarray; Al Lowenstein himself had been caught up in the disarray. Indonesia had turned to violence; four hundred thousand dead in civil war. In India and Pakistan, war had broken out, with a million dead and ten million new refugees.

The churches, the University, labor unions, civil rights leaders, the United Nations, all had disappointing recent histories, but no reason for despair, he told his visitors. We must continue our faith in America and liberal causes and today's young people.

Lucy Morgan visited often, bringing Frank reports from the School of Public Health and other divisions of the medical center. She brought him steaks; she thought he loved steaks.

Frank hired a part-time secretary, Mrs. Sam Teague, paid for by the Z. Smith Reynolds Foundation to help him get his papers in order. Many personal letters he did, himself, typing on a very old standard typewriter -- it must have been a 1930s model, Tom Lambeth says.

One day when Mrs. Teague was away, Frank asked niece Rebecca, who was visiting, to place a call to the U.N., so he could speak to an official there. Something in the morning paper had prompted this. Rebecca placed the call and told a secretary Frank P. Graham wanted to talk.

What was that middle initial? the secretary asked.

Rebecca's heart sank; she had wondered all along if Frank P. Graham would be a forgotten name at the U.N. Not at all. The official did take the call, and made it worthwhile for Frank to make what Rebecca describes as the great effort to walk to the phone for the animated conversation.

His only nephew, realtor Graham Shanks, came to see him as Frank's life neared its close. A novel was in the works about Archie Graham, the older brother, and the two talked about him, and about baseball. Archie had held a record in stolen bases, which Frank held to be a most laudable achievement.

Frank was taken to the hospital in mid-January, 1972, to a small, private room at the end of a corridor. Arnold King visited him there. It was like old times, Frank's mind was lucid, his memory was, as always, superb to the point of being almost unbelievable. Arnold felt Frank never should have left the University, he doubts if he was ever as happy after he left.

Tom Lambeth came by. He mentioned to Frank that Senator Morse says he's the most Christ-like man he has ever known.

He's a good friend, Frank said.

Tom asked him if he was aware that Adlai Stevenson had told him and Joel Fleishman that he would have chosen Frank to be his running mate in 1952, instead of Senator John Sparkman, if the voters of North Carolina had not deprived him of the choice.

President Roosevelt also mentioned my being his running mate, Frank said. You know there were very few white Southern liberals in the Democratic Party then.

While Lambeth was present Frank had asked his doctor, William Blythe -- author Legette Blythe's son -- if he might listen to the Carolina football game on the radio.

Carolina lost, Lambeth recalls, and Frank spoke for several minutes about it having been for Carolina a moral victory.

While in the hospital Frank one morning had Kate phone George Esser and invite him to come by. George was now head of the Southern Regional Council, which Guy Johnson and Howard Odum had wanted Frank to help them found. Frank talked with Esser about Johnson and Vance and Odum, and about John Wheeler, one of the black leaders in Durham.

He told Esser about the day Senator John Kennedy was inaugurated president, about Kennedy finding on his White House desk a plan for

49. Dr. Frank and friends from the neighborhood: A. Jeff Newton III, John Daugherty, Robert A. Rubin, Kevin Daugherty, Dr. Frank, Timothy Newton, Joe Daugherty, unknown, Col. T. F. Taylor. The photo was taken at Col. Taylor's home on Gimghoul Road in 1970 by Lance Richardson, a photographer for the Chapel Hill Weekly. *Photo courtesy of Dr. Louis Rubin.*

desegregrating the country, as prepared and submitted by the Southern Regional Council. Kennedy had liked it, and he and Lyndon had tried to carry it out.

Frank often talked with guests about Al Lowenstein, his son-in-spirit out somewhere in the world, elected to the U.S. Congress, then gerrymandered out of his seat. Frank considered him to be one of the outstanding men of his generation.

The second week not many guests were admitted. The attendants knew little or nothing about the little man in the last room. Tom Wicker, who had been a student at the University and now was a writer, came by with Phillips Russell to pay respects. Wicker recalls that Phillips Russell said something characteristically sharp about Nixon, who was then president.

Now, now, Phillips, Frank said. I've seen Mr. Nixon with his family. He must be a very moral man.

Joel Fleishman also came to see him in the hospital, and brought Professor of Mathematical Statistics Nicholson's son, Brit, in order to determine if Frank's memory was still as accurate as ever. On their arrival Frank was in a coma.

Brit, when did you last see Dr. Graham? Joel asked him.

About twelve years ago, he said, during the Senate campaign.

What was your age?

I was a little boy.

Joel quietly called Dr. Frank out of the coma, as Kate had told him he could. Joel led the young man up close to his bed. Dr. Graham, who is this? he asked.

At once Frank said, Professor Nicholson's son, Brit.

Frank was missed by the children who lived in Miss Kate's neighborhood. After school and on weekends, he had been a pied piper for them, even when he could not walk fast or far.

He would take them to Gimghoul Castle, which was a block or two away, a spooky place even in daytime, a real castle with a turret. Never was anybody home there.

Or he would take them the other direction, to the cemetery.

Spooky, too.

And here lies so-and-so, and there lies so-and-so, he would explain. Here lies a professor of Latin, oh must have been before your parents were born. His wife lies beside him, and I will one day lie beside him.

From graveside to graveside.

On sunny days he would walk that far, to the castle or the cemetery.

He always kept a hat on, too. He was careful about that. He kept it on until he came to a stand of dogwood trees.

He would stand waiting there for a while, beside Marian's grave.

50. The funeral of Dr. Frank Porter Graham.   *Raleigh News and Observer*

Frank Graham Buried

CHAPEL HILL -- Frank Porter Graham, the gentle-voiced former president of the Consolidated University of North Carolina, was buried here Friday.

He was eulogized as a man whose "spirit has drawn here today the deepest tide of pure love that ever came here to wash us clean."

Dr. Robert House, a former chancellor, said of his lifelong friend: "He had already loved the entire university into following him. In his later career, as far as is possible in human limits, Frank Graham achieved his purpose. He loved North Carolina into following him. He loved this nation into following him. He loved the free world into following him. His legacy is that love, one for another, is the real source of strength to build a better world and for peace among men."

That did not mean, House told a memorial service at University Presbyterian Church, that Graham was "a simple idealist with his head in the clouds and his feet off the ground." Said House: "His ground was the moral law. On that he was stern, inflexible and unbeatable. He was a moral genius."

The memorial service followed a 25-minute Presbyterian funeral, spare and devoted to Biblical passages chosen by the family.

Graham was buried beside his wife, Marian Drane Graham, in the old Chapel Hill Cemetery under a headstone that read: "They had faith in youth, and youth responded with their best."

The 85-year-old Graham, who was president of the university for 19 years, died early Wednesday morning after several years of failing health. He was a former U.S. Senator and former United Nations mediator.

The mourners were led by Gov. Bob Scott and Mrs. Scott and Council of State officials.

Former governors Terry Sanford, now president of Duke Univesity, and Judge Dan Moore of the State Supreme Court were there.

Consolidated University President William C. Friday and former President Gordon Gray headed a list of other educator-administrators, including President Kingman Brewster of Yale, Vice President Doublas Hunt of Columbia and chancellors and presidents from North Carolina institutions.

-- ROY PARKER, JR.

The News and Observer, Saturday, Feb. 19, 1972

This tribute to Frank Graham was made in 1969 by Al Lowenstein.

It is as great an honor as I expect I shall ever have to be able to participate in these statements of thanks to this astronaut of the human heart, always risking himself that others may follow with less danger, robust and uncomplaining amongst the discomforts of difficult journeys, always as far ahead of his time and always so much a part of it, always transcending the ordinary limits of geography and custom to adventure on toward new horizons and new opportunities for all his fellow men.

How should we measure how much we owe to such a man, how much our country owes, how much the tired and bruised world? Best simply to say that the least we owe is to try harder to do better for an America at last providing liberty and justice for all, and for a world at last resolving our differences with compassion and peace.

In his will Dr. Frank left his $10,000 estate to the University, the income to go to his sister until her death, and afterward to be used by the University annually to honor Marian Graham.

Death of a Man

By TOM WICKER

IAPEL HILL, N. C., Feb. 18 -- last time I talked with Dr. Frank P. am, it was in the company of his friend and a former teacher of ., Phillips Russell, a man of strong ions. Mr. Russell took to de- icing President Nixon with the iderable spirit that has always ated him.

. Graham, then a frail old man in ng health, grieving the death of Graham, touched Mr. Russell's . "Now, now, Phillips," he said, seen Mr. Nixon with his family. nust be a very moral man."

st this week, a few days before his h at 85, Dr. Frank--as he was liarly known to thousands of sons daughters of the great university he so much to build--was talking with minister about the possibility of life other planets. As the Rev. Vance ron recalled it at the funeral service he University Presbyterian Church morning, Dr. Frank said that, tever other forms of life there ht be, "they cannot know anything ner about God than we know, ause God has revealed his love to and there cannot be anything higher a 'God is love'."

was that gentle heart, that loving it, far more than his great achieve- nts, that made Frank Graham's life radiant. In good times and bad, in ory and fact, in word and deed, he ed his fellow man and in that way loved his God.

As a history teacher the memory of ose lectures still delights an older eration of students; as the president o made the University of North rolina into the light of the South in hard days of the nineteen-thirties forties; as a U.S. Senator ulti- tely defeated in a racist campaign so er that twenty years later it still rks the politics of this state; as one

of those who began the modern civil rights movement under President Tru- man; and in his last active years as a tireless international servant of the United Nations--in all these different and usually thankless tasks, his gentle- ness never withered. He was, Wayne Morse once said, "the most Christlike man I've ever known."

He was nevertheless a hard fighter. When one of his faculty was accused of the heinous crime of lunching with a black man, Dr. Frank calmly told the trustees, "If Professor Erickson has to go on a charge of eating with another human being, then I will have to go first." As a magazine writer com- mented at about that time, Frank Graham had planted "one foot firmly on the Sermon on the Mount and the other on the Bill of Rights."

In its obituary, The Chapel Hill Weekly told how even the formidable John L. Lewis discovered that Dr. Frank's gentle spirit was not mere softness. In a 12-hour session, Mr. Lewis had been brought to an agree- ment to end a wartime strike by Dr. Graham, then an N.L.R.B. negotiator. "Who locked me in with that sweet little S.O.B.?" Mr. Lewis later com- plained.

Still, it was not his deeds nor his strength that most distinguished Dr. Frank. He could salve a student's troubled spirit with a smile and lift men's hearts by example. In the meanest trial of his life, his spirit held him steady and a whole generation of North Carolinians could learn from him what was meant by courage under fire and charity of the soul.

That was in 1950, when he ran for the Senate seat to which he had been appointed by Gov. Kerr Scott, father of

North Carolina's present Governor. In the Democratic primary, despite re- peated charges that he was somehow pro-Communist and unpatriotic, Dr. Frank got more votes than anyone up to then had received for any state office--but with three candidates in the race, he just failed to win a ma- jority. In the runoff, the attack shifted to the worst kind of racist charges, and he was defeated. On the race question as on the human question, Frank Graham was ahead of his time.

Yet, he never struck back with lies and innuendo of his own, nor later denounced the men who had slan- dered him. Dr. Frank did not make the common, fatal error of public men--he never believed his cause was so precious, his victory so necessary, that they could justify any tactic or any means.

So he could stand in the Senate as he was about to leave it and deliver a farewill address unmarked by bitter- ness, infused with a vision of America and of humankind unaltered by his ordeal:

"In this America of our struggles and our hopes," he said, "the least of these our brethren has the freedom to struggle for freedom; where the an- swer to error is not terror, the respect for the past is not reaction and the hope of the future is not revolution; where the integrity of simple people is beyond price and the daily toil of millions is above pomp and power; where the majority is without tyranny, and the minority without fear, and all people have hope."

The hard men, the practical men, the so-called realists will never share or know that vision. But then they will never even know that, whatever the momentary situation, they can win nothing that matters; or that in the everlasting verities of the heart, Frank Graham never lost.

In the love of God and man which transcends all races, colors, creeds, boundaries and curtains, and with a sense of brotherhood with all people whether across the narrow streets, across the hard tracks or across the wide seas, we would, in spite of all illusions, frustrations and fears, pray with faith and work with patience in the long and difficult pilgrimage of the people for peace and freedom.

Frank Porter Graham

PUBLISHER NOTE

This is not a historical perspective or learned essay on the man and his times.

This is, rather, an appreciation. Writ by a man of words, himself; powerful words which make you laugh, or cry, and gather in a picture of a remarkable man.

A product of many years of research, interviews, writing, editing, checking and rewriting, this work is accurate, fair, informative.

At a time which finds the name Graham known chiefly as that of the school and child development center, and the man and his efforts and ideals put away in files, perhaps forgotten, this book might be seen as a necessary portrait of a valuable individual. For some, this book might provide first views of the man; for some, it may stir fond recollections, or bring back pain and regret.

Yet these words are not intended as admonishment, not praise or reproach; a recreation of the spirit of this selfless man is, perhaps, the most needed book that could be hoped for at this time.

Frank Porter Graham, 1887-1972; his home and heart were always open to all who came.

APPENDICES

APPENDIX A

Frank Porter Graham: A Chronology

1886	Born October 14th at Fayetteville, North Carolina, the son of Katherine Sloan and Alexander Graham.
	Graduated from Charlotte High School; attended the Warren Preparatory School.
	Enrolled in the University of North Carolina.
1909	Graduated from the University of North Carolina (A.B. in History).
1910	Received a license to practice law in the state of North Carolina.
1911-1913	Taught English and coached football at Raleigh High School.
1913	Appointed secretary of the Y.M.C.A., University of North Carolina.
1914-1916	Instructor of History, University of North Carolina.
1916	Graduated from Columbia University (M.A. in History).
1917	Enlisted in the U.S. Marine Corps (July 3rd).
1919	Mustered out of the Ma5rine Corps as a first lieutenant (July).
1920-1921	Assistant Professor of History, University of North Carolina; also Dean of Students.
1921	Appointed chairman of a committee to raise funds for state educational institutions; a $20 million bond issue is later authorized.
1921	Appointed Associate Professor of History at UNC.
1922-1923	Graduate student at the University of Chicago.
1923	Wins an Amherst Fellowship; resides in Washington, observing debates in Congress and studying at the Brookings Institution and the Library of Congress.
1924-1925	Studies in England and France on the second year of his Amherst Fellowship

1925	Returns to teaching at the University of North Carolina; travels the state, speaking in favor of freedom of speech in the evolution controversy.
1927	Appointed Professor of History, UNC.
1928-1929	Acting Director of the Institute for Research in Social Science, UNC.
1929	Speaks in favor of the workers involved in the Gastonia strike; drafts "An Industrial Bill of Rights," calling for "the equal right to organize under law."
1930	Elected as the eleventh president of the University of North Carolina (June 9th).
1931	Inauguration as president (November 11th).
1931	Drafted a plan for the consolidation of North Carolina State College for Agriculture and Engineering, Woman's College, and the University of North Carolina.
1932	Married Marian Drane of Edenton, N.C. (July 21st).
1932	Inaguration as president of the Consolidated University of North Carolina (November 10th).
1934	Appointed Chairman of the National Advisory Council of the Cabinet Committee on Economic Security.
1936	Proposes a plan for the reform of amateur athletics in the Southern Conference; provokes a movement by some critics to oust him.
1941-1942	Serves as member of the National Defense Mediation Board.
1942-1946	Member of the National War Labor Board; member the Maritime War Emergency Board.
1945	Appointed Chairman of the Public Hearings Committee of the President's Labor-Management Conference.
1946	Announces a ten-point program for the stimulus of a Southern economic and social renaissance.
1946-1947	Member of the President's Civil Rights Commission.
1947-1948	Appointed as U.S. Representative to the United Nations Committee of Good Offices in the Dutch Indonesian Dispute.
1947-1948	President of the National Association of State Universities.

1948	Truce arranged by Graham is signed between the Netherlands and the Indonesian Republic (Jan. 17th).
1949	Appointed by Governor W. Kerr Scott to fulfill the unexpired term of the late U.S. Senator J. Melville Broughton (March 22nd); resigns as president.
1949	Sworn in as Senator (March 29th); announces for re-election.
1949	Appointed to the Senate Judiciary Committee and the Senate Post Office and Civil Service Committee.
1950	Appointed to the Senate Rules and Administration Committee (after resigning from the Post Office and Civil Service Committee).
1950	Runs first in a field of four candidates in the Democratic primary (May 27th).
1950	Defeated by Willis Smith in a run-off (June 24th).
1950	Ends his term of office as Senator (November 22); returns to Chapel Hill six days later.
1951	Appointed as a labor-management moderator for defense contract disputes in the Alaska Territory.
1951	Appointed Defense Manpower Administrator for the U.S. Department of Labor.
1951	Appointed as United Nations Representative for India and Pakistan (April 11th).
1951	Arrives in Pakistan to negotiate a settlement of the dispute between India and Pakistan over Kashmir (June 29th).
1952-1969	Chairman of the Board, National Sharecroppers Fund.
1954-1963	Serves as a board member of the American Association of the United Nations.
1961-1962	Serves as president of the Board of Directors of the Civil Liberties Foundation.
1962-1964	Chairman, Carolina Charter Tercentenary Committee.
1963-1965	Chairman, National Advisory Committee on Area Development
1967	Death of his wife, Marian (April 27th).
1968	Retires from the staff of the United Nations.
1972	Dies at Chapel Hill, North Carolina (February 16th).

APPENDIX B
LETTER TO MARY ANN CODY

Frank P. Graham
310 East 44th Street
New York 17, N. Y.

27 May, 1963

Miss Mary Ann Cody
Mount Vernon Junior College
Washington, D. C.

Dear Mary Ann Cody,

After being recently in a number of states, including some on the West Coast, speaking at United Nations meetings, I am now catching up in my correspondence.

As requested by you, I am sending these answers regarding the positions which I took in the 1950 Democratic primary on the ten issues listed by you. It might be helpful to amplify the positions which, as you are now aware, were in the main substance, as indicated by your mother, known to her when you were a small child and even earlier. She is most appreciative of your present and growing interest in such matters.

In issue during the campaign were not only the ten issues explicitly listed by you, but also the issues which implicitly had been then a part of a person's commitments during his whole public life.

These definite answers are given herewith without regard to priorities but as the recollections come to mind regarding issues which had developed over the years up to June 1950. The summary follows:

I. Oppositions to all forms of tyranny in America and in the world as definitely expressed in stands and statements against fascism, communism, imperialism - both old and new - and all forms of unfair exploitation of people, east and west, north and south.

This opposition to tyranny was definitely expressed in a resolution written by me at the request of Mr. William Mitch of the C.I.O. [in Birmingham], the Chairman of the Committee on Resolutions of the Southern Conference on Human Welfare, at the meeting in Chattanooga in 1940. This resolution as adopted reads as follows:

"We deplore the rise of dictators anywhere, the oppression of civil
liberties, the persecution of minorities, aggression against small and
weak nations, the violation of human rights, and democratic liberties
of the people by all Fascist, Nazi, Communist, and imperialist powers
alike which resort to force and aggression instead of the processes
of law, freedom, democracy, and international cooperation."

Despite the parliamentary maneuvers of the few members of the far left in the Conference, by whom I had been denounced on account of a fair ruling against one of their parliamentary maneuvers, this resolution was overwhelmingly adoped by the Conference. It was written so as to include in its basic principles not only Finland but also Latvia, Estonia, Lithuania, and any other nations under imperial domination, or which might in the future be threatened or subjugated by a fascist, communist or imperial power.

During the period of its brief existence the Conference never adopted, to my knowledge, a single un-American or pro-Communist or pro-totalitarian resolution, but adoped overwhelmingly resolutions in the best American heritage and hope, such as: (a) for unsegregated meetings; (b) equal justice for labor, Negroes, sharecroppers, tenant farmers, and all disadvantaged minority groups; (c) for fair adjustment of the freight rates which discriminated against Southern farmers and businessmen; (d) for federal aid to the States for schools; (e) for the self-determination and liberation of colonial peoples; and (f) for other humane causes. The main emotional objection to the Conference was not so much that there were a few "reds" in it, but that it was in its composition approximately half black in numbers.

II. For decades, personal and public championship of federal aid to the states for the schools without federal control in order to supplement the basic state and local schoool funds toward equalization of the educational opportunities of the children in all the states. The Southern people, for a long time with approximately one-sixth of the nation's financial ability, have educated approximately one-third of the nation's children. The Southern people invested a larger proportion of their income in the public education of all children than the people in other sections of the country, yet the Southern public schools had not reached the level of the national average. With the outflow of educated talent to other regions, the Southern people have been in the position of carrying the financial load of educating the children when they were non-productive, and then when these young people became productive they were residents in other states and contributed to the creation of wealth in the states of the North and West. It was (and is) important to the other states that the children of the Southern States be better educated. It was (and is) a sound democratic policy that the proportionate imbalance between the regional concentration of wealth and the regional concentration of children be adjusted for the good of the children, the states, the regions and the nation. The children educated by the states become citizens not only of the state but also citizens of the nation, and should be a concern not only of the states but also of the nation. Opposition to federal aid to the states for the schools without federal control is, not in intent, but in actual results, opposition to providing equal educational opportunities for all children in all states. (Spoke for many years in many states before 1950 for federal aid to the states for the schools.)

III. For the promotion of a nation-wide local-state-federal-co-operative program for country-wide public library service in all the counties of the states. (Promoted organization of the Citizen's Library Movement in North Carolina).

IV. For a multiple agricultural program which included: (a) more adequate support and higher development of land-grant colleges and universities, (b) agricultural research, extension and home demonstration; (c) improvement of facilities for the marketing of agricultural produce through the cooperation of private and public, local, state and federal agencies; (d) promotion of agricultural cooperative societies; (e) as much needed supplements to the state-wide good roads system, more adequate rural roads leading to schools, churches and town markets; (f) conservation and improvement of soils as basic to our whole economy; (g) the establishment of fair relations between the prices the farmer pays for his necessities and the prices he receives for his products, with a continuation of the policy of the basic 90 percent of parity, subject to continuous study and any fair and wise adjustments in the interest of the people and in justice to the farmers who produce the food, feed and fibers necessary for the sustenance, clothing and shelter of people and animals as needed; (h) promotion of a nationwide program of rural electrification through the cooperation of local, state and federal agencies; and (i) the development of farm life, not only as a way of agricultural production, but also as a way of life in a more wholesome, beautiful and creative rural civilization as part of the American tradition and hope of a free and abundant society.

V. For adequate support of research in basic fields; the National Science Foundation; and the Oak Ridge Institute for Nuclear Studies [of whose Board was elected the first chairman by the cooperating institutions] through the cooperation of 17 Southern colleges and universities and other agencies.

VI. For a highly productive and socially responsible industrialism as one of the main foundations of an abundant and free society based on: (a) the equal freedom of organization and collective bargaining on the part of labor and management; (b) decent standard of life and labor; (c) decent statutory minimum wages; and (d) amendment of the Taft-Hartley Act so as, for example, to place labor and management on an equal basis with regard to non-communist declarations.

(As a public member of the National War Labor Board, was given the opportunity to interpret the national policy during the war for a reasonable balance between the closed shop and the union shop through the maintenance of a freely accepted and responsible union membership for the duration of the contract. This policy as a stable basis for union-management relations during the war, in connection with both the wage policy of the Board based on Taylor's Little Steel Formula and the price policy of the O.P.A. as directed by Bowles - all these together, with the tireless and patriotic cooperation of labor and management, contributed to an industrial production for America and the Allies unprecedented in all history.)

VII. For a comprehensive program of racial justice: (a) for a constitutional federal law against the remnants of the atrocity of lynching; (b) abolition of the poll tax in the few states in which it has survived, with its unfair policies of accumulation and discrimination; (c) equal suffrage in primaries and general elections in all the states; (d) in view of the fact that only 6 of the 48 states were willing at that time to pass compulsory F.E.P.C. laws, I favored, in line with Brooks Hays, federal sponsorship and leadership in a nationwide program for education, conciliation and cooperation of labor and management, local, state and federal agencies, toward voluntary fair employment practices regardless of race, color or creed or national origin;

(Because of other engagements I did not attend the meeting of the President's Civil Rights Commission held at Dartmouth College in Hanover, N.H. and did not join in voting for a federal compulsory F.E.P.C. My general minority opinion in the body of the Commission's Report covered my general opinion on federal compulsion [in advance of a decision of the Supreme Court outlawing segregation which hitherto had been declared the law of the land in the Southern states]. Also, years before the 1954 Supreme Court decision, in view of the fact that the Armed Serviced autonomously by executive orders were handling wisely and effectively the matter of the integration of the Armed Services, I was opposed to Congressional action in this regard at that time. I had hoped that voluntary integration by the churches and the autonomous integration by the Armed Services would serve for all the states as an example of spiritual and moral progress in the churches and of patriotism in the Armed Services, with proved results in spiritual brotherhood, democratic practice, use of available and competent manpower, cooperative inter-racial teamwork and higher military efficiency on all fronts through desegregation); (e) I stated during the primary campaign that I was opposed to filibusters;

(After the primary I participated with talks on my part totalling less than three hours, not in a filibuster, but in a three-day talking stand with a small group of Senators who supported President Truman's veto of the McCarran International Security because of some its bad provisions. I was one of seven Senators who had voted against the passage of the bill. I was for cloture if there were any prolonged filibuster. During the primary, many friends told me that, if I would publicly state that I would favor filibustering against civil rights legislation, I would probably gain an additional 50,000 votes. I declined to do so. After I was defeated I declined to vote for cloture at a time when no filibuster was in process and in my personal view the cloture was not then applicable.)

(f)   in the years before the 1954 decision of the Supreme Court, when segregation was the law of the land in the Southern states, I maintained that lawful segregation would ultimately be ended and that meantime, within the states without federal compulsion, changes in the minds and hearts of the people in the Southern states should come through religion, education and democratic ideas as set forth in a minority opinion in the body of the report of President Truman's Committee on Civil Rights;   (g) meantime I also held that the states should accept and obey decisions of the Supreme Court applicable in the state as the law of the land. I had suggested to the Executive Committee of the University Board of Trustees that the threefold University of North Carolina accept as its policy the decision of the Supreme Court as handed down in the Oklahoma University case. The Executive Committee, in its wisdom, held, since no application of a Negro was before the Board, and that since the decision in the Oklahoma case was not applicable in North Carolina, that the suggestion was not in order, that the State would deny any such application when made, carry its resistance through the courts, and then accept the decision of the highest court as the law of the land. (This understanding became the wise policy of those who ably administered the University after my time); (h) since the Chapel Hill Presbyterian Church policy, led by our minister, became by word of mouth an issue in the campaign, it may be pertinent to recall a previous observation of Governor Cherry. When some people protested to him as Chairman of the University Board of Trustees that a new president of the University was needed because of his racial attitudes, the Governor observed that the President of the University, in the constitutional separation of church and state, as a state official, faithfully obeyed the law of the State and as a Presbyterian Elder in supporting his minister in his religious views in favor of desegregation of the church [a decade before the Supreme Court decision of 1954], the University President might in his private judgment be obeying the law of God; (i) in carrying out my responsibility as a Senator for making appointments to West Point and Annapolis, and in learning that a too large proportion of North Carolina cadets did not finish their course, I adopted the policy of holding open competitive examinations, conducted by the United States Civil Service, a new venture in an ex-Confederate State, which resulted in a Negro standing fifth among more than fifty odd candidates, and in his appointment as an alternate to West Point becoming an issue in the campaign;

(Hundreds of thousands of handbills with his picture made his appointment an issue in the campaign. Charges were made that though he stood fifth he was appointed to West Point. Some of the local managers of our campaign were accused of misrepresentation when they maintained that no favoritism had been shown the Negro candidate. To refute the false charge of favoritism, several local managers insisted on the number one winner appearing in person. The young man who stood first had been sunning at the seacoast. When he appeared, much tanned, some insisted that he was after all really a mulatto passed off as a white boy. The hundreds of thousands of handbills were used to prove the charge that if I were returned to the Senate, not only would Negroes soon take over West Point, but also they would take over many of the white schools and jobs of white people in the factories and stores. The last days of the campaign were like a forest fire sweeping across the land and stirring the fears of us and the Negro people who intended them no harm in the new age into which the South and the world were already passing. To try to stop it one would have had to renounce one's whole life, which would have been worse than defeat and more disastrous. My only reply would be the one made in Guilford that votes were not wanted from those who did not believe in human dignity.)

(j) as President of the University, in the years before the 1954 decision of the Supreme Court, while strictly obeying the then law of the State, I, with others, championed the freedom of unsegregated public meetings and concerts on the campus, the freedom of students to invite speakers of different ideologies and different races and colors, and the freedom of the teachers to speak and write their views on all matters involving economic, sociological, racial and other vital problems of war, peace and our human predicament, as preparation of our youth and the people of the state for more intelligent and humane grappling with the fateful developments of this age of struggle, challenge and hope for all people everywhere.

(It may be incidentally observed: (1) that, before the Supreme Court decision outlawing segregation on account of race, I held that the influence of religion, the social studies and the broadening sense of democracy, would progressively have their effect on the youth and the people and prepare the way for the ultimate elimination of segregation by the people within the States in accordance with the then law of the land; and (2) that after the Supreme Court decisions of 1954 and 1955, I held that the influence of religion, education and democratic ideas should support the implementation of the Supreme Court decisions and their enforcement by local, state, and, if necessary, federal authorities.)

VIII.   As a long-time member of the American Civil Liberties Union, civil liberties became for some an issue in the campaign. As President of the University I had supported academic freedom of professors and the freedom of the students in inviting the Roosevelts, Norman Thomas, Wendell Wilkie (who was unable to accept), the German Ambassador, the Soviet Ambassador, ex-Governor Eugene Tallmadge, President Mordecai Johnson, Dr. Benjamin Mays, Earl Browder, Frank Knox, etc., to speak in unsegregated open forums. When Norman Thomas was invited several times by the students, a leading Republican protested against the use of the University platform by a man who was then a perennial Socialist candidate for the Presidency. When the students invited Frank Knox, who was then the Republican Candidate for Vice-President, some Democrats protested strongly. The Republican leader, who had protested against Norman Thomas speaking from a University platform, defended Knox's appearance and argued that the University belonged to all the people, Republicans as well as Democrats, etc. When a friend reminded him he had protested against Norman Thomas having the freedom of the University platform, he significantly replied, in good faith and in good humor; "I am beginning to get the idea of a free and open University."

The University was much criticized as having a handful of Communist students in the student body. It was common knowledge that such a small cell existed. I had refused, upon some insistent demands, to take steps to dismiss these students. In some institutions, I have since been informed, cells containing no smaller number than the one in Chapel Hill, operated underground. The small group in Chapel had an open meeting in Gerrard Hall addressed by a visiting speaker. Our student leaders, though strongly opposed to communism, stood guard that no effort would be made to break up the meeting. Students in attendance at the meeting knew more history, economics and politics than the speaker and tore his thesis to threads. For his ignorance and loss of temper, the meeting was a failure and resulted in a loss of ground for his cause in Chapel Hill. The only Communist speaker invited by the students who was denied a University platform, was one then under indictment in the federal courts for treason. Upon informal legal advice, the Chancellor rightfully denied a campus platform to him as possibly involving the University in the violation of a federal statute. I, of course, publicly supported Chancellor House in this position.

IX.   Regarding the charge that I was soft on communism, as shown by membership in alleged "communist front" organizations, it was pertinent to point that I had made personal and public statement, separately and jointly, against communism, fascism and imperialism. Though I had the highest respect for the integrity, patriotism and the many distinguished public services of my good friend, Henry A. Wallace, I joined Secretary Harold Ickes and others in denouncing the Progressive Party, which sponsored and supported his candidacy for the Presidency against Truman. I was denounced by some communists in America as the "tool of the Southern mill barons" at the very time I was being charged by spokesmen of the Southern textile industry as a foe of the textile industry. In reality the championship of wise social legislation regarding the equal freedom of organization, hours of work, child labor and minimum wages, was in friendship for the textile industry, which included workers no less than managers. Pravda and Izvestia, spokesmen for the Kremlin, denounced me as a tool of Wall Street and an agent of the Pentagon.

There were many irresponsible listings of alleged communist front organizations. The responsible list was made by the Department of Justice under Executive Order 9835 after study by the F.B.I. and other agencies.

I was never a member of any organization, which, after the study made under Executive Order 9835, was placed on the Attorney General's list. Regarding the four so listed, of which I had been a member, I was not a member for considerable time before they were so listed. By some irresponsible listing, I was listed as a member of some organizations that I had never heard of and some on whose mailing list I happened, on their initiative, to be included without my having joined. I was even listed as a member of organizations which I had definitely declined to join or sponsor.

Among the organizations I had sponsored at one time or another, in one case I favored the self-determination of the people of the democratically organized Spanish Republic and opposed interference by either fascists or communists, both the time Franco was actively supported by Hitler and Mussolini and at the time Stalin's aid was received in shameful default of aid from the western democracies. In all situations I favored the free self-determination of the people of Spain and against interference by France, Mussolini, Hitler and Stalin. I continue to stand on this principle. In response to the invitation of my good friend, President Emeritus William A. Nielson of Smith College, and as advised by editorials in the New York Times and the New York World Telegram, I joined the American Committee for the Protection of the Foreign Born. Long before it was placed on the Attorney General's list, both he and I had ceased to be members of this Committee.

Regarding the salute to the Red Army, in which I joined, it is seldom pointed out that this salute was led by Secretary Henry L. Stimson, Cordell Hull, General Douglas McArthur, King George V, and Governors of States, when soldiers of the Red Army, as defenders of the soil of their motherland, were holding the gates at Stalingrad against the armies of Hitler. Whenever I take a stand for Justice to Negroes, sharecroppers and disadvantaged minority groups, out come the old charges about communist fronts, which, however, fail in their purpose to shut us up on the vital issues of the day. If you are interested in more detail about "communist fronts" Steve Lesher may share with you the answers I gave him with more precise details..

I did not and will never renounce any stand I have taken for equal human freedom. The best way to participate and help in humane causes is to join in voluntary association with patriotic people of good faith and good will and work actively in good causes as part of the heritage, genius and hope of America. The only way to avoid not being in an organization which some sincere but misguided people might infiltrate for their own purposes is never to join any voluntary organization. One way to work is to join and oppose efforts of subversion, if any, however covert. Voluntary associations for the fulfillment of our Judaic-Christian heritage and the American dream is of the very essence of Americanism. The overwhelming number of those who join are fellow travellers of their religious hopes and authentic Americanism, and are not fellow travellers of fascism, communism or imperialism. The wave of the future is self-determination, liberty, equality and brotherhood, and not totalitarianism, racialism or colonialism, old or new. (For interpretation of views before and since 1954 decision, you might care to read speeches made in North Carolina, Winthrop College, Auburn, Alabama, and the article in The Virginia Quarterly Review, Winter Issue, 1962.)

X. For responsible self-determination of people in the Pacific Islands under control of the United States as well as all colonial peoples anywhere; for free choice by the people of Puerto Rico; and for the admission of Alaska and Hawaii into the Union of States. (See Senate statement on Alaska and Hawaii)

XI. For reciprocal trade agreements without emasculation by amendments and reservations pressed for by high protectionist interests. (See Senate speech for Reciprocal Trade Agreements)

XII. Adequate national defense meantime in a bi-polar world of peril with unremitting struggle for universal disarmament and collective security. After World War II the United States demobilized its powerful armies, put much of its fleet in mothballs, and offered the Marshall Plan to all the nations of Europe as a basis for co-operation in economic recovery and progress, and offered to share its then monopoly of atomic power for humane purposes through the United Nations. In view of the rejection of these developments by Stalin, and in the face of unfulfilled promises for self-determination by the people of Eastern Europe, the take-over of Poland, Rumania, Bulgaria, Hungary, Albania and Czechoslovakia and the threat to Greece, Turkey and Western Europe, a chain of U.S. military bases were established in a defensive effort to contain the massive power reaching across the heartland of the earth.

XIII. Under Articles 51 and 52 of the United Nations Charter, I was for support of the Organization of the American States, so as to establish a multilateral collective security in the Western Hemisphere as a step in the evolution of the Monroe Doctrine from the unilateral responsibility of the United States into a multilateral responsibility of the Organization of the American States for defense against aggression, [for] freedom, peace and progress in the Western Hemisphere.

XIV. For Point 4 and foreign aid as a way to help through mutual aid, technically underdeveloped countries to develop their own natural and human resources for the freer, fairer and more productive life of their people.

XV. Under Articles 51 and 52 of the United Nations Charter, I favored the Atlantic Union for defense against aggression and for collective security, mutual aid, freedom, peace and humane progress. It was made clear in the Senate debates that the Atlantic Pact was not for support of the colonialism of allies in Africa or Asia but was defense against aggression in Europe. The alternative, as developed in the United States Senate, was between, on one hand, the United States going it alone as Fortress America, and, on the other hand, working in co-operation with the States in the O.A.S. and in the Atlantic Pact to contain aggression, defend freedom and maintain the peace meantime with the hope that there would evolve a more experienced, stronger and more effective United Nations. (You might wish to read a talk I made in the Senate for the Atlantic Pact.)

XVI. For (a) the support or the United Nations and all its specialized agencies; and (b) for a stronger and more effective United Nations by (1) the continuous struggle for effective universal disarmament; (2) a stand-by international police force; (3) economic development programs in all underdeveloped regions as part of the production as the basis for a better and more creative life for all people and all their children; (4) the progressive fulfillment of the Unlversal Declaration of human rights regardless of race or region, color, creed or economic condition; (5) for responsible self-determination of people, whether under the old or new colonialism; (6) universal membership of all peace-loving nations; and (7) development of the rule of law instead of the rule of war as a basis for peace, justice, well-being and progress on the earth as the God-given home of the family of man. In closing, Mary Ann, I feel, in trying to provide background and material for your working on your term paper, I have over-burdened you with much detail of which, however, substance is composed. I have omitted many failures and frustrations. Otherwise I would have over-loaded this statement, already a burden for even your young eyes, needed no doubt now for your preparation long in advance for exams.

With appreciation of your interest in public affairs, and with best wishes,

Sincerely yours,

[Frank Graham]

APPENDIX C
COMMENCEMENT ADDRESS, JUNE 6, 1966, CHAPEL HILL, N. C.

The Content of the Diploma

The diplomas you receive this day hold many things of substance and spirit. Contained therein are your mothers, fathers and families, here tonight and at home, who sacrificed that you might be here; the teachers and schoolmates of earlier years who spurred you on your way here; the friendships of your college years, precious beyond price; the spacious libraries which opened for you the cultural treasures gathered from all ages and all lands; modern laboratories for testing old theories and finding new truths; discussions in dormitories, fraternities and in the shops and homes of the friendly folk of Chapel Hill; vigorous interchange in the student legislature and in the lively columns of the Daily Tar Heel; dialogues in classrooms with fellow students under the situmulus of professors distinguished in the world of scholarship, teaching and research; spiritual renewals at high levels in the comradeship of religious associations, ministers, priests and rabbis, as you reach upward with the towers and steeples of Chapel Hill toward the life of the spirit; sixteen years of your own hard scholastic work; your struggles and your dreams; and not least of all the people who founded, builded, endowed and supported this university for your years of all-round development here - all these are packed in the meaning of the diploma you receive tonight. May you ever be worthy of the noble name it bears as your alma mater for all time to come.

Deeply Mindful of the Great Histories and
Values of all Colleges and Universities

Commencement day marks not only the real commencement of life's tests of the higher education of youth, but also the annual rebirth of America in the legions of youth who graduate from all the colleges and universities these June days in this land of hope and in the world of peril. We are deeply mindful of the great histories, struggles and values of all our sister colleges and universities, publicly supported, church related and privately endowed. On this night, as appropriate to this occasion, we confine ourselves to the heritage and hopes of this University in Chapel Hill.

This commencement occasion moves me to say to the Class of 1966, as you leave this place, that however far you may go on life's ways, alma mater will ever reach out across all the miles and years to hold you close in her great spirit. As on the playing field, so ever in the venturesome game of life she would have you play the game so hard and clean that if you lose, you will win something bigger than the game, and if you win, you will not lose something greater than the victory.

Her Heritage and Hopes are Part
of Your Heritage and Hopes

Since the heritage and hopes of this place have become a part of your own life, we will recall for you come bits of its early history and present hopes. To be unaware of the depth of our heritage is to impair the foundations of the height of our hopes.

In this American institution in North Carolina, in the forest of Orange, in Chapel Hill, voted by American universities for several decades to be at the front in the South, have been blended for you here traditions as old as the American Revolution, whose veterans founded this university, and hopes as young as the youth gathered here. In Chapel Hill are rock walls more ancient than the moss which covers them and historic halls more classic than the ivy which keeps them ever fresh with nature's own renewing life. In these surroundings of history and beauty, light and liberty, you have been challenged to stretch the mind to the height of your individual ability and to the depth of the inner person for nobler creations of the human spirit. It has become your resposibility to test thoroughly, to organize logically, to think and write clearly, and to judge fairly, and, with the opportunity, on your own initiative, to evaluate what is sound in your learning, honorable in your citizenship, true in your heritage, and best in our American hopes. Your college life has thus become not only the place for the joyous development of the whole personality and the wholesome life, but also the training ground for continuing your general learning, for increasing your special skill, and for participation in the civic affairs of your generation. The campus democracy will now deepen for you in the larger commonwealth as a more hopefully creative part in the adventurous business of making a nobler nation in the wider world, in need of the best which youth has to give to all mankind.

Foretold at Halifax in the revolutionary Constitution of 1776, chartered in Fayetteville in 1789, its cornerstone laid here by General William R. Davie on October 12th, 1793, and opened as the University of the people, January 15, 1795, the life of this university has been an embattled struggle from the last decade of the 18th century to the 6th decade of the 20th century. In each of the 43 generations of students, there have ever been loyal people, who, in the midst of the battles, have become sincerely concerned about the impact of the struggles upon the image of this university as reflected in the mirror of the times, as the university sought to prepare youth and the people for a freer and fairer life.

In the limits of this occasion we will take random glimpses of a few persons and episodes representative of the struggles in her now dimmer but not to be forgotten basic first century and her now latest more vivid year.

We catch a view of the first President, Joseph Caldwell, buried under the oaks on this campus, who, in the days of a highly valid but too exclusive emphasis on the classics, struggled to emphasize the no less valid meaning of science and to open for youthful minds glimpses of the then largely unexplored universe, when he brought from England and established in Chapel Hill the first astronomical observatory in any American University. He thus dimly foreshadowed the age of outer space, over whose explorations an alumnus of this University, James Webb, now presides in the leadership of venturesome pioneers, who, after glimpses in the Morehead Planetarum, blaze the hazardous trails in the infinite reaches of the expanding universe.

President Caldwell and Two of His Students,
Archibald de Bow Murphey and John Motley Morehead

During Caldwell's influential years at Chapel Hill there were at various times many most remarkable young men. One was Archibald de Bow Murphey, who drafted a plan for public education and state develpment, which, if the plan, on the grounds if its alleged radicalism, had not been rejected by privilege and reaction, would have placed North Carolina at the forefront of the American States, instead of for decades being called the "Rip Van Winkle of the States".

Another was John Motley Morehead, the first, who favored the gradual emancipation of the slaves, the right of free Negroes to vote, founded a college for women, and, as Governor, championed the establishment of a school for the blind and the building of the first railroad in North Carolina to connect the sharply divided east and west.

In vision and progress he was the forerunner of his grandson, John Motley Morehead, who was the builder of an industrial enterprise, which reaches across the world in this generation, and the founder of an endowment for excellence in scholarship at his alma mater which will reach across all the generations to come.

In the decades after Morehead's student days, when spending public funds for public elementary schools was considered a form of dangerous radicalism, it was on the groundwork of ideas laid by Murphey that sons of the University, Yancey, Hill and Cherry, let the fight for founding the first public schools in our State. When, under the pressures of the Civil War, it was proposed that the money for public schools be used in the war effort, another son, our first State Superintendent of Public Instruction, Calvin H. Wiley, successfully cried out against using up the seed corn of the State's future hopes.

Under President Swain the Largest
Student Body Next to that of Yale

In pre-Civil War years, under President Swain, attracted by her fame, there came to Chapel Hill from the wide region from Virginia to Texas, more students than were in any American college or university except Yale.

The Dismissal of Professor
Hedrick of Salisbury

It must be confessed that in the tense times of the approach toward the Civil War, a courageous Univesity professor of chemistry, Ben Hedrick from Salisbury, favored the election of John C. Freemont, the first Republican candidate for President. He was dismissed by the Trustees. Hinson Rowan Helper, a resident of Salisbury, had written "The Impending Crisis in the South", which, despite statisical fallacies, emphasized that slavery was a block to Southern progress and a heavy load on the back of the vast majority of the Southern people. Because of widespread demands, joined in by some University alumni, he left the State under the intolerance of the law to ban the book.

The Vote Against Secession and the
Later Stand Against Invasion of
the South.

After the States in the lower South had seceded, many sons of this university led the people of North Carolina in voting against secession. However, when the call came for the invasion of the Southern States by Federal armies, North Carolina joined the Confederacy and provided more soldiers than any other state. The sons of this university provided more volunteers and suffered more casualties than any college or university on either side of that titanic conflict. The spirit of the sons and our people was revealed, when, on a high ridge of valor at Gettysburg, Isaac Erwin Avery of Morganton, as he lay dying, wrote on the back of a blood stained envelope, "Tell my father that I fell with my face to the foe."

The historic and personal relationship of the people and their university, through the generations is exemplified in such facts as follows: The grandfather of that soldier was Waightstill Avery, who inserted in the North Carolina Constitution of 1776 the provision for one or more universities. He was named "Waightstill" because his parents of many sons were waiting still on the Lord for the daughter who did not come. Yet, a great-granddaughter of Waightstill Avery later did come -- Gladys Avery Tillett of Charlotte, a graduate of the Woman's College and of this University. With her face toward to the foes of equal rights of women, she has, by valorous persistence, wrought a revolution in the foreign policy of the United States from an established policy of abstaining from voting, to the new policy of voting for conventions on human rights in the United Nations.

Mrs. Spencer and the Reopening
of the University

Nine decades earlier it was an indomitable woman, Mrs. Cornelia Phillips Spencer, who, when the University was closed in the period of "Reconstruction", stayed on in Chapel Hill amid the desolation which followed the Civil War and amid the weeds which had taken over the campus. She persistently wrote to "her boys", long leaders in the State, to reopen the University. They gathered on a hopefull mission in Raleigh in 1875. She waited with high hopes in Chapel Hill. From them came to her the simple message that it was voted that day to reopen the University. With filial joy, this valiant woman climbed the stairs of the Old South Building into the belfry. With the aid of a broken rope she rang the bell which had not rung for five years in Chapel Hill. As the old bell rang out clear and true in tones of the spirit which carried accross the State, the people of North Carolina were on the march again with faces forward to this day.

The Great Educational Crusade
and Its High Peak Under Aycock

As Mrs. Spencer was the mother of the reopening, President Kemp P. Battle was the father. He gathered funds, selected a strong faculty, and won the first annual State appropriation. Under him gathered in Chapel Hill in the early 1880's one of the most remarkable groups of young idealists ever to gather in the same student community on any campus. Note well the names: Charles B.

Aycock, Edwin A. Alderman, Charles D. McIver, James Y. Joyner, N.C.S. Noble, Horace Williams, Robert Pell, A. W. McAllister, A.A.F. Seawell, Josephus Daniels in the summer Law School, and their fellow student peers.

Without a Marshall Plan for recovery from the ruins of war, with the handicaps of discriminatory freight rates against Southern agriculture and industry, with the responsibility of the Southern people for providing for the disabled Confederate veterans and for helping to provide for the disabled Union veterans, these young men, challenged by it all, highly resolved that they would rebuild a broken society, then heavy-laden with poverty and illiteracy. Two of them, Alderman and McIver, on their graduating evening, talked the long night through as to how they would use their lives to that purpose. As Alderman later said, they decided toward sunrise, by a light that was never seen on land or sea, to give their lives to education. They carried on their great crusade that the way out and up from poverty and ignorance was through the schoolhouse door. School houses, and soon teachers colleges, began rising across the State from the sand dunes to the mountain coves. As a part of the educational crusade, the Southern industrial revolution, the agricultural depression, and the farmers' revolt, and in response to the militant leadership of Colonel Leonidas Polk, and the Wautauga Club, there was founded at Raleigh the North Carolina State College, well on the way to becoming another M.I.T. in the nation, as a part of the land grant college movement which worked a democratic revolution in higher education, whose impact was felt aross the State, the nation, and is being felt around the world today. Also as a part of the same educational crusade, the awakening of the people, the woman's movement, and in response to the dynamic eloquence of Charles D. McIver, there was founded in Greensboro, the Woman's College, whose graduates, under his successors, have creatively helped through the churches, the homes, the schools, the farms, offices and civic enterprises, to make North Carolina a more productive, wholesome and beautiful place in which to live and serve the needs of the people in all the succeeding generations. This fairest daughter of the Old North State, on the way for some time to becoming another Bryn Mawr in the nation, is now on the eve of a new efflorescence as the University of North Carolina in Greensboro, under an able and gallant leadership in the four-fold University of the people in Chapel Hill, Raleigh, Greensboro and Charlotte.

The Answer of Charles B. Aycock to Unfair Proposals

The educational crusade reached a high peak at the turn of the century in the administration of Charles B. Aycock, North Carolina's great Educational Governor. While speaking for the public schools in Birmingham, Alabama, he fell dead on the plaform immediately after saying those prophetic words which he had said many times in North Carolina, and I quote: "For the equal right of every child to burgeon out all that is in him."

On one occasion he was heavily advised on the grounds of political expediency to lead his party (1) for the indefinite postponement of the year 1908 as the termination date for ending the exclusion of voters on account of race and (2) that funds for the separate public schools be approtioned in proportion to the taxes paid by the respective races. As much in sorrow as in indignation, he replied that, if such measure were adopted by his party for the sake of political power, that they would break his campaign pledge given all over North Carolina and that he would resign as Governor in protest at what would have beeen his broken word, the dishonor of his party and the shame of his State, which he loved too much to betray. The bi-racial structure which he championed at that stage, is now equitably passing away, but the keeping of his word that education not color should be the qualification for voting -- though later misused -- and that public funds for schools should not be apportioned according to racial sources but according to the number of children, will live in the grateful remembrance of the people, who loved him and honor him to this day.

Those who today look down on the work of Charles B. Aycock and Booker T. Washington, as they grappled with the issues of their day, should acknowledge that while they are looking down they are standing on the shoulders of the men upon whom they are looking down, and should rather be looking up to achieve correspondingly in our day what such leaders as Aycock and Washington achieved in their day.

A Leap from President Battle to 1966

Time does not permit me to follow the observations just made on the administrations of President Caldwell, Swain and Battle with observations on the adminstrations of Presidents Winston, Alderman, Venable, Edward K. Graham, Harry W. Chase, and their successors, with their distinctive contributions to the life, growth, freedom, eminence and service of this University. We now leave them for other times.

Accordingly, I take a long leap from the Battle adminstration, when Aycock and his fellow college mates went forth to war on poverty and ignorance, to the year 1966 to make a few, and, I trust, helpful observations on the issue of open student forums in our State-supported colleges and universities. My own personal position on the basic issues was set forth in talks made at the invitation of students at the North Carolina State University in Raleigh, the Administration of the University of North Carolina in Greensboro, and the Model Student Legislature. This position, of course, still stands.

While freshly resourced in some representative bits of the University's first and basic century, I pray your patience and understanding while I take the minimum time necessary to make, I trust, a balanced and fair analysis in seeking to find a common ground for our whole University family..

In the situation, which has developed from forces and trends in the State and from the resulting circumstances, the Chancellor was the only person with the delegated authority to make the decision now in issue; and the representatative student leaders were, it seems, in practical terms, the only persons who could test the constitutional principles involves in this case.

Many on both sides have long been known to me. On the basis of that knowlege I am sure that the positions, which they respectively hold, are honestly held by the leaders on both sides.

One of the Basic Issues

In cutting through a tangle of many complex facts, a basic issue is found to have arisen from the fact that Mr. Herbert Aptheker, a communist theoretician, and Mr. Frank Wilkinson, a pleader of the fifth amendment against self-incrimination in an alleged security situation, both of whom have spoken this past spring semester without untoward incidents, on many college campuses, when invited by a group of responsible university student leaders, were denied the right to speak during the last spring semester on the campus at Chapel Hill.

The Acting Chancellor, Dr. J. Carlyle Sitterson, In Reaching His Decision Followed the Procedures Prescribed by the Board of Trustees.

In reaching his decision, the Acting Chancellor followed procedures adopted by the Board of Trustees, as he understood them, and made his decision under the responsibility which had been delegated to him by the Trustees. He appointed and consulted a well balanced faculty-student committee for advice in the matter. He also consulted the Faculty Advisory Committee, who are regularly elected by the faculty for advice on vitally important matters. The two committees make up two of the University's honor rolls.

Also, I am moved to say that the Governor, the members of the Board of Trustees, The President, many members of the faculty, the former Editor-in-Chief of the *Daily Tar Heel*, many members of the student body, and a very large body of citizens of the State, in their support of Chancellor Sitterson and his decision in the case, are all sincere in their concern and their support.

Chancellor Sitterson

Since Chancellor Sitterson is the focus of this situation, I am moved, as a citizen and an alumnus, a twin status which even an ex-President does not lose in matters of state-wide public policy, to speak out of my knowledge of him. There is no need for this on his part but it is appropriate on the part of an alumnus and citizen.

I have know Chancellor Carlyle Sitterson and his wife since they were children. They both come from homes of religion and learning, light and liberty, and loyalty and devotion to this University. Those homes have been strongholds of freedom, and, with other such families all over the State, they have long been a source of freedom, strength and support of this University. His integrity, high scholarship, campus leadership, teaching experience and administrative ability, provided the background for his recommendations by President Friday and unanimous election by the Trustees as Chancellor of the University of North Carolina at Chapel Hill.

The Student Leaders in This Case

Since the student leaders, on their own initiative, are the source of the action now pending in the courts, I am also moved to make the following observations.

The group of student leaders in this case is composed of the former and present Presidents of the Student Body, elected in campus-wide elections, the President of the Y.M.C.A., the Di-Phi Literary Society, the Carolina Political Union, and the Carolina Forum, all elected by their respective associations, and the present Editor-in-Chief of <u>The Daily Tar Heel</u> -- all these represent long established student organizations on the campus of the University at Chapel Hill. The two members of the Steering Committee of the Students of a Democratic Society represent a recent organization established at Chapel Hill and in colleges in many part of the country. All these student leaders are, I believe, responsible and sincere in their concern and in their action in this case.

The Student Body, in electing their present President, who made one of the main planks in his campaign for election the right of having student-sponsored, responsible, balanced and free open forums, were aware of his vigorous position on this matter and were sincere in their support of him.

The student leaders, instead of resorting to sit-ins, resorted to sitting of the highest court, in accordance with due process of law and the American Bill of Rights.

The Position of the North Carolina Chapters of the American Association of University Professors in the Universities and Colleges of North Carolina.

The North Carolina Chapter of the American Association of University Professors, whose membership includes institutions in all sections of the State, and whose President is Dr. C. E. Boulware of North Carolina College in Durham, joined in the action of the students. The main concern of this Association in colleges all over the United States, is the preservation of academic freedom. They have long held and supported in the leading universities and colleges of this country the position that student-sponsored, responsible, balanced, free and open student forums are one of the basic principles of academic freedom in America and serve an important educational purpose. They are concerned, I understand, that while spokesmen for the extreme right, the conservative and the liberal views were permitted to speak this past spring semester on the campus at Chapel Hill, two spokesmen for the extreme left were prohibited from speaking this last spring semester on the campus at Chapel Hill. Furthermore, they are concerned that, while spokesmen for the extreme left were allowed to speak to classes and special groups on the invitation of professors, that the two speakers in question in this case were not allowed to speak upon the invitation of elected student leaders, representing the whole student body and long established student associations, with their traditional freedom for responsible, balanced and free open forums.

The Position of the North Carolina Chapter of the Civil Liberties Union

The North Carolina Chapter of the Civil Liberties Union has joined in the action of the students. Their original concern, as is also the concern of the student leaders and the Chapters of the Association of University Professors, is with civil liberties, in accordance with the American Bill of Rights. The Civil Liberties Union has a membership that includes highly respected citizens as far east as Wilmington and Wagram, and as far west as Boone, and includes specialists on civil liberties in North Carolina colleges and universities. Their

Chairman is Charles F. Lambeth, Jr. of Thomasville, whose father was a leading Methodist, a graduate and long time trustee of Duke University, and whose mother was of a family of ministers, professors, editors and historians, who were devoted alumni and alumnae of Wake Forest and Meredith Colleges.

The concern of members of this North Carolina Chapter of Civil Liberties in this case is with the questions as to possible violation of the constitution of the United States, which guarantees to its citizens: (1) in the First Amendment, freedom of speech and assembly; (2) the right to plead the Fifth Amendment in certain circumstances; (3) the right to equal protection of the laws in the Fourteenth Amendment; and (4) the right not to be attainted by a discriminatory classification, as provided in Article 1, Section 9 of the Constitution.

Since these questions and these issues are now in the hands of the court, it is well that the case for the State and the University is in the hands of such distinguished and able lawyers as the State Attorney-General, the Honorable Mr. Bruton; and William T. Joyner. William T. Joyner is both a loyal son of the University and of James Y. Joyner, who went forth from Chapel Hill in the 1880's with Alderman, McIver, Daniels and Aycock, whose strong right arm he became in the great education crusade for a freer and fairer society in North Carolina.

It is also well that the case for the Association of University Professors, the Civil Liberties Union and the Student Leaders, is in the respectively able hands of Professor William Van Alstine of Duke University, a constitutional specialist in academic freedom; Professor Dan Pollitt, a constitutional specialist in civil liberties in the Law School at Chapel Hill; and McNeill Smith, long a champion of equal justice under the Constitution. He, like other members of the Civil Liberties Union, such as R. Mayne Albright and Charles F. Lambeth, were promoters of traditionally responsible and balanced free and open student forums at Chapel Hill, which provided the ways for the exercise of individual initiative in their educational growth and knowledge of the world in which they were to play their self-reliant and responsible parts.

The list of student leaders; the members of the Association of University Professors; and the members of the North Carolina Chapter of Civil Liberties, are three of the honor rolls of our State.

In a Situation in Which Leaders on Both Sides are Believers
in and Committed to the American Bill of Rights, the Need
Now is not for Taking Hostile Sides but Rather the Need is
for a Clarification by the Highest Courts of the Relevancy
of the Principles of the Bill of Rights, to Whose Side all
Sides May Rally on a Reconciling Common Ground.

It appears that there was a carryover of influence in the fact that before a decision made by the Trustees prohibiting the two speakers in question from speaking (a decision made pending the establishment of regulations regarding far left wing speakers) the then Dean Sitterson supported Chancellor Sharp, who was in favor of allowing them to speak. It was after action by the Trustees, which delegated authority to him as Acting Chancellor, that he made his decision in deference to the previous action of the Trustees, and also in his interpretation, under the circumstances, of the meaning "of serving an educational advantage".

Since the leaders of the two sides believe in and are committed to the American Bill of Rights, the need now is not for hostile lineups of sides. Rather the need is for the determination and clarification by the highest courts of the relevancy of the American Bill of Rights, to the side of which all sides may rally on a reconciling common ground.

Rising above any question of the sincere zeal of youth in their democratic faith in the education values of balanced open student forums; rising above any lack of clarity regarding the carry-over of the influence of the speaker ban law, its modification, the action of the Trustees under the law, and the decision of the Chancellor in his interpretation of, and in his deference to, the action of the Trustees; and rising above any proposals for a State-wide campaign for the revival of the original speaker ban law -- rising above them all is the grandeur of the American Bill of Rights and the majesty of the courts in their responsible clarification, application and determination of the relevancy of the American Bill of Rights as a basic cornerstone of the rightful freedom of individuals, of minorities, and of all the people in our State and in our Nation.

This clarification and determination by the highest courts will, in the long run, be a real and enduring service to Governors, Legislators, Trustees, Presidents, Chancellors, Professors and Students of all our State institutions and by implication to all colleges and universities in the State and the Nation. This clarification and determination will be of service also to professors who may hereafter be considering becoming members of our four-fold University and state colleges, and not least important of all, for the information and understanding of the people of the State.

With the Issue Decided by the Highest Court,
a Reconciling Common Ground is Found for a
Rendezvous of the People with Both Our Great
Heritage of Freedom and Their Higher Destiny of
Service to Truth, Youth and the Commonwealth.

With any lingering or indirect influences of the speaker ban law and its modification eliminated insofar as found in violation of the American Bill of Rights by the highest courts in their free discretion and independent wisdom, what a present and future prospect calls to our people for a rendezvous with both their heritage of freedom and their higher destiny of service in this land!

In this land, once so heavy laden with poverty and illiteracy, now renewing its productive life with the growing cooperation of the races on the rising basis of equal justice and opportunity, the people of the South, against heavy odds, have increasingly made their recovery and are rising to the opportunity of this hour. In the old South, whose people played a decisive part in the creation of this Republic, where human slavery made one of the last stands in the modern world, and where industrialism made fresh beginnings on productive soil, we have the lessons in the tragedies of one and the opportunities in the power of the other to help build a nobler civilization than has yet characterized the relations of the religious communions, labor and management, the races and all the nations. As the school houses open wider with equal opportunity, the mills move into the waste places, and the rivers come rushing from the hillsides with the power for the electrification of our homes, towns, farms and factories, we will place in the center of it all the children of today, upon whose hopes will move forward the civilization of tomorrow in the spirit of Him who said, "suffer the little children to come unto me and forbid them not for such is the Kingdom of God."

Here in North Carolina, under a gracious and invigorating Southern sun, in this pleasant land from the mountains to the sea, through the cooperation of the four-fold University of North Carolina, Duke University, the Research Triangle, all the colleges, publicly supported, church-related and privately endowed, community colleges, technical institutes, industrial education centers, the public and private elementary and secondary schools, the North Carolina Fund, the Center for the Performing Arts, and all the humane institutions and the productive agencies of the people's life and welfare, the opportunities are as boundless as the aptitudes, imagination and high resolve of the people. The opportunity is nothing less than building by the people in this blessed land through this manifold free cooperation under able and devoted leaders, trustees, administrators, professors and students, one of the great educational, agricultural, industrial, medical, humane and spritual centers of the modern world.

The Need for a Non-Partisan Peoples' Muster of Understanding to the Side of Our Embattled Universities and Colleges.

Against such a development, some special interest will possibly seek again to trade on the popular fears and resentments growing out of students' and professors' active interest in, and lawful petitions for, equal opportunities of all Americans. As in other crises, such as the depression; the threats to the schools, colleges and universities; the need of roads, medical education and state-wide hospital care, there must be organized again at the grass roots in all the counties a non-partisan people's movement for the people's understanding of the necessity of the freedom and support of the universities, so basic to the freedom and welfare of the people. Free and responsible student open forums are necessary for their understanding of the kind of a world in which youth has to live, work, vote and play their responsible parts. Freedom is necessary for industrial and agricultural research and extension, and for the equal rights of collective cooperation between labor and management, which together have produced an economic abundance in America unprecendented in human history.

Freedom is necessary for the widening of the base of the general health and social welfare in order to lift the level of human liberty. All these interrelated freedoms are necessary for the noblest creation of the human spirit in building that great civilization in North Carolina for which voices are calling from generations gone, from the generation living, and from generations yet unborn. Since all basic freedoms are interrelated, the people, when informed and aroused, will rally to the side of the embattled universities and colleges against the false charges that they are breeding grounds of atheism and communism.

For meeting head on these charges made against the historic freedom and present hopes of our universities and colleges, you, your excellency, as Chairman of the Board of Trustees, out of your own ancestral inheritance and your personal knowledge, you, Mr. President, and you, Mr. Chancellor, and all those who constructively share your heavy responsibilities, need the understanding and help of the legions of people of good will in our State. As we all now rally to the side of the whole University, the Chairman of the Board of Trustees, in their great trust, the President, in his vision of the widening of the four-fold University of the people, unfolding for more affluent times, the Chancellor, the professors and the students, the people, in the long run, not by cutting and tearing down, but rather by building up with adequate investments in youth, will create the way out and up for a more productive, freer and fairer North Carolina.

The Misdirected Charges of Atheism and of Communism Against the Freedom of the Colleges and Universities, Whose Freedom is the Opposite of all Forms of Totalitarianism

Regarding the charge of atheism, let us recall that many honest young minds in the colleges have in times past effectively grappled with (1) the Copernican dethronement of the earth as the center of the universe, (2) the Darwinian evolutionary identification of man with animals, (3) the alleged overriding of spiritual power by Marxist economic determinism, (4) the Freudian subjection of the conscious mind to primitive drives and subconscious forces, and (5) the modification of absolute theories by the theory of relativity. It has come to pass that youthful minds in the colleges are grappling with the idea of the death of God, as now honestly put forward by some theologians.

With full freedom of thought and dissent, some of the most distinguished scientists in our universities, such as Einstein, found that a universe without God would be more inconceivable and the subject of more skepticism than a universe with God.

At the very time that some theologians are proclaiming that God is dead, many preeminent scientists and professors in the universities, as citizens of the general community or as members of religious communions, are finding God alternatively, or in combination, in (1) the design, order and majesty of the universe; (2) the fact, in spite of the cruelties of nature and man and the incomprehensibility of the suffering of the innocent and the power of the ruthless, that there is a moral sovereignty which undergirds the nature of man and nations, whose moral laws cannot be ultimately defied without damage to human beings and to nations; (3) the intimations and revelations of the spiritual power of the great seers of history, East and West; (4) the spiritual lightning of the great Hebrew prophets which flashes fom the inner presence of God, and their moral thunder, which resounds across the centuries, to help in the struggles of individuals over human frailties for the good life and social justice; or in (5) the supreme revelation of both the humanity and divinity in Him who preached the gospel to the poor, ministered to the sick and hungry, redeemed the fallen with forgiveness, selected a member of a despised people as the example of brotherhood, said, "I and the Father are one and ye are my brethren", "As I am in this world so are ye", "know the truth and the truth will make you free", made merry at the wedding feast, ate with publicans and sinners, drove the money changers from the temple, and against all counsel of expediency set His face steadfast to take the Jerusalem road, was crucified, suffered and died, and made the Cross a symbol of love and sacrifice with its call to heroism and compassion in the sharing and giving of life, and rose in spiritual power for all persons as children of one God and brothers of all people in one world neighborhood of human brotherhood.

Resourced in such a spiritual heritage, a mother, when suddenly told of the death of her son, while serving with the Peace Corps in the high Andes, was asked in the midst of her overwhelming grief, what she had to say. She said simply, "I am glad that he was happy in being where he wanted to be in the service of others." Something more than materialism and something higher than an accidental collocation of atoms spoke in the love of that mother and the service of that son.

The Charge That the University
is Soft on Communism

The charge that the university is soft on Communism is no more justified than that the university is a center of atheism. The fact that the students wish to hear communists speak in their responsible and fairly balanced open forums along with speakers who represent the extreme right, the conservative and the liberal points of view, does not mean that they are soft on communism, but simply means they wish to understand the nature of the world of their generation. In overwhelming numbers they have faith not only in responsible student open forums, but also they have faith in themselves, the values of freedom and the robustness of our American democracy. This charge is made by some, because, in the conception of universities' responsible teachers and interpreters, people include, rightfully, not only the financially affluent, the socially privileged and the politically powerful, but also the minority religious groups, the small business men, the small farm families, industrial, agricultural and migrant workers, colored people, and the disinherited of the earth. This charge, made in the very midst of the universities' struggle in behalf of the freedom of the mind, the equal dignity of the individual human person, civil liberties, the freedom of assembly, speech, publications and the responsible student open forums, is a charge made in historical reverse. Civil liberties, academic freedom and open forums are prohibited in Communist societies and are promoted in free societies. When both Hittler and Stalin were on their road to totalitarian tyranny, they found across their road to power autonomous organizations which were the creations of successive chapters of almost 2000 years of the history of the rise of liberty in the Western world. The institutions which blocked their way were churches, parliaments, universities, corporations, labor unions, voluntary associations of the people, and open forums. In order to rise to totalitarian power, both Communism and Fascism had to crush, subjugate or restrict the freedom of all these historic autonomous institutions of the people.

The Responsible Freedom of Universities
a Sacred Trust

One of the most precious of these autonomous institutions was born in the Middle Ages. With the fall and disintegration of the Roman Empire, as the transmitter of the classical legacies to the West, it was then that the classical intellectual heritage of the academy of Plato, the lyceum of Aristotle, the libraries, museums and institutions of Alexandria, and the colleges of rhetoric of Quintillian of Rome, were largely lost in the Western world. During the Dark Ages the flickering light of learning was kept burning in the monasteries, and the vigorous minds of the conquering barbarians at a necessarily lower level were tutored by the church.

With the papal reintegrations and the slow recovery of Europe, the rise of trade, towns and the middle class, and the rise of scholasticism in reponse to the spreading intellectual ferment of the times, given impetus by the great Islamic intellectual revival, universities were founded in the later Middle Ages. Great universities were founded and conducted by professors. Great universities were founded and conducted by students. Professors and students together became the most essential parts of our medieval and modern universities. Administrators represent not only the authority of trustees but also embody the academic freedom of professors and the self-government of students in the free community of scholars, long established in the tradition of the University world. The universities, along with the parliaments and the cathedrals, still tower across the centuries as among the noblest creations of the human spirit. The academic freedom of the community of scholars became the sacred trust of the trustees, the administrators, the faculty, the students and the people.

Their freedom may be temporarily impaired at times by ecclesiastical and state authorities, but not without heavy damage to the universities, the churches, the state and the people. Thus we observe that almost 2,000 years of the history of the rise of autonomous institutions of the people, and 750 years of medieval and modern universities were reversed in the rise of totalitarian tyranny and in the rise of movements to impair the responsible freedom of professors and the responsible open forums of the students. The fact that there have been since the inflexible iron tyranny of Stalin, some real advances in the common life of the great Russian people, in the midst of the moral imperative of an honorable peaceful coexistence, in no way lessens our continuing need for emphasis on the values of autonomous organizations, civil liberties and the American Bill of Rights, especially in view of the continuation of much of the substance of totalitarianism in the Soviet Union today, which still prohibits the freedom of these institutions.

Not only so, but also North Carolina, which was the first State to authorize its delegates to vote for a Declaration of Independence at Philadelphia, became involved in struggles for the very principles for which the American Revolution was fought, such as the freedom of religion, the press, speech, assembly and open forums. Thus also there became involved in North Carolina the validity of the American Bill of Rights. Yet it was North Carolina which refused to ratify the Constitution of the United States until her leaders were assured that the Bill of Rights would at the first feasible opportunity be made a valid and vital part of the Constitution of the United States. It is not in the heritage and hope of the people of North Carolina to turn to totalitarian ways and thereby turn their backs on (1) our Judaic-Christian-Greco-Roman-European-British-American heritage, (2) the principles of the American Revolution, and (3) the American Bill of Rights. They are all the very antitheses of Communism and Fascism. It is therefore contrary to our heritage to charge that the universities are the breeding ground of atheism and communism. The real objection held by some interests to this university community is not that it is a center of atheism and communism, but that its people take seriously our Judaic-Christian heritage and our revolutionary historic Americanism. Our advancing democracy at its humane best seeks to help make the world free for differences so that freedom of differences may become the source of progress and that progress means not the exploitation or annihilation of people but the cooperation of nations for peace in the world.

It is wholesome from time to time to recur to the fundamental principle of human freedom, for which the American Revolution was fought, the Constitution framed, the Bill of Rights formulated, and this University founded, as a child of the Revolution to help fulfill.

We must make clear to ourselves and the world that the great autonomous organizations of the people, the historic freedom of universities, and the guarantees of our Constitution, are not only the past and historic, but the present and living source of America's faith in herself, the world's faith in America and America's moral influence and power in the partnership of nations for freedom, justice and peace in the world, in this age of mortal peril and immortal hope for all people on the earth in the home of the family of man.

APPENDIX D:

Southern Youth Movement in Lawful Assemblies and Petitions

There is a rightful place in an open and free democracy for the views and lawful activities of conservatives, liberals and radicals. In this reciprocal exchange and testing of ideas in open struggle of the people for freedom, justice and well-being, is the democratic meaning, humane progress and advancing hope of a free society. In the anxieties and hopes of this struggle some spokesmen of the extreme right sometimes in effect not only label as un-American the basic principles of our historic Americanism, but also sometimes label as Communistic the noblest idealism of the prophetic Hebraic-Christian heritage. These spokesmen of the extreme right would in effect teach our youth an unhistorical Americanism and mistakenly credit our most authentic Americanism to Communism, which in actual life is a ruthless totalitarianism.

By the same inverse logic, the spokesmen of the left put the label of "freedom loving peoples' democracies" on this totalitarian tyranny, which, with all its achievements in science, technology, mass education and vast production, sometimes includes in its program terrorism, firing squads, and concentration camps and prohibits open political discussions, free elections, due process of law and freedom of assembly, speech, the press and religion.

The Southern youth movement in lawful assemblies and petitions for the same service for the same price in stores which sell their goods and services to all people, did not have its origin in Moscow. Its origin is in the democratic idealism of the American Declaration of Independence, whose revolutionary words for human freedom and equality went ringing around the world and are still singing in the valiant hearts and the unfulfilled hopes of the people in two hemispheres. Its farther headwaters are in the Judean hills where Jesus, as the supreme incarnation of the Divine Lord, lived and died for the equal freedom, dignity and hope of all human beings as children of one God and brothers of all people.

The petitions, songs and prayers of these non-violent youth, with the Bible and the Constitution in their minds, religious hymns and patriotic songs on their lips, and love and brotherhood in their hearts, are not seeking to overthrow the Republic or to overturn the lawful rights of persons and property. Rather they are standing on American foundations in the prophetic Judaic-Christian tradition for the further fulfillment of the noble heritage of freedom learned in American history, and the greater hope of equal dignity and human rights, promised in their religion of human brotherhood.

When their non-violent actions have gone beyond being assemblies, petitions, songs and prayers, into being sit-ins, contrary to local customs, ordinance and laws, their purpose, in most cases, has not been basically to disobey the local laws governing stores which sell goods and services to all people, but mainly to test and reveal, even through dedicated imprisonment if necessary, what is the basic law under the Constitution as interpreted by the courts. In sitting down they were in their hearts and hopes standing up for the American dream. They have, in the main, been intent upon developing only a sufficient series of test cases so that a representative number of them would both touch the conscience of the people and reach the Supreme Court for judicial determination.

This land of liberty and constitutional democracy is based on civil liberties, equal suffrage, free elections of representatives of the people, fundamental rights, open courts and due process of law. The cases testing basic human rights under the Constitution, when determined by the courts, impose upon all people as law abiding and responsible citizens in a free society, the duty to obey the decisions of the Supreme Court while they stand as the supreme law of the land in all States.

As long as the schools, colleges and churches preserve and advance their freedom to transmit and fulfill their intellectual and spiritual heritage and hope, any subversive elements of the extreme left or the extreme right will be exposed in their mistaken pretensions and dissolved in the rigorous currents of our spiritual heritage and the robust hopes of the American dream. It is the suppression of the rightful freedom of the extreme right or left which gives them appealing power. It is the exposure to light and liberty which reveal their pretensions of freedom and their designs of tyranny over the minds and lives of the people. In one case it is the design of the tyranny and privilege of a minority class; in the other case it is the design and privilege of a minority party. In both cases is the tyranny of an inner and monolithic few over the ideas, work, lives and destiny of the whole people.

The American workers in autonomous and responsible freedom of organization against exploitation, defeated and dissolved subversive elements in the vigorous currents of their own resilient moral commitments to their inner faith and their own historic Americanism. The American Negroes, despite historic wrongs and present frustrations, have, with their religious faith and democratic hopes, resisted the lures and promises of Communism, have fought and died in battles against both Fascism and Communism and struggle today to test and fulfill the law of the land for themselves and all their children. America, which has taught all her children the hope of the American dream, cannot, without reversing the course of her history to her own undoing, ask any Americans to deny and betray their religious heritage and their democratic hope.

APPENDIX E:

The United Nations in the Atomic Age
[1957]

In this time of hazard and hope for all the peoples of the earth it my be helpful to stand off and take a look at the United Nations in depth and in breadth. Let us view the United Nations both in the vertical perspective of the long past of the human race and in the horizontal perspective of the present precarious world of the family of man.

A World Imperiled by Atomic Power in the Hands of Man in the Absolute National State

Man by nature has the capacity for good and evil. Atomic power by nature in the hands of man has the potentials for good and evil. A threat graver for the survival of the human species on this planet than the prehistoric dinosaurs or the massive glaciers, which extinguished much of the life on the earth, is atomic power in the hands of man in the absolute national state.

The people of the national states carry stored away deep in their sub-conscious natures the primitive inheritance of hundreds of millions of years as animals, hundreds of thousands of years as savages, and scores of thousands of years as barbarians. In the providence of nature and nature's God there is stored away deep in the nature and inheritance of man a divine spark of infinite capacity and hope. Along with the physical descent of man from lower species is the spiritual ascent of man in his slowly deepening consciousness the child of one God and the brother of all people toward the developing family of man. The evolving brotherhood within the nation and in the family of nations has not yet become the family of man.

Meantime the explosive potential of atomic energy in the uncontrolled power of nations can blow the world to pieces. For the first time in history the people of one generation have the capacity to destroy all the people on the earth and bring to an end all the heritage of all the generations gone and all the hopes of all the generations yet unborn and consequently never to be born.

Man needs religion and the inner resources of the human spirit for sublimating the savage impulses deep in the nature of man and for fulfilling his creative capacities for freedom, dignity, and his spiritual aspirations. So the nations need the United Nations to restrain and guide the nations which are too often irresponsible in their sovereignties, explosive in their national emotions, and unlimited in their power. In this perspective of the primitive human inheritance of millions of years, the nations need the United Nations for their own survival and for the fulfillment of their higher capacities for the freedom of peoples and the peace of nations.

A World Police State or a More Effective United Nations

Let us move forward from the perspective of millions of years and view the need for the United Nations in the perspective of the last five thousand years. We observe the political evolution of states across the last five thousand years from tribal states to city states to empire states to feudal states of ancient and medieval times to the nation states of modern times. In this age of the possible central consolidation of the means of production, distribution, communication and security across vast continents and seas, we are now confronted with the fateful alternative as to whether the next transition will be from the nation states to a world police state or to the more effective cooperation of nation states in a more adequate United Nations for the more inclusive collective security of freedom, justice, compassion and peace on the earth. In this perspective of five thousand years an effective United Nations has become the moral imperative of a world to be made safe for democracy, free for differences, and secure for justice and peace.

The Interdependence of Scientific Ideas and Economic Revolutions

In the last five hundred years two great economic revolutions made the nations parts of one commercially and industrially interdependent world. These two economic revolutions illustrate the vast practical importance of ideas, pure theories, philosophical speculation and basic research. The great commercial revolution, with its expanding global interchange of travel and trade, was made possible by scientific fact toward which the mind of man was groping in his scientific speculation that the earth itself might be a great magnet. The pivoted needle of the mariner's compass pointing true north aud south in response to the invisible electromagnetic lines of force running through the earth, magnetic pole to pole, made possible the discovery of America, the rounding of Africa by sea to Asia, and a great economic revolution. An idea became mechanized, the mechanism brought on the great commercial revolution. On the pivoting of a little needle the medieval world turned into the modern world and the resulting revolution made the nations part of one commercially interdependent world.

Several hundred years later the idea of the latent power of heat in the mind of Professor Joseph Black of the University of Glasgow became in the inventive hands of James Watts the expansive power of steam in the engine which wrought the great industrial revolution and made the nations part of one industrially interdependent world. The dynamic mechanical framework flung around the earth by steam, electricity, gas and oil powered engines gathered up wars and depressions anywhere and involved human beings everywhere.

In such a world a Slavic youth pulled a trigger on June 26, 1914. I do not mean to suggest that the pull of that trigger caused the first World War. We learned that we were living in the kind of a world in which the pull of a trigger caught up on the wires of the world precipitated the release of pent up economic, social, political, psychological and military forces. In less than four years two million American boys had crossed an ocean and ten million of the finest youth were killed on the battlefields of three continents.

Into this kind of a world came another idea from the speculations and researches of men and women in universities and laboratories. The idea of the nuclear nature of the atom once a pure theory became a mechanism, the motive force of the atomic revolution, and made all the nations parts of one fatefully interdependent world. There can now be no isolation from the seas around, the continents beyond, or the skies above. In the vertical depth of the perspective of millions of years, five thousand years, five hundred years, the last thirteen years, the United Nations has become a must for the survival of the human race.

The United Nations a Moral Imperative for Human Survival in the Present World

Let us now look at the United Nations in the perspective of horizontal breadth reaching around the earth in these days of a precariously balanced bi-polar global peace.

On this imperiled earth live two billion six hundred million people. Over half the people live in Asia, more than two hundred million more live in Africa, over two-thirds of the people of the world are colored. What the United States and the United Nations do for the equal freedom and dignity of colored people has a bearing on what the nations and the colored peoples do about freedom in the world and human survival on the earth.

The time bombs with their remnants of racialism, not yet supplanted by the practice of the equal freedom and dignity of all people; and the remnants of colonialism, not yet replaced by the responsible self-determination of people; and the remnants of the old exploitive capitalism, not yet replaced by the socially responsible industrialism, can, with their fuses lighted by fear and hate, blow to bits the nations of the earth. In such an explosive world the United Nations is the one forum in which the people of all races, religions, colors and creeds can meet together on an equal basis and talk the hottest issue through for conciliation and cooperation instead of shooting it out in hate and annihilation.

Whether in the perspective of the long past of the human race or in the perspective of the present needs of all peoples, the United Nations becomes the moral imperative for human survival on the earth. It is fortunate that, at the very time atomic power made its entrance into history and a world revolution encompassed the earth, the United Nations made its entrance on the stage of the world. The people of the United States have learned the hard way that their historic splendid isolation did not keep them out of the first World War; staying out of the League of Nations did not keep us out of the second World War. People of all parties decided that instead of staying on the outside and being drawn into world wars after they start, we would join the United Nations and seek more effectively on the inside to try to prevent the beginning of a third world war.

The Values, Frustrations and Needs of the United Nations

The United Nations with all its frustrations and faults has been a safety valve for the pent-up resentments and hazardous impulses of nations; has restrained and guided sovereign nations; and has so far helped to prevent the beginning of the third world war. It is better that the delegates of eighty-one nations even shout at each other in the open forum of the world than that scores of millions of youths shoot at each other on the battlefields of the earth. The United Nations has helped to cool off a half a dozen spots on the earth where a local fire might have become a global conflagration. Quietly and undramatically the organs and the specialized agencies of the United Nations are seeking to relieve human miseries, desperation and misunderstanding which make for war. They are carrying on the "moral equivalent of war" in humane campaigns against poverty, hunger, illiteracy, disease, colonialism, discrimination, armaments, and the war system itself. For its more effective work the United Nations in its frustrations and failures needs:

(1) the establishment of an international police force;

(2) the withholding of the veto in the areas of the peaceful settlement of disputes, membership and disarmament in cases on which seven members on the Security Council and two-thirds of the General Assembly join in a recommendation; and

(3) the inauguration of large programs of technical assistance and economic development as a practical way to supplant step by step the old vicious circle of fear, armaments, war and annihilation with a new circle of faith, economic development, effective disarmament and international cooperation in peace for a life more free, fair and equal for all people. Just as the cession of our western lands by the historic original states to the United States and the acquisition of the Louisiana territory widened the values and strengthened the meaning of the United States, so it is now timely to consider the long-run wisdom of the cession of the Jurisdiction of Antarctica and outer space to the United Nations and thus widen and strengthen the meaning of the United Nations in its great responsibility and value for the survival of man on the earth.

Though the rays of light break through the clouds of our time, thermo-nuclear power still casts its lengthening shadows across the earth, darkening the homes and hopes of men. The earth's clock, with its atomic--hydrogen--electronic parts, is fast ticking away toward the midnight of man's desperation or toward the morning of his hopes. In this age the ways of human destiny fatefully fork down the road of drift toward universal annihilation or up the road toward more effective cooperation through the United Nations. The dynamic international mechanical framework girdling the globe and the hopeful international political organization encompassing the earth need the moral reinforcement of the spiritual communions of all people as sons of God and brothers of men as the most practical and necessary way of human freedom, progress and survival on the earth as the God-given home of the family of man.

Frank P. Graham

APPENDIX F

THE UNIVERSITY TODAY

The Inaugural Address Delivered November 11, 1931

By Frank P. Graham
Eleventh President of the University of North Carolina

The local occasion which brings us together is submerged in the international occasion which focuses today the thought of the world upon the coming of peace. A University is so dynamic in its life that no occasion, however local or however international, is outside the range of its radiation. The campus and the world interact upon each other with generative and regenerative power. A university is more than intellectually dynamic, it is vitally organic with the life streams of the culture of the ages and the present hopes of the people. With a rootage as deep as the race and as wide as the world, the university grows in local soil for the finding of truth for all and the development of youth in whom are gathered both the local and international hopes of mankind.

A modern university is such a vital and manifold institution, has been so integrated into the structure of western civiliation, unbroken in their interconnection since the twelfth century, is so intimately a part of the context of every real problem of the modern world, that any life strand found at hand anywhere running through the life of the world enters into the texture of the modern university. We may work out from that strand into the complex life of the university and back again into the tangled life of the world.

ARMISTICE DAY AND THE UNIVERSITY

This is the forenoon of November 11, 1931, the fourteenth Armistice Day. As we, in Chapel Hill, go back to the armistice hour of that first day we find as the minute hand moved close to the hour, a young man, not long from the classrooms and playing fields of this University, was struck down at the head of his men and lay dying as the armistice hour struck the peace for a war-wrecked world. He was one of the tens of thousands of college men killed where danger stretched its farthest front, one of the ten millions of the fittest men on earth killed in four years of war. Greater than the gigantic figures of death, disease, and physical destruction is the uncountable loss of creative intellectual and spiritual power. All gone the training, the potential discoveries, inventions, literature, ideas, and dreams of youth done to death. Disillusionment to those who killed them! With all the heroism and idealism of the war, came also the moral and spiritual damages suffered far from the battlefront by millions caught in the awful backwash of the war and the wreckage of the values of human life and personality. Upon the backs of those who fought the war and whose work sustains a broken and bewildered world are now loaded the crushing costs of the war to be paid by them, their children and their children's children.

Today, as the sun makes its way across the world to the armistice hour, the people of Europe and America become still and silent as they remember their dead and the peace that came. It ties us to all mankind as we listen to the deep stillness of the millions in their silent commemorative aspiration for peace. Here in this beautiful Kenan Memorial Stadium we were silent and joined in the stillness of the peoples in a spiritual fellowship of the hope for peace on earth and goodwill toward men. We would be untrue to the spirit of this University, which has ever given and will ever give her life and her youth to every call that comes to the idealism and heroism of youth, if we did not link the purpose of this day to the purpose of this University and schools everywhere.

The colleges and universities, by virtue of their humane purpose and the very nature of their social being, have the responsibility of helping to build a world in which the call to the idealism and heroism of youth should never again be a call to war. It is their function to make realistically intelligent and morally heroic the aspirations and work of mankind toward a warless world, vivid with the unfolding possibilities of coöperative work and play, valorous with the adventures of physical and social mastery, and beautiful with the creations of the human spirit.

THE COLLEGE

To these high ends stands the University. At the center of the University is the college of liberal arts. In these recent decades the college of liberal arts, as a result of its own incoherence, the advance of the junior college, and the encroachments of the professional and vocational schools, has been subjected to a severe defensive reëxamination as to its place in the scheme of higher education. Several fundamental and dramatic experiments are now under way involving both the personalities of the experimenters and the function of the college. Scores of other experiments involving the purpose of the college in general and the curriculum and teaching methods in particular give a various and cumulative content to what has been called "a movement" for the college of liberal arts. The history of the college of liberal arts, whether as the denominational college which heroically blazed the trail for all the others, or as the privately endowed independent college, or as the central college of the modern university, private or state, gives solid ground for such reinvigoration of the college of arts and sciences. The college of arts and sciences, the foundation college for the professional and graduate schools and service province of them all, has a kingdom of its own and a purpose within its own high nature. This purpose, toward which it has in various forms been groping for centuries, is the development of the more complete human being, a unified victorious personality, increasingly equipped to understand himself and the world in which he is to play his useful and coöperative part. The struggle of the college to find its place and purpose has helped both to reflect and develop the spirit of the age. Any sound reconsideration of the curriculum of the college should be from the approaches of historical experience, the unchanging values of the whole personality, and the needs of the changing times.

1. The Background of the Curriculum

Amid its mediæval origins the liberal arts were subordinated to the ecclesiastical ends of preparation for the next world. With the Renaissance, despite its vivid implication in the affairs of this world, its recovery of old ideas, leading to discoveries of a new world and a new way to an old world, a new earth and the new heavens, yet the widening interests of the universities centered largely in the ancient learning as containing all learning. Learning for the next world gave way in part to learning from the classic past. The scientific revolution of the last three centuries brought the minds of the men of the universities from their absorption in the next world and their preoccupation with the ancient culture to a concern for the present and the mastery of this earth and the forces of nature. It came to be thought that the human intellect, with its new sciences, could go beyond the learning of the ancients and bring heaven to earth now, whether in the New Atlantis or in New Worlds for Old.

In these three periods of cultural history--scholastic, humanistic, and scientific--we find curricular adjustments in slow response to the intellectual emphasis of the age. In the mediæval university, though the secular process was under way, we still found in this stronghold of scholasticism scorn of the body and this world. Incidentally, it may be said that physical education is yet to break through the scholastic doors and get into the curriculum of this University and many American universities of the twentieth century. During the Renaissance the revived classics had a difficult time winning a place in the curriculum, and there are those today who would throw them out altogether. With the rise of the new science, the scholastics and the humanists, who became dominant in the universities, combined to delay the recognition of science on a basis of curricular equality with the humanities. But there can be no mistaking the masterful tones of science today in the university and in the world. In response to the increasing complexity of modern society there has arisen in turn the new group of social sciences. The humanists and the natural scientists have given questioning admission to the newer social sciences. Neither paleontology, as a natural-scientific introduction to the study of anthropology, nor anthropology as a social-scientific introduction to the study of archaeology and history, is in the curriculum of this University and many other universities. This questioning is a valid process, but more and more the new social sciences will prove their saving value in this complex and baffling age.

2. The Body as Basic to the Whole Personality

In so far as the curriculum failed to meet the physical needs of youth in the mediæval university and the aesthetic and spiritual needs of youth in modern America, it was, and is, incomplete in meeting the needs of the whole human being. The ideal of the liberal college is to develop the whole personality. It is the high witness of the race in the ideal of the Greek philosophers on down to the findings of the modern psychologist and biologist that youthful training should be based on the unity of the human being. William James said that every experience involved the neural mechanism. Professor Conklin, from his Princeton and Woods Hole biological laboratory, says, "More and more science is recognizing the unity of the entire organism; structure and function, body and mind, are parts of one living whole." Neglect of the body, then, is a neglect of an instrument of thought and feeling. The whole personality participates for better or worse in every physical or mental or emotional expression of the human being. Damage to the body cuts down the intellectual and emotional capacities. Deficiencies in the training of the physical senses short-circuit much of the beauty and the glory of the world. Resiliency of the body brings resiliency of the mind. Generous energies make for the liberal spirit. Yet the college would miss its purpose in exalting the physical and athletic to the subordination of the intellectual and spiritual. Athletics should be a means on the way to something higher. Physical education, with its courses in physiology and hygiene, its gymnasium, playing fields, intramural sports, and the promotion of both indoor and outdoor volunteer play, would constitute the wholesome groundwork of both the general physical well-being and college sports. The varsity teams would then be the democratic and natural but the none-the-less crowned products of a community participation in athletics. The college would then work through the body, through sports and sportsmanship, hardihood, courage, and fair play to a higher human code, and to the imaginative release of the human spirit through sport into the building of a more beautiful personality.

3. Intellectual Content and Training

With the recognition of the indispensible values of the body, the college of liberal arts can then justly and more successfully insist on that excellence in intellectual training which is one of its basic concerns. The body will be better equipped and more alert to respond to a trained mind. This basic need for trained minds recurringly raises the question as to what are the best subjects for intellectual discipline and excellence. This question takes us, as we have noticed, into the historical midst of the fifteenth and sixteenth century struggle as to the comparative intellectual and spiritual values of the sacred and secular learning and the seventeenth, eighteenth and nineteenth century battles of the classics and the sciences. It also takes us into the midst of the nineteenth century rivalry between the ancient and modern languages and between the elective system and required courses once considered essential for formal discipline. It finds us now in the very center of the twentieth century curricular pull between the humanities, natural sciences and older social sciences on one side and the newer social sciences on the other.

In these days, when we hear on one side that the liberal arts college in the university should be abolished and university work be made immediately professional and vocational or of senior college and graduate grade, and on the other side that the liberal arts education should not only be divorced from any specific connection with the professions and vocations but should not include any subject that has any utilitarian value, it is well for us not to be dogmatic, but to try to keep our historical perspective and preserve our cultural balance. Well on in the nineteenth century we hear James Russell Lowell say that a university should be a place where nothing useful is taught and Ezra Cornell say that a university should be a place where any student could study anything he wanted to know. As we listen to the dead masters of the arts and sciences speaking on the subject of the content, distribution, and values of the liberal courses--Francis Bacon, Milton, Goethe, Cardinal Newman, John Stuart Mill, Huxley, Charles W. Eliot, Gilman, Harper, James R. Angel, Benjamin Ide Wheeler, Charles R. Van Hise, David Starr Jordan, and Edwin A. Alderman--or the living teachers, thinkers and experimenters in the field of a liberal education, we may dare to bring their liberal view to modern developments. We may sum them up essentially in saying that a liberal education should include those matters every human being should know, as a human organism, as an intelligent citizen, and as a spiritual personality, about himself, his body, his mind, and his emotions; the race, its origin and historical development; the economic and political struction of society and its human implications; some languages, the essence of the great literatures, arts, philosophies, and religions of mankind; with some limitations on the breadth on the distribution of courses and some provision for the depth of concentration in the field of a special interest. The physical and mathematical sciences, the biological sciences, the social sciences, and the humanities constitute the main divisions in America's most daring and dramatic curricular adventure. Many American colleges are now working out the values of some such curriculum. It is important that we do not merely imitate. We can, as we tentatively explore the curriculum, keep our minds open to these welcome experiments out of which are to come values, we believe, for all our colleges and universities.

In the mastery of these liberal subjects, if reënforced by master teachers with laboratory, observatory, library, music hall, theatre, studio, gallery, museum, and the world of nature, will come limitless opportunities for mental discipline and student self-education in exactness in observation, relentless analysis, logical organization of materials and ideas, clear exposition, appreciation of truth, beauty, and moral heroism, and practice in expressing in various art forms more beautifully what is deep in the mind and soul of youth.

4. The Campus

Supplementing the classroom, the library, and the laboratory is the campus. Sometimes, unfortunately, the campus and its activities supplant the classroom, the library and the laboratory. Sometimes they doubtless serve partly to make up for the lack of imaginative vitality and the opportunity to participate creatively in the learning process. These activities are vivid with personalities and the warm current of youthful life, with opportunities for leadership and cooperation, and challenging the problems of freedom and self-government. The campus should not supplant or merely supplement, but can, with well-balanced activities and wise and sympathetic guidance, organically reënforce the purpose of the college to develop the whole human being, the integrated view, and the creative life.

5. The Integrated View and Spiritual Values

Above campus activities, curriculum and content, above intellectual power itself, is the spirit of culture, the integrated view, the understanding mind that sees in deep perspective and in wide relation. There is no magic in the liberal arts course to make the liberal mind. A student may master the words and syntax of a language and miss the majesty and beauty of the literature. He may work daily in the stacks and miss the decisive significance of the library as the reservoir of the race from which the streams of history gather momentum and direction. He may make an efficient routine of work in the laboratory and fail to realize that in quiet laboratories work the scholars who are blazing now the obscure trails which are to become the highways of the world's life. He may with his microscope identify the particles of an electron and miss the personality next to him in the laboratory. He may with his telescope get a sense of the sweep of the universe and fail to develop the imaginative sympathy that senses for him the struggle and sweep of mankind through history. He may learn historical facts and miss the influence of the moral heroism of Socrates or a Wilson or the spiritual beauty of Saint Francis or a Florence Nightingale. He may discover or dig out facts and have no sense of humility or opportunity in the presence of the implications of the discovery of truth for mankind. The teacher's opportunity comes in the opportunity to help the student develop not only mental discipline, mastery of content, and intellectual excellence, but also an attitude of mind, an intelligent response to heroic situations, and an appreciative assimilation into the core of his own character the nobility in the lives of those whom he meets in books and in life. The liberal education would give both depth and breadth to the mind and would embrace in its deepening process of integration the spiritual values of human personality.

This wholeness of view includes within its range not only the unity of the courses and groups of courses which constitute the content of the liberal arts and sciences, but also the unity of the race and more and more the unity of the universe. Departments of knowledge, despite elaborate separation, overlap and merge with other departments. Conklin says, for example, that psychology and education are branches of biology because they are all studies of living things. Then, for examples, physics is geological, biological, and chemical in nature. Astronomical and mathematical physics, with its seventeenth century universe of a fixed reference frame and immutable laws of nature, which God Himself respected, carried over its influence and contributed to the political conception of a constitution of fundamental law and the inalienable rights of man which the king himself, with his claim of divine rights, had to respect. The mechanical conception of the universe reënforced by a mechanical civilization, went over into the preconception of a mechanically self-balancing economic system operating automatically according to immutable economic laws. There is the trace of this mechanical influence as a strand in the weaving of the classical economics of the nineteenth century, the behavioristic psychology of the twentieth century and varying forms of the mechanistic philosophy in the last two centuries. Biology, with its theory of evolution, reënforced the preconceptions of a free competitive society and of the philosophy of war. Thus we see from these fragmentary and often fugitive bits of influences the deep interrelation of physics, mathematics, biology, psychology, economic and political theories, and a philosophy of life. This view of the many strands and influences that go into the making of our lives and our philosophy that can come from the new curriculum of the college is essential not only to a student's better understanding of himself and the most acute problems of the modern age, but is essential also to a view of the universe.

We listen to a great American physicist as he traces the steps in the gradual integration of the six formerly rigorously separated branches of physics on the way to becoming one great whole. The professor of theoretical physics in the University of Berlin recently writes that the study of philosophy, once in scientific disrepute, is coming back with a new meaning and a wide power. Professor Planck points out that, as scientific research by its conquest of the world of sense "simplifies the world picture of physics, the structure of the physical moves further and further away from the world of sense." What Professor Planck points out as the increasing simplification of the world picture becomes the basis for a more complete view of the universe. We deeply need the values in the general view of the great philosophers. The scientist and philosopher are approaching a more respectful meeting in the presence of the mystery of life and the universe. Haldane moves from matter to mechanism to life to personality to spirituality. Personality, as an evolutionary achievement, reveals the spiritual quality of the materialistic process. From physics we go into metaphysics. Matter becomes energy, and energy brings us to the borderland of a universe, seen and unseen, the reverberations of whose moral sovereignty are in the inner man in answer to the intuitions and aspirations of the human spirit.

As is life, so in college, subjects, ideas, and processes cannot be kept in separate departments. We should in college, if for no other reason than convenience, have departments of subjects but not compartments of knowledge. The very fluidity of ideas and the organic nature of life processes make it necessary that in our very respect for specialization and the value of departments we should from time to time reëxamine the curriculum. Let us welcome the scores of experiments underway all over America and not adopt any of them by way of imitation but adapt what is good as we venture on our own account according to our own needs. In no other way that by the integrated view can we understand the wider implications of the specialized knowledge. Only with the whole view can we build up correlative social control of the new forces and mechanisms let loose upon the world by specialized knowledge with the power to destroy or rebuild the structure of the modern world.

These are the high stakes for which the college would play its part. Its conception of the unity of learning, the unity of life, and the unity of the universe makes for a sense of the spiritual potentiality of the total personality. This integrated view makes for a sense of the spiritual essence of civilization, even in its gathered fragments transmitted more and more from age to age with the possibility of being transformed into the Kingdom of God according to the pattern of Him who was the master teacher of the inner way of the unified life.

THE PROFESSIONAL SCHOOLS

In the rebuilding of the civilization of the Kingdom, we need not only the specialized knowledge and the integrated way of life but also specialized ways of making a living. The college is based on the idea of Jesus that man does not live by bread alone; but we must remember that the first petition in the Lord's Prayer is "Give us this day our daily bread." Youth, to play a significant part in the world's life, needs a specialized skill, a vocation, a profession. The vocational and professional schools came in America largely outside the universities on account of the gaps in the university structure. This specialized skill in law, medicine, pharmacy, agriculture, engineering, education, business, journalism, and public administration and welfare was learned by the apprentice on the job. But as the professions and vocation became more complex, proprietary schools of law, medicine, pharmacy, and business arose to meet a real life need. Schools of religion have a rightful place in the modern university. The School of Religion at our next-door neighbor, Duke University, has high potential value to the whole South. In time the joint processes of specialization and synthesis in all fields of knowledge resulted in the incorporation of all professional schools and some high-grade vocational schools within the framework of the university.

The university needs the professional schools with their specialized knowledge, equipment, and skills, their high standards of scholarship, their spirit of work, thoroughness, and excellence. The professional schools, assimilated into the organic structure of the university, need the university with its wide variety of skills, interests, and contacts, its general resources, and wholeness of view. Consider the reciprocal contributions of Osler, Welch, and Hopkins, the Pound group and Harvard, the Russell group and Columbia, Shailer Mathews and Chicago.

The professional schools, while raising the standards of specialized scholarship, need to be concerned more and more with the liberal cultural equipment of the master. The teacher in the professional schools is in a strategic position to preserve and carry forward the liberal culture and the general view. He can bring to a focus on the most highly technical case all the historical, economic, social, psychological, political, or philosophic influences which converge upon it with implicating power. In the law schools there is the beginning of the recognition of the value of the liberal reënforcement of the most highly techincal knowledge. For example, a professor who received his liberal arts training in a Southern university, his doctorate in economics in the Middle West, is teaching torts in the law school of an Eastern university. Another who has the liberal arts degree, the doctorate of philosophy in economics and politics, and two law degrees, is, despite his youth, already a productive scholar and able teacher of law. A new professor of pharmacy in this University has a liberal training as the foundation of, and doctorate of philosophy on top of, his special scientific training. Without making a fetish of degrees, this liberal training is basic to a wholesome attitude of mind in professional training. Some of the most scholarly and liberally cultured minds in America are in schools of engineering, commerce, agriculture, education and other highly professional schools. Many also who have never seen a college have a spirit of the rarest culture distilled from nature, books, and life. These men have been careful not to set method over against liberal learning. With a view to cultural and human implications of the most specialized knowledge, they find themselves in the midst of work and culture, surging life, and the difficult but at times thrilling, processes of rebuilding a world.

A teacher in an East Carolina city communicated the flame within his heart to men and women who transformed communities, became teachers, superintendents of schools, and presidents of several Southern colleges and universities. A permanently crippled but useful ex-Confederate, no longer master of slaves but master of botany and chemistry, scientifically remade old plantations, built mills, endowed a college, and became the source of hope to people over a wide area. A later youth trained culturally in the South and vocationally in the North brought back into the Southern piedmont a kit of tools and a youthful dream for a venturesome part in refounding the structure of our Southern civilization. A young lawyer in a public religious meeting standing up for freedom of scientific inquiry against the tides that rolled in upon him, stood unmoved in the tumult, steadfast in the strength of science, history, the humanities, and the religion of Jesus which mustered to his almost lonely side. Many business men in these hard times are draining their reserves and are taking their losses standing up in order that people may have work and food. Editors, with courage for opprobrium and financial loss, have fought the fight of the inarticulate peoples and of despised minorities. Physicians daily minister to the bodies, minds, and spirits of broken men. Rabbis, priests, and preachers come out of lonely vigils to sustain the sympathies, courage, and faith of men in cruel times. To lawyers, doctors, pharmacists, teachers, journalists, manufacturers, business men, scientific engineers, social engineers, farmers, statesmen, and ministers of religion; to them with the depth of a specialized mastery and the cultural breadth of an imaginative mind, there open professional opportunies as wide as the needs of the people.

THE GRADUATE SCHOOL

But a group of professional schools around the college do not make a university. Without a graduate school there can be no university. Postgraduate courses do not make a greaduate school. The American Association of Universities, essentially an association of graduate schools, founded in 1900 by Presidents Eliot, Gilman, and Harper in the interest of excellence in graduate research, holds as one of its present requirements for membership that a university be equipped in faculty, laboratories, general library, and special source materials to give the degree of doctor of philosophy in five departments. However adequate be the laboratories and supplies, departmental libraries and source materials, carrells, seminar rooms, and all the valuable facilities for thorough research, without great scholars the whole apparatus of research may become as so much sounding brass. There can be no great graduate school and no great university without great teachers. A good part of a lifetime given by day and by night on scant income to the deep exploration of a field is the price of the scholarship of the master. No smattering and no sham; only thoroughness and excellence among the masters. Several groups of these masters, distinguised in different fields, prevent unchecked specialization in any one field. These various groups of eminent scholars, seekers for truth, and teachers, by the very interrelation of fields, intellectual interchange, and coördination on the level of graduate excellence are integrated in the university. The university guidance of graduate work should make impossible research in ultra-scholastic and utilitarian trivialities, but at the same time should not by a routine uniformity or traditional control cramp the vigorous and autonomous life of schools and departments. Tradition and routine should give way to excellence. The quality of the college, the professional schools, and the whole university is renewed from and advanced by the excellence of the graduate school. The college of arts and sciences is the youthful heart of the university, the professional schools are its skillful arm, and the graduate school is its crowning glory.

1. Research and Teaching

The two particular functions of the graduate school are to train students in research and to prepare students to teach. The two functions, though separate in their techniques, reënforce each other in the unity of the graduate purpose for the advancement of knowledge and the well-being of the race. In some universities three-fourths of the graduate students become teachers. A great teacher, without publication of his researches, is sometimes an apparently unrecognized gift of God to his generation. Yet research is a resource of the teacher. There is a sense of reverent humility in him who has to dig in the sources for his own facts and ideas. There is often a contagious enthusiasm communicated to the students by the teacher who comes fresh from the mine bringing the ore in the hands that dug it out. Research on the part of the teacher in the humanities and sciences deepens the content and insight of the teacher and makes available fresh resources for other teachers; develops the scholarly research spirit in many students, and thus widens the association and the interchange of the ideas of teachers and scholars around the earth who, by their patient discovery and teaching of truth, are doing their hopeful bit toward the gradual making of a better world.

2. Research on Its Own Account

Research, apart from teaching, has values on its own account. It was James Madison's patient and thorough researches into the structure of the Ancient Western European and Colonial governments that enabled him as a practical statesman in a critical period, to guide the framing of the constitution of the United States. Hertz, the German research scholar, standing on the pure researches of the English professor, Clerk Maxwell, discovered the idea out of which Marconi, the Italian, invented the mechanism for wireless telegraphy. The researches and hypotheses of Copernicus, Galileo, and Kepler helped to make possible the theory of gravitation which came from the integrating mind of Isaac Newton, or as President Walter Dill Scott called him, Professor Newton of Cambridge University. The American Professor Michelson, by his researches, helped to prepare the way for the revolutionary theory of the German Professor Einstein.

3. The Utility of Scientific Research

If we were to recapitulate with President Scott the list of the names of the men whose researches in pure science have not only explored the far reaches of the universe and the inside of the atom but have also discovered the scientific principle on which is erected the technological structure of our modern industrial civilization, we would call, for the most part, the names of college professors and quiet relentless seekers for truth in university laboratories. He has estimated that college and university research make possible in a normal time the production of more wealth in America in one year than has been spent on all the colleges and universities since John Harvard founded the college under the elms in Cambridge. It has also been estimated that the result of college and university research in the pure sciences as the basis for sanitary and hydraulic engineering, personal and public health, save in America the lives of one million people a year.

4. The Graduate School and Organized Research

In the complicated modern world it was inevitable that research should be organized in institutes, councils, and big universities. Mr. Vernon Kellogg has pointed out that the research organizations are dependent on the colleges and universities for manning and recruiting their staffs. The graduate school is par excellence the training ground for research, organized and unorganized. In graduate research there is no immediate profit motive, and the student has the unadulterated scientific freedom necessary for training in research. Deeply specialized as is research, it should for that very reason keep its connection with all divisions of graduate work and never narrow its special eye to the wider implications of the smallest bit of truth found in the laboratory of library stacks or tentatively guessed on a walk about the campus or in some lonely nook in the woods or where you will. In the meagerly equipped laboratories of this University before the twentieth century and since, the researches of unpretentious scholars in the natural science have been recognized for their value to learning and mankind by scholars on four continents.

5. Research in the Social Sciences

The social sciences, of course, are lagging behind the natural sciences. For the most part they have risen in recent times. Scholars in the social sciences have a tremendous task to bring their researches up to the needs of the times. Individuals in graduate schools and organizations here and there are doing heroic work, with civilization itself as the stakes of social mastery. On account of the complicated nature of our social structure, institutes for research in the social sciences are being organized mainly and naturally within the universities as, for example, the Institute of Human Relations at Yale. The Institute for Research in the Social Sciences here is an indispensable reënforcement of the graduate resources and impulses of the University in the unexplored fields of the social sciences. Together with the pioneer department of rural social-economics, the departments of economics, education, history, sociology, psychology, and the law school, it is making realistic studies and significant contributions to the better understanding of the human and social implications of our economic, political, and legal structure. The Institute has had considerable regard for interractial relations with all their problems of human injustice and unequal opportunity in the present South. These researches in interracial relations are based on the human attitude that, with all our racial solidarities and pragmatic expedients of social separation, the two great races have fundamentally a common destiny in building a nobler civilization and that, if we go up, we go up together. The University Press has made these researches available for the people of the South and has carried forward an intellectual exchange with scholars and institutions over the world. Five of the books from this press are on the League of Nations list for international intellectual coöperation.

a. Research, Integrated Thinking, and War

Scholars, colleges, universities, and research agencies all over the world need to join their intellectual and spiritual resources in research and make specialized and integrated studies of the problems whose social consequences reach around the world and down the ages. The World War and the world economic depression have taken their toll in human lives, human well-being, and happiness beyond measurement or imagination. Wars and depression throw their cruel and sinister shadows across the homes of the people on all the continents of this earth. We, who, in our scientific price, consider that we have mastered the earth, stand baffled in the midst of these two mighty foes of every locality and all mankind. The very fact of recurring wars and recurring depressions raises a question as to the quality of our education and the sincerity of our religion. The people in a world in which such depressions and wars can recur are not yet intellectual and spiritual in the control of their institutions. The nature of the wars and depressions illustrates the complex structure of life and the world. They make necessary greater depths in specialization and a new integrations of old and new knowledge in all fields for a better understanding of the problems and the processes of solution. The explanation that war is caused by economic interests is too simple to be true to the complex nature of human beings and human society. The human being carries around as part of his structure and heritage biological, psychological, anthropological, historical, economic, political, philosophical and spiritual equipment. Human society is as complex as the human life implicated in its framework. Wars may come from springs deep in the structure of human beings or deep in the structure of human society or in both. It is the heroic task of biology, psychology, and all the social sciences to try to light up the origins of war and work out its social control and abolition. On the surface it is clear that science and technology have with power engines, farms, factories, stores, banks, ocean lanes, rails, cables and concrete roads, flung across the earth the mechanical framework of a mighty economic structure. A pistol shot in Sarajevo or a stock market crash in Wall Street causes repercussions around the world. A Slavic student, in killing a German Archduke, precipitated national antagonisms, imperial ambitions, economic rivalries, and released the human passions and the dynamic energies of the peoples of two hemispheres which caused two million American soldiers to cross an ocean and left ten million dead on the battlefields of three continents. Press a trigger in a village or press a button in an office and you may release pent-up forces that involve the nations and civilization. This interdependent world economic structure has thrust through the national boundaries which would hedge it about. Out of regard for the values of nationality, we should not set nationalism over against mankind but rather work through the nations and all available international organizations for the preservation of the nations and the salvation of the human race. The social scientist is up against an almost impenetrable jungle in many regions of knowledge. He finds himself on the fringe of the wilderness in an internationally lawless world. From the pure research in colleges and universities have come the scientific findings and ideas which became the technological basis of modern civilization. From the colleges and universities must come the findings and thinking which will become the basis for a more intelligent understanding, guidance, and control of the processes out of which come wars and depressions.

b. Research, Integrated Thinking and the Depression

Research and integrated thinking are desperately needed now to be brought to bear on the great depression. The rhythm of life and business, the high and low swing of the business cycle, unregulated over-production, the hang-over of handicraft ideas with their controls in the age of the power engine, the dislocation of agriculture and the sickness of the coal and cotton industries, the placing of pecuniary considerations above the industrial and the industrial above the human and spiritual, destructive competition, prohibitive tariffs, the breakdown in the system and ethics of distribution and consumption, ultra-nationalist politics in an interdependent economic world, the great fear and insecurity of the people, armaments, reparations and international debts, unemployment, hunger amid plenty, the misery and despair of the millions everywhere, demand the most realistic consideration and high thinking of business men, statesmen, and scholars in the universities. Nothing less than an international enlistment of the most specially and liberally equipped minds and the most spiritually resourced personalities is needed against the darkness of this hour.

The colleges and universities stand strategic and the crossroads of a recurring transition in the history of modern times. They have, to our tragic cost, equipped us with only fragmentary views of human beings and human society. The universities are often slow to meet the needs of the age. In the transition from mediæval to modern times, with its focus of forces involving the disintegration of the feudal order, the commercial revolution, and the religious revolt, the universities tardily admitted to curricular equality the revived ancient learning which was the intellectual ferment of it all. Close to the beginning of the last century the Western world stood in the presence of the steam power revolution. The universities were slow to give cultural equality to the new sciences which, in their own laboratories, were to rediscover and conquer the earth, and refound the technological basis of modern society. Modern democracies stand face to face today with communist and fascist dictatorships. The people of the Western world, already in the midst of the social challenge of of the electrical and gas power revolutions, find themselves overwhelmed with three other great influences: the consequences of the World War, the world moral confusion, and the world economic depression. The stakes are too great and catastrophic developments are too swift for the universities to stand aside or wait upon tradition for their course or vested interests for their cue. In the face of revolutions, dictatorships, and catastrophe, America, through the schools, colleges and universities, must learn to be true to her inner Americanism of freedom of the mind and equality of opportunity for all people.

What the classics meant intellectually in Renaissance times, and what the natural sciences have meant technologically in the industrial age, suggest something of what the social sciences in the twentieth century can mean humanly in the making of a nobler America and more beautiful world in which men and women can do their day's work and dream dreams for their children. Scholars of the first rank in all nations enlisted in high research can lay out the groundwork for the better coöperation of the nations in international diplomacy, disarmament, finance, commerce, culture, scientific and social mastery, and catch the imagination and heroism of youth in the high adventures of the human spirit for the saving of the nations and the succor of the peoples of the earth who ask for the chance to earn their daily bread.

THE UNIVERSITY AND THE PEOPLE

1. The Extension Division

It is the function of the state university not only to find its bits of truth and teach the truth gathered from scholars everywhere, but to carry this truth to the people that they may take it into their lives and help to make it prevail in the world of affairs. It is the ideal of the University Extension Division to make the resources of the universities, the discoveries of science, and the finding of the social scientists available for the people of the commonwealth. The members of the general faculty, the special faculty, the special library, special lectures, courses in class and by correspondence, bureaus, institutes, interscholastic activities involving athletics, debates, classics, music, plays, and playwriting, and in an independent and far-reaching way the general library and the library school all serve to carry or send the University to the people. The public schools, teachers, men's civic clubs, professional associations, women's clubs and associations, and people in towns, on farms, and in remote mountain coves, all tap the life that is here. The universities should set their faces like flint against what is clearly trivial, merely current, or only novel. Yet the American state university should not, from a fear to assert its own soul against what in its life would be a new Toryism of exclusive culture, high tuition, and intellectual stratification, be misled into a mere imitation of European traditions and institutions. The state university comes from the people and should go out to the people. The intellectual life of the university should be quickened by contact and interchange with the people. They have a common destiny in the adventure of building a better state. The state university cannot, as the university of the people, be an institution of a class, whether based on section, blood, money, creed, or intellectual background. Deep injustice anywhere in the commonwealth leaves its psychic scars upon university life. The state university can never lose the common touch without treason to its own nature and without drying up the springs from which flow the living waters of its own life. The state university is the university of all the people. It takes no side, but democracy and justice are on the side where it belongs. The university is organic with the life of the people, and the currents of its life would flow back into the life of the people with transforming excellence and creative power. There should be no lowering of standards in the extension process. Its standards and opportunities shall be second to none and open to all to the end that we build a commonwealth in which shall be preserved democracy without vulgarity and excellence without arrogance.

2. The Schools of the People

The public schools are now and will increasingly be the community center of university extension and adult education. The University will not only extend and share its life with the public schools and the people but University men, as citizens, if true to the traditions of this University made by men who can fight no more – Murphey, Yancey, Wiley, Vance, Alderman, McIver, and Aycock – will fight for the schools of the people.

The University is resourced in the public schools and the public schools are resourced in the University. The go up or down together. Now is the time in the midst of depression, unemployment, and educational defeatism for the Extension Division and the public schools to envisage and lay out the plans for a future all-inclusive educational program in the communities for the continuous education of all the people as a way to use wisely the advancing leisure, to substitute cultural content for merely mechanical contacts, natural creative play for artificial and empty excitement, and to lay the intellectual groundwork for a more general and intelligent understanding of and participation in the affairs of the world and its opportunities for a larger mastery of human destiny. Land to the west for more than two hundred years helped to keep open and free our American life. The land is closed but the schools are open and will help to make us free. Along the converging roads of the public schools, adult education, and university extension, lies one hope of our American democracy struggling for a higher mastery. We cannot, in these critical times, which test in our budgets what we really believe in, cut the schools and pinch our way out. With the inclusive and continuous education of all our people we must socially invest, we must build, we must create our way out from depression into a higher prosperity and from poverty into a nobler power.

THE FREEDOM OF THE UNIVERSITY

Along with culture and democracy must go freedom. Without freedom there can be neither true culture nor real democracy. Without freedom there can be no university. Freedom in a university runs a various course and has a wide meaning. It means the freedom of students with their growing sense of responsibility and student citizenship to govern themselves in campus affairs, and the right of lawful assembly and free discussions by any students of any issues and views whatever. This campus freedom carries with it a high moral responsibility. For the faculty, freedom means the right of the faculty to control the curriculum, scholastic standards, and especially matters pertaining to intellectual excellence; to teach and speak freely, not as propagandists, but as scholars and seekers for the truth with a clear sense of responsibility for the truth and a deep sense of the teacher's part in the development of the whole youthful personality; to organize their own independent association for discussion and statement of views, and as a basic part of the university's life to help shape university policies by votes, representation, advice, and, may we hope, a larger sharing in the life of the people of the state. For the administrative head, freedom means to take full responsibility in his own sphere and make decisions in the long-run view of all the circumstances, to express views, without illusions as to their influence but with some sense of fairness, humility, and tolerance, on those issues that concern the whole people, asking no quarter and fearing no special interest. Freedom of the trustees means the freedom to represent the public interests independent of any party, faction or interests; to receive endowments for this meagerly endowed University from any honest source without fear or favor or strings attached beyond an honorable rsponsibility, and the freedom to make the institution, within the limits of their responsibility to the people and its own high nature, an autonomous institution in its administration, faculty, standards, admissions, excellence, and the budget which is basic to them all.

Freedom of the university means the freedom to study not only the biological implications of the physical structure of a fish but also the human implications of the economic structure of society. It means freedom from the prejudices of section, race, or creed; it means a free compasion of her sons for all people in need of justice and brotherhood. It means the freedom of the liberated spirit to understand sympathetically those who misunderstand freedom and would strike it down. It means the freedom for consideration of the plight of unorganized and inarticulate peoples in an unorganized world in which powerful combinations and high pressure lobbies work their special will on the general life. In the university should be found the free voice not only for the unvoiced millions but also for the unpopular and even for the hated minorities. Its platform should never be an agency of partisan propoganda but should ever be a fair forum of free opinion. Freedom should never mean a loss of the sense of lawful and moral responsibility to the trustees and the people from whom the university came and to whom her life returns manifold.

But this freedom of the university should not be mistaken for approval of those who are merely sophisticated or who superficially exploit the passing currents or great human causes, or who fundamentally debase the deep human passions and poison the springs from which flow the waters of life. Such an abuse of freedom has the scorn of scholars whose intellectual integrity and wholesome life are a source of freedom. True freedom of self-expression does not lead either to self-exploitation or to self-deterioration but rather leads to the self-realization of the whole personality for the good life. No abuse of freedom, however, should cause us to strike down freedom of speech or publication, the fresh resources of a free university, a free religion, and a free state.

Finally, freedom of the university means freedom of the scholar to find and report the truth honestly, without interference by the university, the state, or any interests whatever. If a scholar be enlisted by the state for research on a mooted issue, though such scholarly and independent report may be imputed to the University as an institution by powerful lobbies opposed to the report, the University will stand by the right of the scholar to make the report, whatever be the consequences. The real destruction of the University would come from the university administration's interference, or any other interference, with the report. Without such freedom of research we would have no university and no democracy.

These conceptions of the various forms of the freedom of the university are stated for the sake of fairness. The only present recourse for changing such conceptions is to change the University administration. This is not said defiantly but in all friendliness and simply as a matter of openness and clearness. It is said with no personal concern, for it is our faith that whatever the administration, the freedom of the University, gathering momentum across a century, and the democracy of the people, sometimes sleeping but never dead, will rise in majesty to reassert the intellectual integrity and the moral autonomy of the University of North Carolina.

This integrity, democracy, and freedom of the University comes out of its own nature. The idea and structure of the University evolve through the centuries under the impact of social needs and youthful hopes. The college and the campus, the professional schools, the graduate school, the library and laboratories, playhouse and music hall, the institute of research and the press, the library school and the democratic extension of the University's life throughout the commonwealth, are all gradually and organically being integrated into the idea and structure of this university of the people. In such a free university we will learn to see in every significant situation—personal, local, national, or international—the composing elements, whether geographic, biological, psychological, historical, economic, social, political, intellectual, or spiritual, or all. This organic university, with its humanities, natural sciences, and social sciences, has the rootage of its growth in the experience of the race, the aspirations of the human personality, and the needs of a changing age. Out of the very organic structure and quality of the university issue its democracy and its freedom.

CONCLUSION

Roll Call of Presidents and Muster of Sons

Out of the past, historic with struggles of freedom and democracy, come figures, living and dead, to stand by us in this inaugural hour in the woods where Davie, the founder, in the eighteenth century stood under the poplar and raised the standard of a people's hope. The lives of the presidents reassure us all with their spiritual presence and power: Caldwell, the first president, in whose administration for the first time in America a modern language was given curricular equality with an ancient language and the first observatory was established in an American college, and whose communicated social passion sent Murphey to lay the foundation of the state's publc schools, and Morehead to build railways to bind the East and West in bonds of iron; Swain, in whose time the University advanced to a high leadership in the South, and who, in the closing war days and reconstruction, was a conciliatory spirit in an age of hate; Battle, dauntless father of the reopening of the University, deviser of a separate group of graduate courses in the curriculum fifty years ago, and founder of the first university summer school in America, whose gay kindliness will ever pervade this place and whose noble spirit still walks in these woods; Winston, lying stricken in this village today, a casualty of the life militant, champion of religious freedom and educational democracy who synthesized the classical and scientific, the cultural and vocational, in his own varied and brilliant life; Alderman, lately and deeply lamented, who in his last days with something of a premonition of the end returned in filial memories to alma mater, her sons, and her scenes where his eloquence long stirred the creative imagination of the people of a commonwealth and caught the ear of the people of a nation; Venable with his passion for soundness of scholarship and integrity of life, the symbol of the group of scientific scholars whose research and teaching won recognition among the scholars of the world, with us still in modest retirement these later years gathering flowers from his garden for his friends in the village where he once gathered truth from test tubes for all mankind; Graham, major prophet of university extension and interpreter of culture and democracy to the people, his name memorialized in a students' building on the campus whose ideals he helped to mold and whose life he passionately extended all over the state as he identified a democratic state university with the life of the people whose sustaining power has returned a hundred fold since his going; and Chase, under whose leadership came the greatest material expansion and intellectual advance, whose administration gathered up the momentum and values of the past, added high values of his own, and worked a synthesis of many, champion of the freedom of scientific inquiry in testing times, genial, leader and friend, now president of the University of Illinois but always at home in Chapel Hill. These chieftains and the hosts of her sons always muster in spiritual power in every hour of her need. Into the soul of the place has entered the spirit of an heroic woman, symbol of all mothers and women whose hopes and prayers have wrought mightily under these oaks.

With the University today stand all the state and denominational schools, colleges, and the neighbor university. Not in antagonism but in all friendliness and rivalry in excellence we would work in this region and build her together one of the great intellectual and spiritual centers of the world.

Chapel Hill

In Chapel Hill among a friendly folk, this old University, the first state university to open its doors, stands on a hill set in the midst of beautiful forests under skies that give their color and their charm to the life of youth gathered here. Traditions grow here with the ivy on the historic buildings and the moss on the ancient oaks. Friendships form here for the human pilgrimage. There is music in the air of the place. To the artist's touch flowers grow beautifully from the soil and plays come simply from the life of the people. Above the traffic of the hour church spires reach toward the life of the spirit. Into this life, with its ideals, failures, and high courage, comes youth with his body and his mind, his hopes and his dreams. Scholars muster here the intellectual and spritual resources of the race for the development of the whole personality of the poorest boy, and would make the University of North Carolina a stronghold of liberal learning with outposts of research along all the frontiers of the world. Great teachers on this hill kindle the fires that burn for him and light up the heavens of the commonwealth with the hopes of light and liberty for all mankind.

APPENDIX G.

Archibald "Moonlight" Graham

Dr. Frank is said to have idolized his older brother Archibald, pictured above (first player at left of back row). Archie, nicknamed "Moonlight," was featured in the movie "Field of Dreams" and was played, as an older man, by Burt Lancaster. Archie went on to play ball for the New York Giants, but for one inning only, possibly the shortest major league career of any.
North Carolina Collection, UNC Library

'Field of Dreams' brings posthumous fame to the 'other' Graham brother -- Archibald

By TOM MOORE
The Chapel Hill Herald

CHAPEL HILL -- In life, Frank Porter Graham, the great southern liberal who served as U.S. Senator and president of the University of North Carolina, was the more famous brother.

But posthumously Archibald Graham is gaining ground, thanks to the hit movie, "Field of Dreams."

The film, a baseball fairy tale in which Shoeless Joe Jackson and other members of the blacklisted Chicago White Sox team of 1919 come back as ghosts to play ball on an Iowa farm, features Archibald "Moonlight" Graham as a character because he briefly played major league baseball before becoming a physician.

In fact, Moonlight Graham, portrayed in the movie by Burt Lancaster as a kindly old doctor, had one of the briefest careers in major league history.

According to *The Baseball Encyclopedia,* he played one inning as the right fielder for the 1905 New York Giants, the team that won the National League pennant and World Series that year under the management of the legendary John McGraw.

Graham, who earlier played center field for UNC's varsity baseball team, was put in late in the Giants' June 29 game against the Brooklyn Dodgers. The Giants won 11-1.

And Graham never even got to bat. "I would have liked that; just once to stare down the pitcher," Graham says in "Field of Dreams."

In the film Graham gets his turn at the plate. It's the one forgivable liberty the filmmakers take with his life.

For unexplained reasons, Moonlight Graham's one game has been moved to 1922. The film also portrays him as pursuing a professional baseball career before going to medical school, and he is made a native of Chisholm, Minn., the small mining town where the real Moonlight Graham worked as a doctor specializing in eye problems for most of his life.

Shoeless Joe, the W.P. Kinsella novel that is the basis for "Field of Dreams," gets the facts right. But it does not mention his famous brother or give details about his minor league and college baseball career.

Moonlight Graham, who was born in Fayetteville in 1878 and died in Chisholm in 1965, played minor league ball in Scranton, Penn., in the summers of 1903 and 1904, according to records provided by Graham at the University of North Carolina at Chapel Hill Alumni Association headquarters. He also was a member of the N.Y. Giants team in 1905 and 1906.

He began playing professional baseball after receiving a medical certificate at the University of Maryland, using his salary to help finance post-graduate studies at Johns Hopkins University in the off-seasons, said Joe Herzenberg, a historian working on a biography of the late Frank Porter Graham.

"Archie was an accomplished baseball player, and his baseball skills were a great source of pride for the Graham family," Herzenberg said.

The source for his baseball nickname "Moonlight" is no longer known -- because his wife is dead and he had no children. But it could be a reference to Graham's playing baseball to help finance his academic pursuits, Herzenberg said.

Graham's minor league records are lost and UNC's Sports Information Office does not have his records for the 1900, 1901 and 1902 seasons he played at UNC. Graham was enrolled in UNC's medical school during his last season at UNC, according to the 1902 *Yackety Yack* student yearbook.

And he played varsity baseball and varsity football at the University of Maryland while working on his medical degree there in 1903 and 1904.

Graham worked briefly as a doctor in New York City, then moved to Chisholm.

There he married his wife, Alicia Madden, ran unsuccessfully for mayor in 1920, and did pioneering research in eye diseases and blood pressure, according to information supplied by Graham.

Frank Porter Graham, who idolized his older brother, attempted to follow in Archie's footsteps, but his baseball career only went as far as UNC's varsity team, Herzenberg said.

"He wasn't as tall as Archie and consequently wasn't nearly as good a player," Herzenberg said.

May 22, 1989, courtesy The Chapel Hill Herald

APPENDIX H

Hubert S. Robinson, Sr.
Campaign Pamphlet

Statement from the Candidate

I hope you will take time to read the statements below about my career which have been prepared by my friends.

It is my humble conviction that I am qualified by training and experience to serve on the Board of Aldermen, a position which I regard as a sacred trust.

As a citizen of Chapel Hill for 23 years, I have tried to be alert and active in all movements for the betterment of our community. I am deeply grateful and appreciative of the many opportunities the community has given me to serve.

If you feel that I can further serve you as a member of the Board of Aldermen, it will be a pleasure to give all I have to prove worthy of your support.

It is heartening to remember that, as opportunity has been given to one of my race to serve in such a capacity, it has been observed far and wide that community relationships have been bettered.

I shall be happy to talk to anyone or any group concerning my candidacy. Your support and your vote will be greatly appreciated.—Hubert Robinson, Sr.

Statement by Friends
of Candidate Robinson

Hubert S. Robinson, Sr., was born in Hogansville, Ga., a town of about 3,000 inhabitants, July 17, 1893. His father was Ike Robinson, the first Negro merchant in that small town. At a very early age both of his parents died and he was left in the care of an elderly grandmother.

He attended public school in Hogansville, later attending State Normal School, Montgomery, Ala. After leaving school his jobs included driving a grocery wagon, auto mechanic, carrying the mail from Hogansville to Greenville, a distance of 16 miles, by horse and buggy, and opearting a taxi-cab. He served as chauffeur for the Governor of Georgia when the Chief Executive visited Hogansville.

As a young man he left Hogansville and settled in the twin towns of West Point, Ga., and Lannett, Ala. He married and became very active in the community life there. He joined the Methodist Church and served as a Steward, Trustee, President of the Epworth League, and Teller of Units. When the church was destroyed by a tornado, he was a leader in a movement to raise funds for a new church that cost $22,000.

He was Secretary of the School Board for six years, and he and his wife worked hard for the support of the school. A supplement had to be raised each year to help pay the teachers. This was provided by a small monthly donation asked of the students and by plays and minstrels presented in the nearby towns. Most of the recreation and entertainment of the twin towns was under Hubert's sponsorship.

Hubert came to Chapel Hill from West Point, Ga., where for two years he had served as chauffeur for the late Mr. Phillip Lanier. When Mr. Lanier died his sister, the late Mrs. E. C. Branson of Chapel Hill, encouraged Hubert to seek a job as chauffeur and handyman for Dr. Frank P. Graham, who had just been elected president of the University.

Hubert worked for Dr. Graham throughout the 19 years he was president of the University, after which he took a job in the Morehead Planetarium where he is now employed.

Hubert's community activities in Chapel Hill include organization of the Civic Club, which was instrumental in securing the addition to the Orange County School, now Northside Elementary School, and the Negro Community Center. When the Community Center was completed, it was turned over to the Navy for the duration of World War II. After that it was turned back to the colored people.

The Child Care Committee elected him as chairman of the operating committee of the Center, a position he held for seven years.

During World War II, he served as auxiliary fireman, took a course in poisonous gases, and received a certificate of membership in the U. S. Citizens Service Corps for work in Red Cross Sewing Rooms. He also served as a member of the O.P.A. Price Panel, checking all colored grocery stores in Chapel Hill once a week to see that they were complying with government regulations.

For six years he was part-time attendance officer for Orange County Training School, during which time he had 11 cases in court. That job afforded some unusual experiences in dealing with children and their parents. Police Chief Sloan gave him 100 per cent cooperation in solving some of the problems encountered on this job.

Hubert has also been as actively engaged in school work. He served on the Advisory School Board for seven years, as President of-the P.T.A. for three years and as Treasurer for seven years. In 20 years he has missed only three P.T.A. meetings.

Other community activities include the establishment of the H. M. Holmes Nursery School, under the Landrum Act, and chairman of the War Fund Drive in 1941 when $361.00 was raised. Almost every other charity drive in Chapel Hill among the colored people has been headed by him at some time.

In 1948 he was appointed the only Negro on a committee to make a study of the needs of Orange County. The work of this very important committee required 13 trips to Hillsboro. One of the important recommendations of this committee was the building of a new court house for Orange

County. For this committee appointment he has been very proud.

He is humbly grateful for the opportunity to have served this community in helping to promote certain progressive measures, including paved streets, mail delivery in the Negro sections of town, and part-time Negro policemen.

As Master of the Masons, President of the Chapel Hill Investment Corporation, Treasurer of the P.T.A., Vice-President of the Chapel Hill Mutual Burial Association, and member of the Executive Board of the Red Cross, he leads a very active civic life.

As a family man, he is the father of five children, two of whom have graduated from college. Hubert, Jr., is now employed by the Welfare Department in Greensboro, and Ernestine is teaching school in Rocky Mount. Harold is in the Marines and the other son, Frank, is a freshman at A and T College. The youngest daughter, Beatrice, is a second-year high school student. His wife is the former Miss Addie Belle Palmer, a registered nurse. His two hobbies are a diary, which he has been keeping for 21 years, and woodwork, which he does in his shop, located in his backyard.

Brief Sketch

of Hubert Robinson, Sr.

Native of Hogansville, Ga.

Educated in public schools and at State Normal School, Montgomery, Ala.

Resident of Chapel Hill for 23 years.

Throughout this period has been active in civic, church, and fraternal groups.

His activities have included:

Chairman of the operating committee of the Negro Community Center for seven years.

President of the Orange County Training School P.T.A. and treasurer of P.T.A.

Chairman of the Board of Trustees, First Baptist Church.

Member of Executive Board, Chapel Hill Red Cross.

Master of the Prince Hall Masonic Lodge, Chapel Hill.

President of Chapel Hill Investment Corporation.

Member of Advisory Board to the Chapel Hill School Board.

Member of Study Group appointed by County Commissioners to study needs of Orange County. Out of this study came plans for the new Courthouse in Hillsboro.

Attendance officer for Orange County Training School for six years.

Member of OPA Price Panel during World War II.

Vice President Chapel Hill Community Council.

Hubert S. Robinson, Sr.

Candidate for

Board of Aldermen

of Chapel Hill

In May 5 Election

Your Support and Vote
Will Be Greatly Appreciated

The campaign pamphlet of Hubert Robinson for the Chapel Hill board of aldermen. He was successful in his bid.

FRANK PORTER GRAHAM AND SOUTHERN POLITICS:
Without Tears and With a Smile or Two
by Edwin Yoder

My first awareness of Frank Graham is still as vivid as if it had occurred only yesterday. It dates, of course, to the summer of 1950, my 16th year. Others know more than I of the events of that time, but I must say a brief word or two about it. For me, that summer brimmed with memorable moments of worry, inspiration and excitement, of tragedy and even a bit of low comedy.

My late father, a much-revered small-town schoolmaster, was typical of many people who were inspired to go to uncommon lengths of involvement in Dr. Graham's behalf. He was nothing if not a political man, yet as a public servant he adhered to a strict code of impartiality. He insisted, for instance, that a man who irritated him serve for years as the chairman of his school board--in part, I am sure, because the man was a Republican and, moreover, a "rotten" kind of Republican as my father would have said, to be distinguished from the "honest" one.

But to return to my story: I was startled one morning to see, on the rear floorboard of his car, a stack of political posters. It was the first and only time I ever saw political advertising in his possesssion. I still recall the headline-sized type: DON'T BE FOOLED, it said, BY THE BIGGEST POLITICAL LIES IN NORTH CAROLINA HISTORY. Where he had obtained them, and where they were bound on that hot late spring morning, I either did not ask or have forgotten. They were, in any case, Frank Graham posters; and the second primary campaign was heating up to its disgraceful denouement.

Frank Graham was, all but uniquely, a figure who stirred risky loyalties in people like my father. Our little town, and our otherwise neighborly neighborhood, were as bitterly divided as the state itself. Even the pleasant summer custom of pot-luck garden suppers had been curtailed after an unpleasant scene in which unacceptable things had been said about

Dr. Graham in my father's presence. With th compression of his lips so familiar to me, had said, "Sonny, I am afraid we must home." And we went, even before the eati was finished. No figure other than Dr. Fra could have aroused such passionate commi ment -- and this was, more interestingly, at personal remove. My father had two old brothers, scholars who had been closer to Fra Graham's age and generation than he. So far I know he himself was not personally close. was what Frank Graham represented that ma tered.

I recall, some days later, addressing stacks penny postcards in the dead of night, in th back office of my father's close friend an political collaborator, William Shakespeare Ha ris, the local postmaster. He and my father, an sometimes L. P. Best, in those days constitute the liberal cell of Mebane, virtually in i entirety. Anyway, my father and I and M Shake and his son Sandy addressed those card to registered voters (Mr. Shake was, conve niently, a registrar and had the voting lists i his possession). What would have been said ha that scene been revealed I do not know possibly nothing. But for the schoolmaster an the postmaster to be conspiring, like Nicode mus, by night was, again, not risk-free. Tha was another measure of the intensity of feelin in those days. But the campaign as seen fro my hometown was not without a certain comi relief.

I was working at my first newspaper job, o a long-vanished sheet known as *The Meban Journal*. My editor, employer and mentor wa the jovial and in many ways generous Randolp S. Hancock, a Falstaffian bundle of boilerplate prejudices, cheerfully unconcealed. I was, give my distant Germanic derivation, known to hin as "von Yoder." Chapel Hill was, of course "red hill." Many other epithets hardly suitable for repetition here were plentifully, if no meanly, applied for Hancock had a great stock them, even though he was in many ways a prisingly urbane man. Yet to the acute but used embarrassment of my father (who was teful for Hancock's patronage of his son), the tor of the Journal, a few days before the cond primary, burst forth in a front-page umn. Hancock went on at length about the epy, dangerous characters he had seen and ard during his days as a journalism student at lumbia, spewing their evil foreign doctrines m soapboxes in the parks of Manhattan. eir contagious fare, he recalled, was espe- lly communism and racial mixing, which of urse in his book went inextricably together. cNeill Smith's memory of the eastern North rolina countryman who deplored "commu- sm, socialism, and running around at night," tches the flavor of it.) The point of this creed s one we heard all too much of that summer: at the dear but sappy Dr. Graham had nocently imbibed these dangerous doctrines in e same place and time, more or less, probably ile working at his doctorate at Columbia.

That memorable summer prepared me, and e-disposed me, long before I ever met Frank rter Graham personally, to believe him to be special man. In his later years I came to know m fairly well. As a close friend of his nephew d my Chapel Hill classmate Graham Shanks, nce even served as Dr. Graham's backup as st man in Graham's wedding in Akron, Ohio. mention it because it was there that I tnessed the casting of his celebrated spell. As we were gathered at one of the pre- edding parties, with everyone else quaffing ampagne or something stronger, but Dr. Frank gh on water or lemonade, the following scene curred. One of the bridesmaids was a girl med Pollock, from somewhere deep in eastern orth Carolina. "'Young lady," Dr. Frank asked, o you know where that wonderful old English me of yours came from?" She confessed that e didn't. "One day," Dr. Frank continued, "the ing of England was passing through one of the

royal forests and found a great tree blocking his way. A man of great strength in his entourage volunteered to remove it, and uprooted it by brute force, whereupon the King renamed him Sir John Pull-Oak. The Pollocks of North Carolina were once Pull-Oaks!"

Other fondly remembered scenes come back. Dr. Graham did not approve when the Carlyle Commission on the structure of higher educa- tion recommended co-education at Woman's College in Greensboro. He had, after all, fought hard at the time of university consolidation in 1933 to keep Woman's College a *woman's* college. As we were walking along with Fred and Fran Weaver toward the commencement luncheon at Lenoir Hall that year, Dr. Graham, who was with us, caught my arm in the pump-handle-action wrestler's grip of his. From Polk Place to the very doors of Lenoir, he never let go. All the while he begged, he insisted, he implored, looking up at me with those riveting eyes, that I simply must denounce co-education in Greensboro.

His single-minded focus and intensity did not brook inattention. Even some years later when he was too feeble to be out among the walks and trees of Chapel Hill, he would hold court in his bathrobe in the little sunroom at his sister Kate Sanders' house. He was still reviewing his old battles with the Indians over Kashmir. One day he said to me with great emphasis: "Ed, if they don't do justice there, I am going to have to ask for time to speak to the General Assembly and tell the truth about all their broken promises."

Here, then, was a small man, pint-sized really, who aroused huge loyalties, even at a distance and even when they entailed risk; who charmed bridesmaids with romantic etymolo- gies; whose steely will, when absorbed in a cause or purpose, was unyielding. That is the man Frank Graham as I remember him, and cherish the memory.

A selection from a lecture given by Ed Yoder at a 1990 weekend seminar on Frank Graham. One of America's most thoughtful journalists and social critics, he is a syndicated columnist with the Washington Post Writers Group and has received the Pulitzer Prize for his commentary.